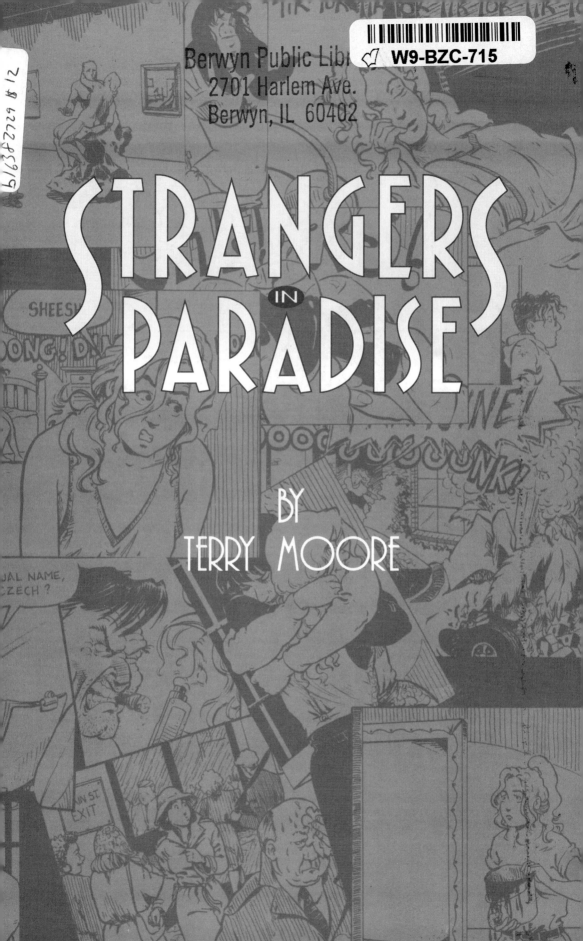

STRANGERS IN PARADISE

BY
TERRY MOORE

Under this picture, which ran on the inside front cover of the first issue of **Strangers In Paradise**, I admitted this was my first comic book and thanked a number of people who had helped me in one way or another. It was just last year but that seems so long ago now. Since that humble beginning I, like most all comic book creators, have become incredibly rich and powerful and now have factories all over the world cranking out Strangers In Paradise comics, lunchboxes, action figures and all the rest of the more than 4300 specialty items you've all grown to know and love. The SiP theme parks have expanded into 32 countries, rivaling even the BoneParks empire. I'm very popular in France.

All that from just three comics. Jeez, why didn't anybody tell me it was this *easy* ?!

...Heh heh, well I can dream, can't I? Truth is, I'm *still* in debt from last years big push to break into the comic book business and although SiP received critical acclaim, it had little bitty, microscopic print runs compared to the really big comics...like **Barbie**.

But that's okay, because all I really wanted to do was lose myself in this story about 2 girls and a guy who gets to know them. And I did.

I've never known a field to embrace the newcomers and help them along like the comics business. My continued thanks and gratitude go out to **Diana Schutz, Charles Phillips, Jeff Novotny, Tom Fassbender and James Eisele, Mark Herr, Carol and Sonny Denbow, Neil Gaiman, Bob Kahan, Wayne Markley, Jeff, Dave and Teri, Bill Stoddard** and my home buds at **Bedrock City Comics, Richard Evans** and **Bob Allen.**

The Collected Strangers in Paradise Volume No.1, 11th printing, October 2001 published by Abstract Studio, P.O. Box 271487, Houston, TX 77277-1487. All contents are © 1995 Terry Moore. Any similarities between any of the characters, names or establishments is purely coincidential and unintended. Nothing in this book may be reproduced without the express written consent of Terry Moore, except for purposes of review and promotion. This book contains some previously published material.
Printed in Canada ISBN 1-892597-00-4

Contents

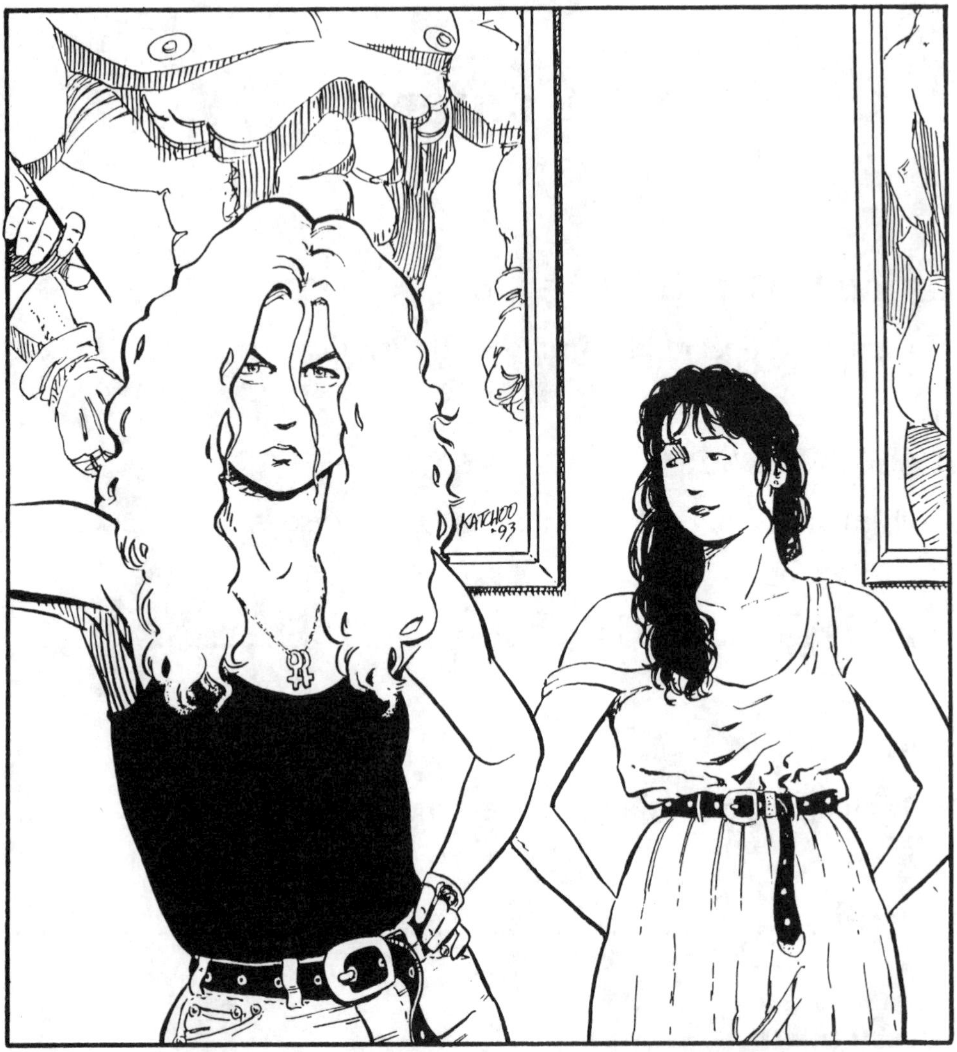
KATCHOO '93

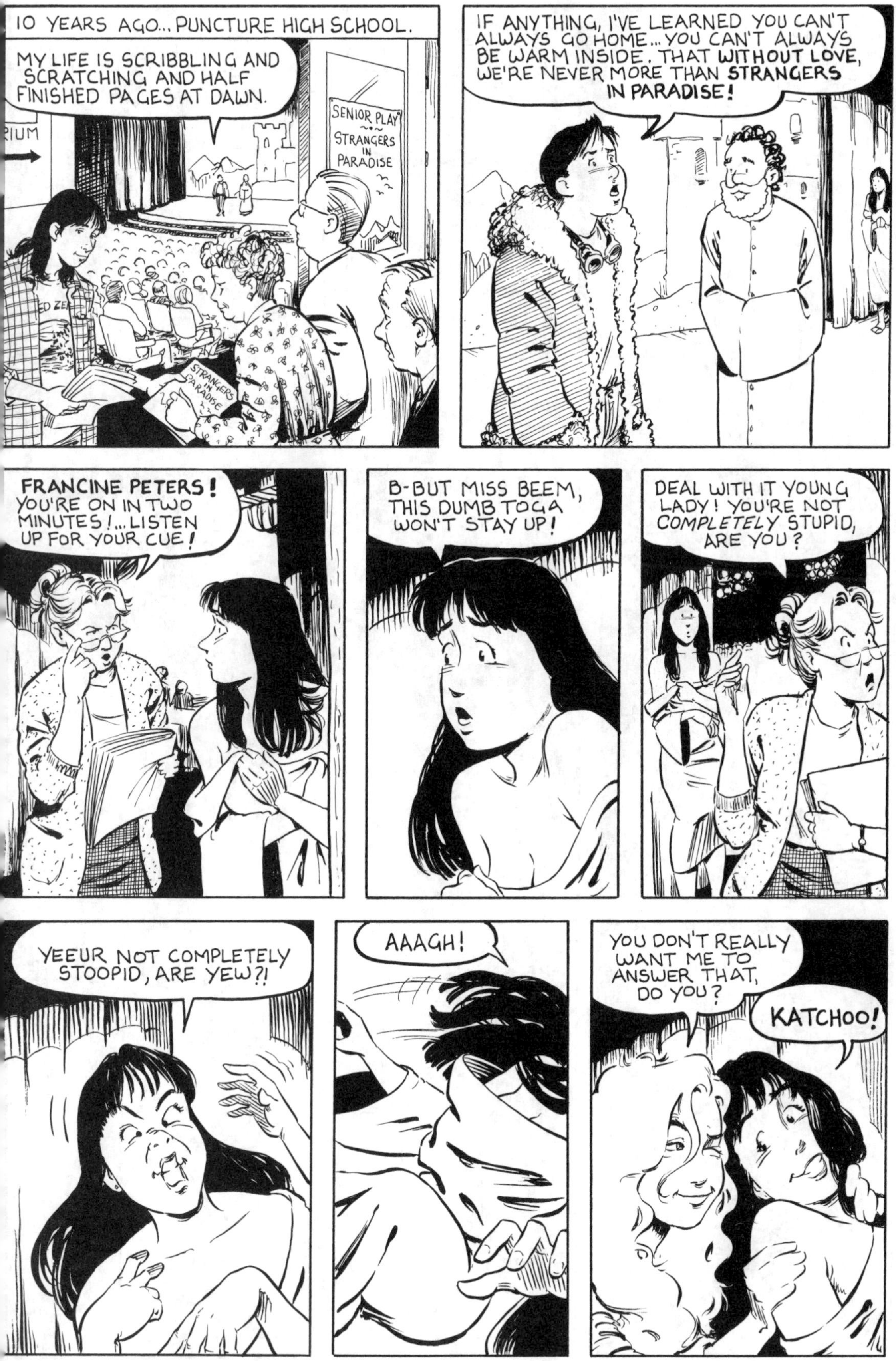
10 YEARS AGO... PUNCTURE HIGH SCHOOL.
MY LIFE IS SCRIBBLING AND SCRATCHING AND HALF FINISHED PAGES AT DAWN.
SENIOR PLAY STRANGERS IN PARADISE
STRANGERS IN PARADISE
IF ANYTHING, I'VE LEARNED YOU CAN'T ALWAYS GO HOME... YOU CAN'T ALWAYS BE WARM INSIDE. THAT WITHOUT LOVE, WE'RE NEVER MORE THAN STRANGERS IN PARADISE!
FRANCINE PETERS! YOU'RE ON IN TWO MINUTES!... LISTEN UP FOR YOUR CUE!
B-BUT MISS BEEM, THIS DUMB TOGA WON'T STAY UP!
DEAL WITH IT YOUNG LADY! YOU'RE NOT COMPLETELY STUPID, ARE YOU?
YEEUR NOT COMPLETELY STOOPID, ARE YEW?!
AAAGH!
YOU DON'T REALLY WANT ME TO ANSWER THAT, DO YOU?
KATCHOO!

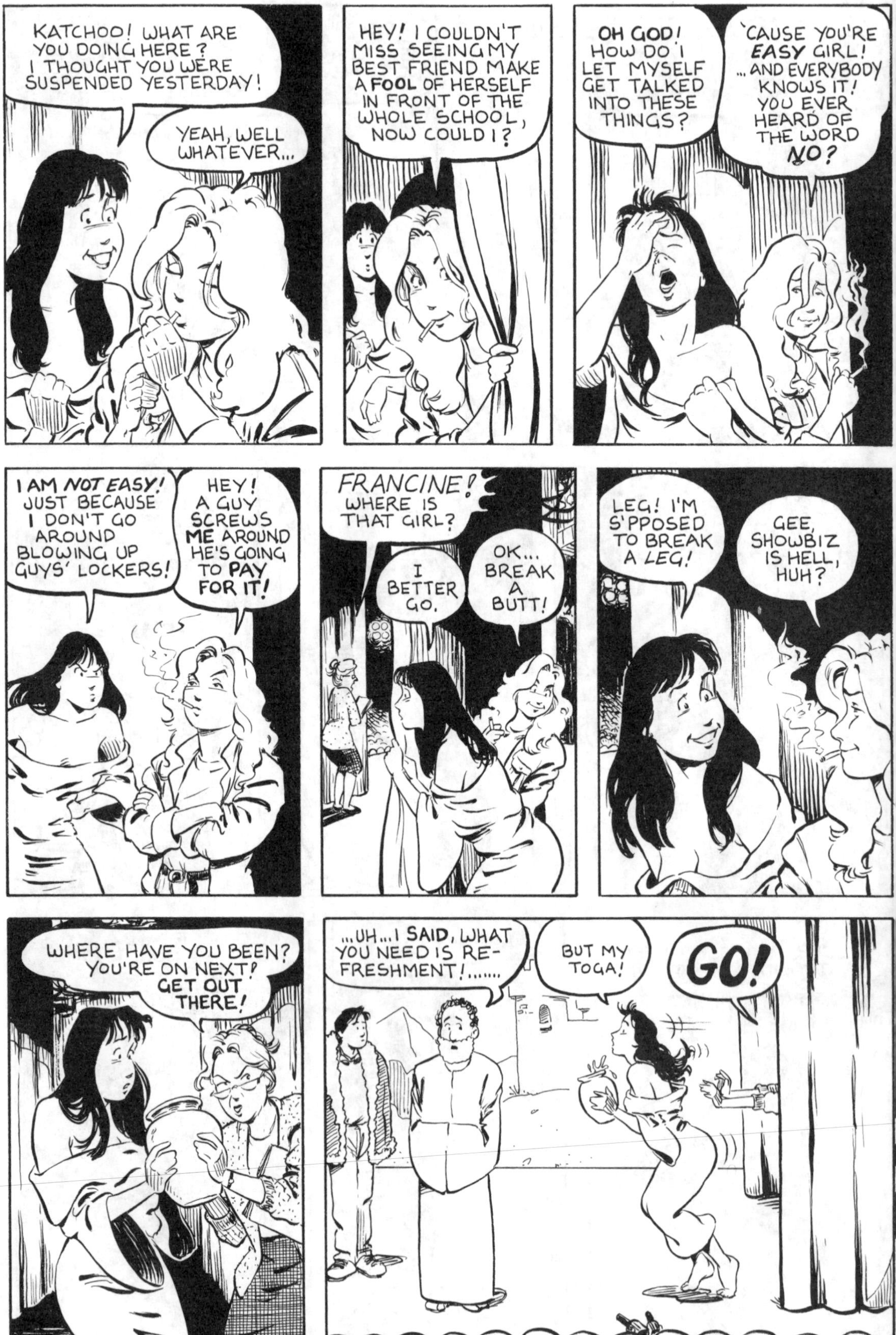

KATCHOO! WHAT ARE YOU DOING HERE? I THOUGHT YOU WERE SUSPENDED YESTERDAY!
YEAH, WELL WHATEVER...
HEY! I COULDN'T MISS SEEING MY BEST FRIEND MAKE A FOOL OF HERSELF IN FRONT OF THE WHOLE SCHOOL, NOW COULD I?
OH GOD! HOW DO I LET MYSELF GET TALKED INTO THESE THINGS?
'CAUSE YOU'RE EASY GIRL! ...AND EVERYBODY KNOWS IT! YOU EVER HEARD OF THE WORD NO?
I AM NOT EASY! JUST BECAUSE I DON'T GO AROUND BLOWING UP GUYS' LOCKERS!
HEY! A GUY SCREWS ME AROUND HE'S GOING TO PAY FOR IT!
FRANCINE! WHERE IS THAT GIRL?
I BETTER GO.
OK... BREAK A BUTT!
LEG! I'M S'PPOSED TO BREAK A LEG!
GEE, SHOWBIZ IS HELL, HUH?
WHERE HAVE YOU BEEN? YOU'RE ON NEXT! GET OUT THERE!
...UH...I SAID, WHAT YOU NEED IS RE-FRESHMENT!.......
BUT MY TOGA!
GO!

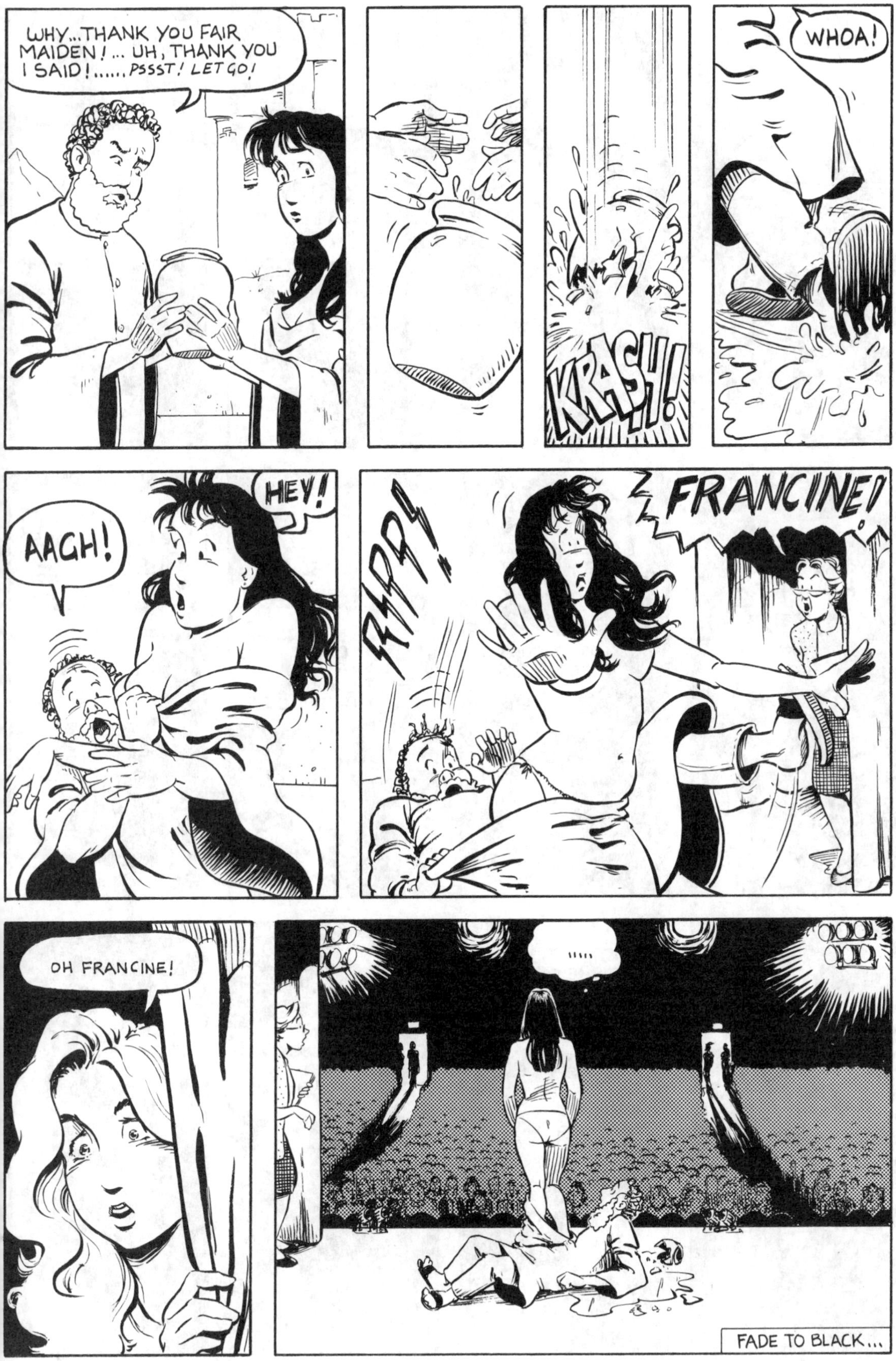
WHY...THANK YOU FAIR MAIDEN! ... UH, THANK YOU I SAID!...... PSSST! LET GO!
KRASH!
WHOA!
AAGH!
HEY!
RIPP!
FRANCINE!
OH FRANCINE!
.....
FADE TO BLACK...

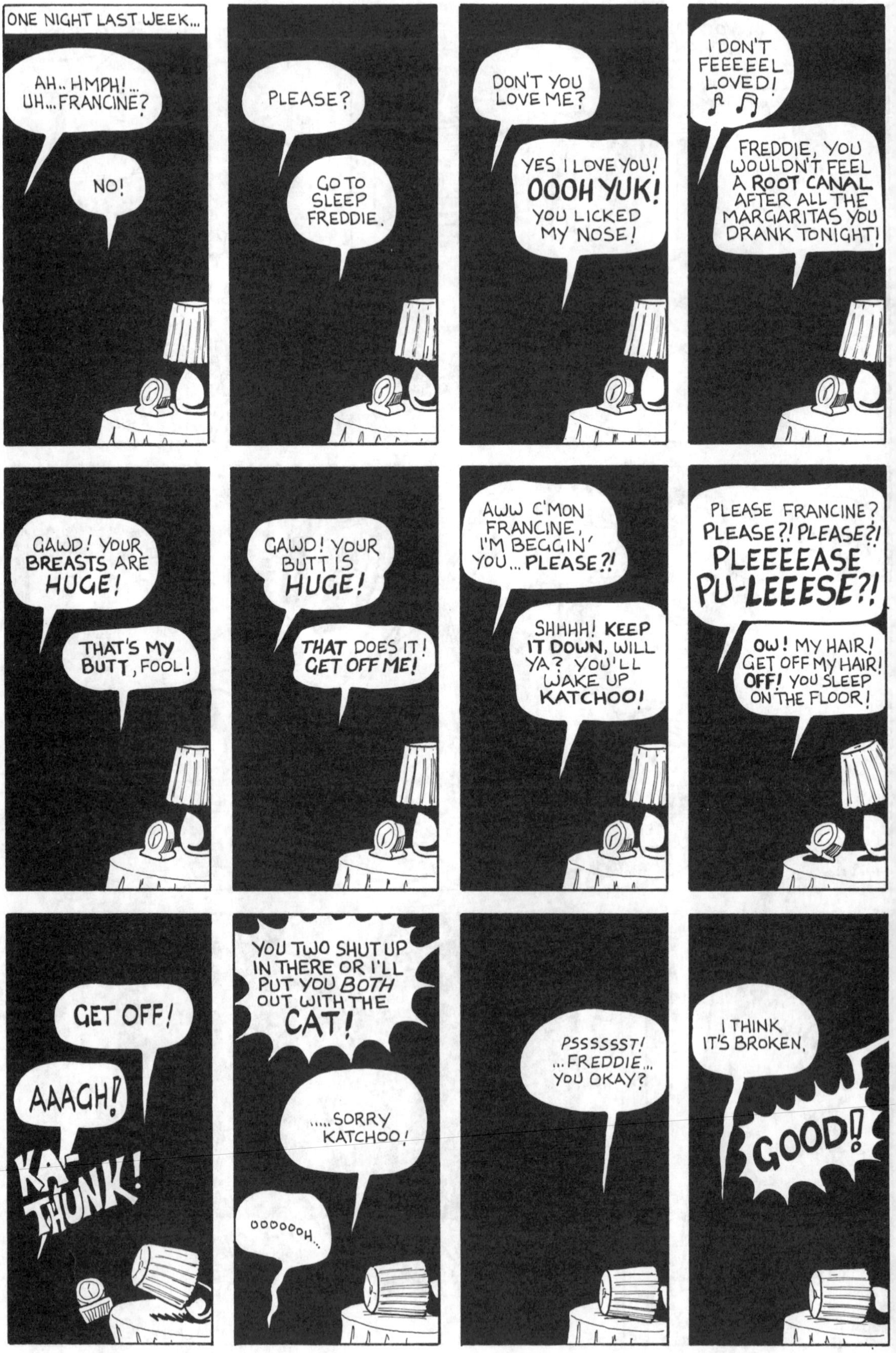

ONE NIGHT LAST WEEK...
AH.. HMPH!... UH... FRANCINE?
NO!
PLEASE?
GO TO SLEEP FREDDIE.
DON'T YOU LOVE ME?
YES I LOVE YOU! OOOH YUK! YOU LICKED MY NOSE!
I DON'T FEEEEEL LOVED!
FREDDIE, YOU WOULDN'T FEEL A ROOT CANAL AFTER ALL THE MARGARITAS YOU DRANK TONIGHT!
GAWD! YOUR BREASTS ARE HUGE!
THAT'S MY BUTT, FOOL!
GAWD! YOUR BUTT IS HUGE!
THAT DOES IT! GET OFF ME!
AWW C'MON FRANCINE, I'M BEGGIN' YOU... PLEASE?!
SHHHH! KEEP IT DOWN, WILL YA? YOU'LL WAKE UP KATCHOO!
PLEASE FRANCINE? PLEASE?! PLEASE?! PLEEEEASE PU-LEEESE?!
OW! MY HAIR! GET OFF MY HAIR! OFF! YOU SLEEP ON THE FLOOR!
GET OFF!
AAAGH!
KA-THUNK!
YOU TWO SHUT UP IN THERE OR I'LL PUT YOU BOTH OUT WITH THE CAT!
.....SORRY KATCHOO!
OOOOOOH...
PSSSSSST! ...FREDDIE... YOU OKAY?
I THINK IT'S BROKEN.
GOOD!!

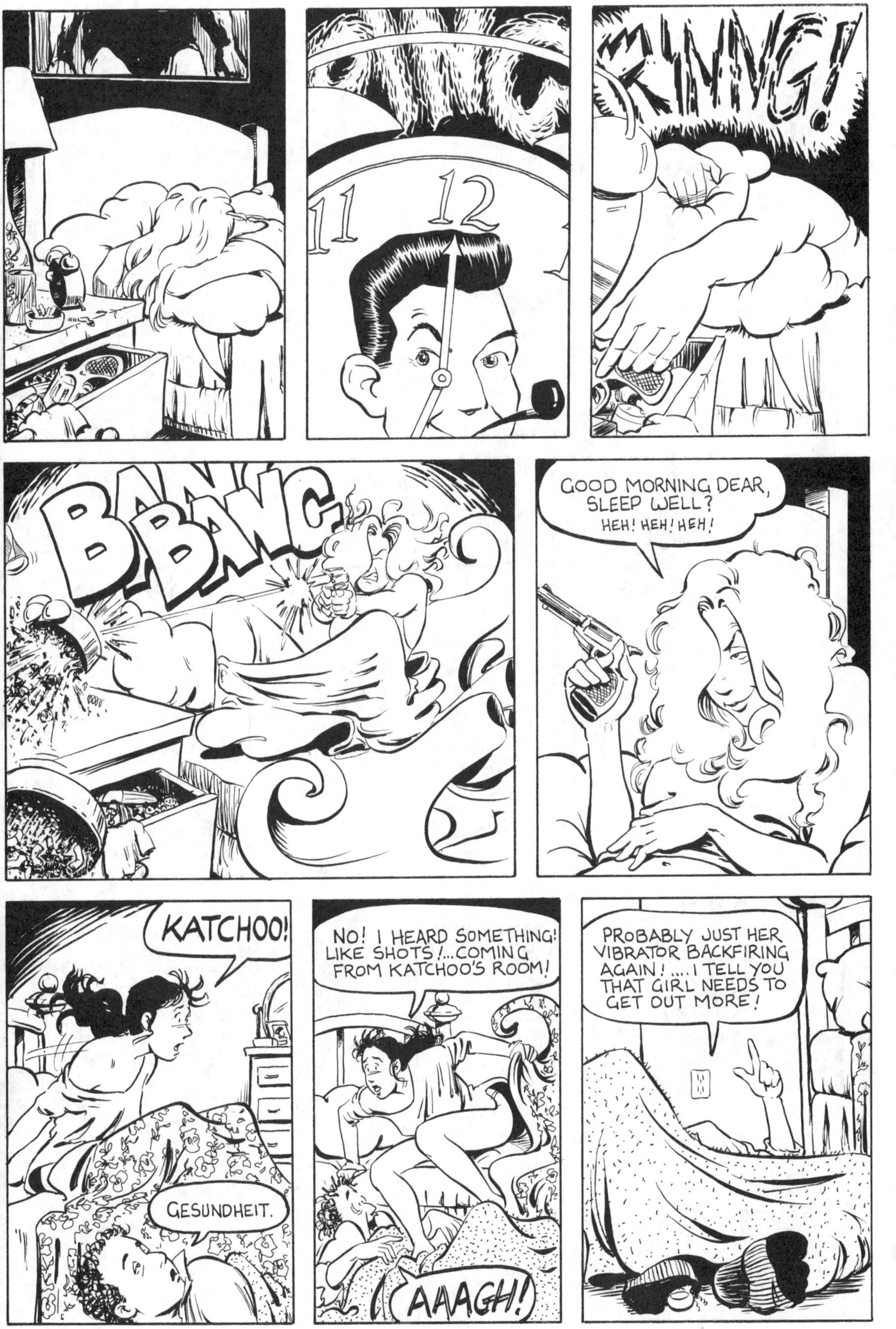
RING!
BANG BANG
GOOD MORNING DEAR, SLEEP WELL? HEH! HEH! HEH!
KATCHOO!
GESUNDHEIT.
NO! I HEARD SOMETHING! LIKE SHOTS!...COMING FROM KATCHOO'S ROOM!
AAAGH!
PROBABLY JUST HER VIBRATOR BACKFIRING AGAIN! ....I TELL YOU THAT GIRL NEEDS TO GET OUT MORE!

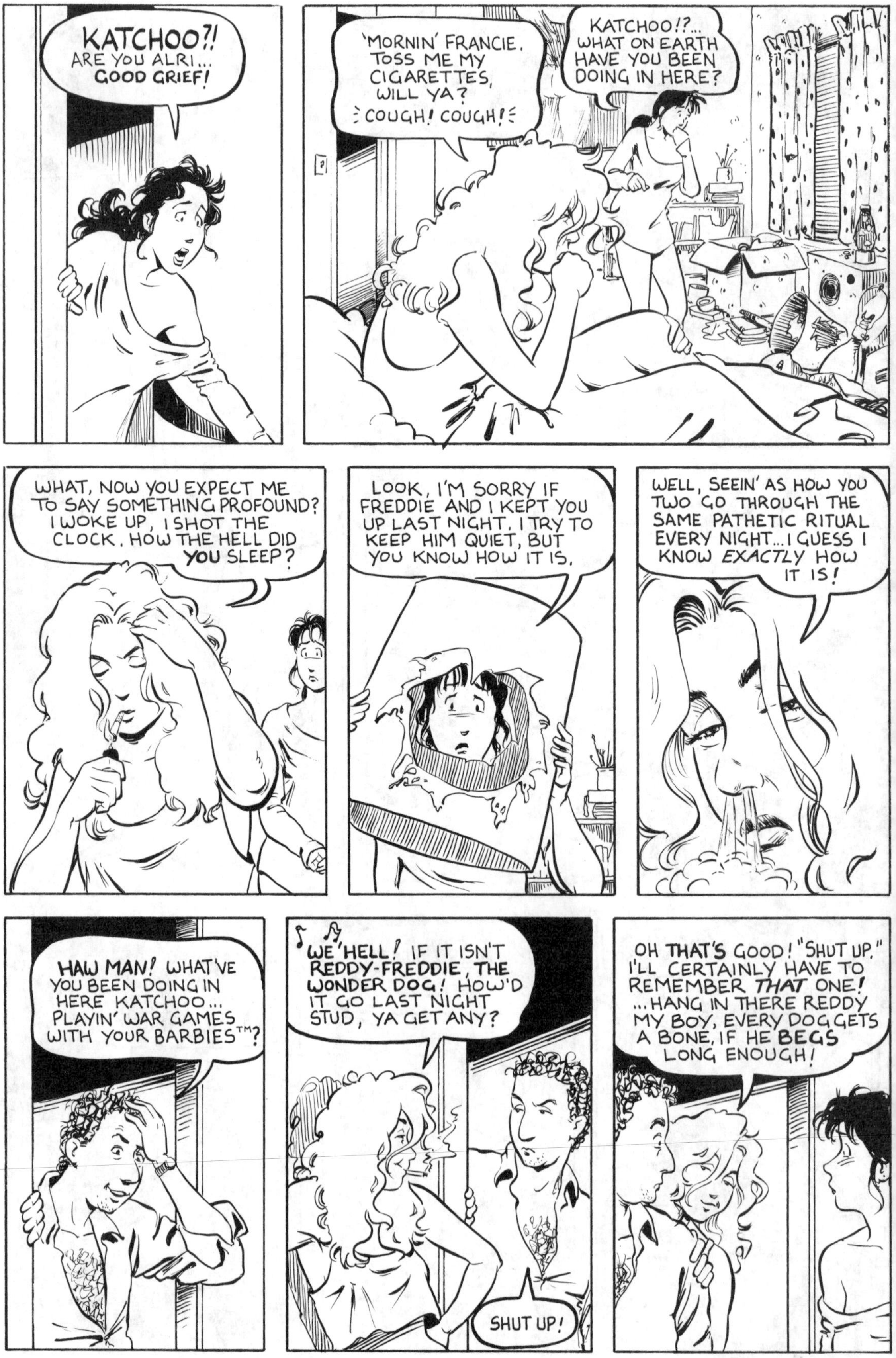
KATCHOO?! ARE YOU ALRI... GOOD GRIEF!
'MORNIN' FRANCIE. TOSS ME MY CIGARETTES, WILL YA? COUGH! COUGH!
KATCHOO!?... WHAT ON EARTH HAVE YOU BEEN DOING IN HERE?
WHAT, NOW YOU EXPECT ME TO SAY SOMETHING PROFOUND? I WOKE UP, I SHOT THE CLOCK. HOW THE HELL DID YOU SLEEP?
LOOK, I'M SORRY IF FREDDIE AND I KEPT YOU UP LAST NIGHT. I TRY TO KEEP HIM QUIET, BUT YOU KNOW HOW IT IS.
WELL, SEEIN' AS HOW YOU TWO GO THROUGH THE SAME PATHETIC RITUAL EVERY NIGHT... I GUESS I KNOW EXACTLY HOW IT IS!
HAW MAN! WHAT'VE YOU BEEN DOING IN HERE KATCHOO... PLAYIN' WAR GAMES WITH YOUR BARBIES™?
WE'HELL! IF IT ISN'T REDDY-FREDDIE, THE WONDER DOG! HOW'D IT GO LAST NIGHT STUD, YA GET ANY?
SHUT UP!
OH THAT'S GOOD! "SHUT UP." I'LL CERTAINLY HAVE TO REMEMBER THAT ONE! ...HANG IN THERE REDDY MY BOY, EVERY DOG GETS A BONE, IF HE BEGS LONG ENOUGH!

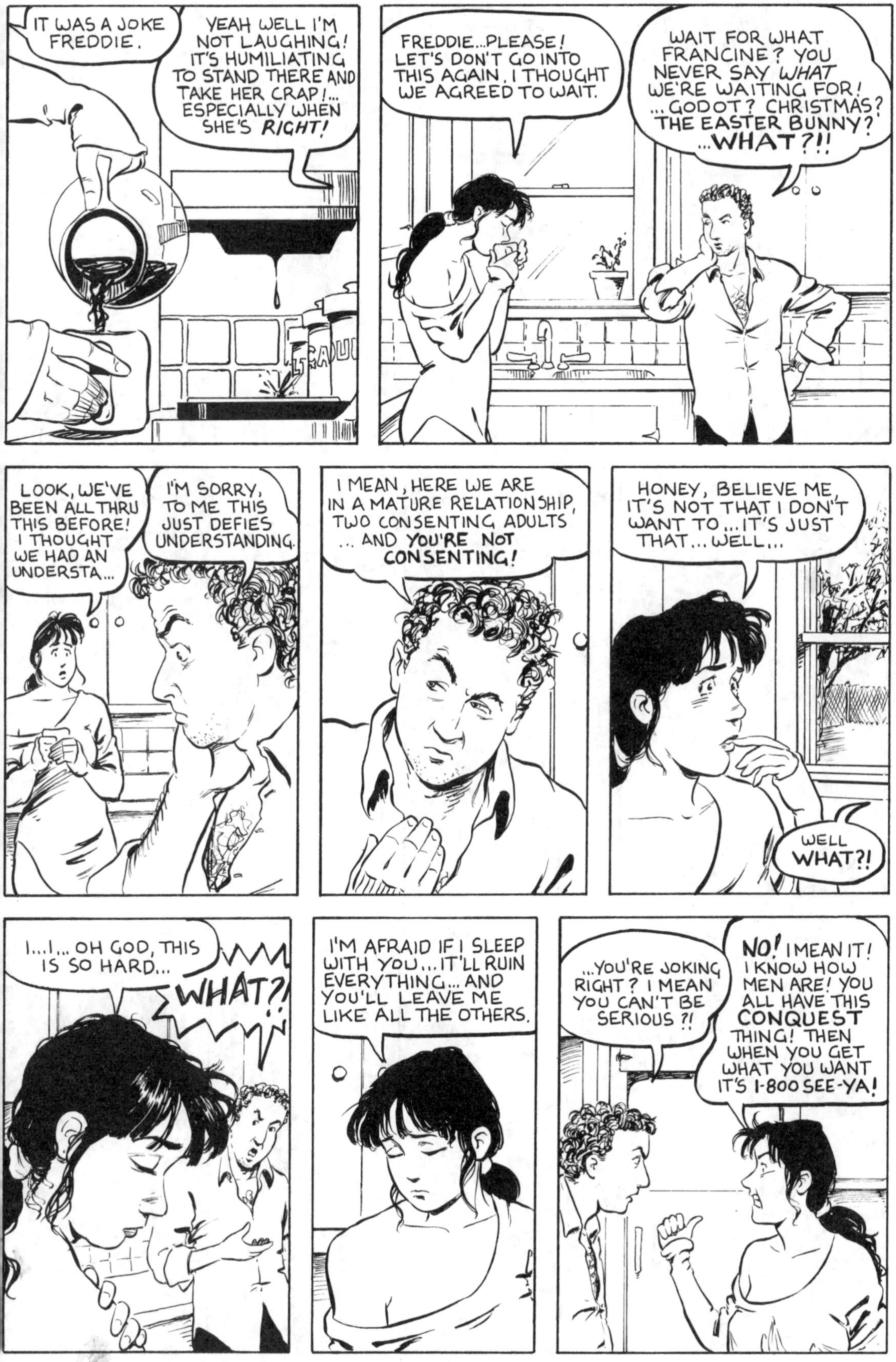
IT WAS A JOKE FREDDIE.
YEAH WELL I'M NOT LAUGHING! IT'S HUMILIATING TO STAND THERE AND TAKE HER CRAP!... ESPECIALLY WHEN SHE'S RIGHT!
FREDDIE...PLEASE! LET'S DON'T GO INTO THIS AGAIN. I THOUGHT WE AGREED TO WAIT.
WAIT FOR WHAT FRANCINE? YOU NEVER SAY WHAT WE'RE WAITING FOR! ...GODOT? CHRISTMAS? THE EASTER BUNNY? ...WHAT?!!
LOOK, WE'VE BEEN ALL THRU THIS BEFORE! I THOUGHT WE HAD AN UNDERSTA...
I'M SORRY, TO ME THIS JUST DEFIES UNDERSTANDING.
I MEAN, HERE WE ARE IN A MATURE RELATIONSHIP, TWO CONSENTING ADULTS ... AND YOU'RE NOT CONSENTING!
HONEY, BELIEVE ME, IT'S NOT THAT I DON'T WANT TO...IT'S JUST THAT...WELL...
WELL WHAT?!
I...I...OH GOD, THIS IS SO HARD...
WHAT?!
I'M AFRAID IF I SLEEP WITH YOU...IT'LL RUIN EVERYTHING... AND YOU'LL LEAVE ME LIKE ALL THE OTHERS.
...YOU'RE JOKING RIGHT? I MEAN YOU CAN'T BE SERIOUS?!
NO! I MEAN IT! I KNOW HOW MEN ARE! YOU ALL HAVE THIS CONQUEST THING! THEN WHEN YOU GET WHAT YOU WANT IT'S 1-800 SEE-YA!

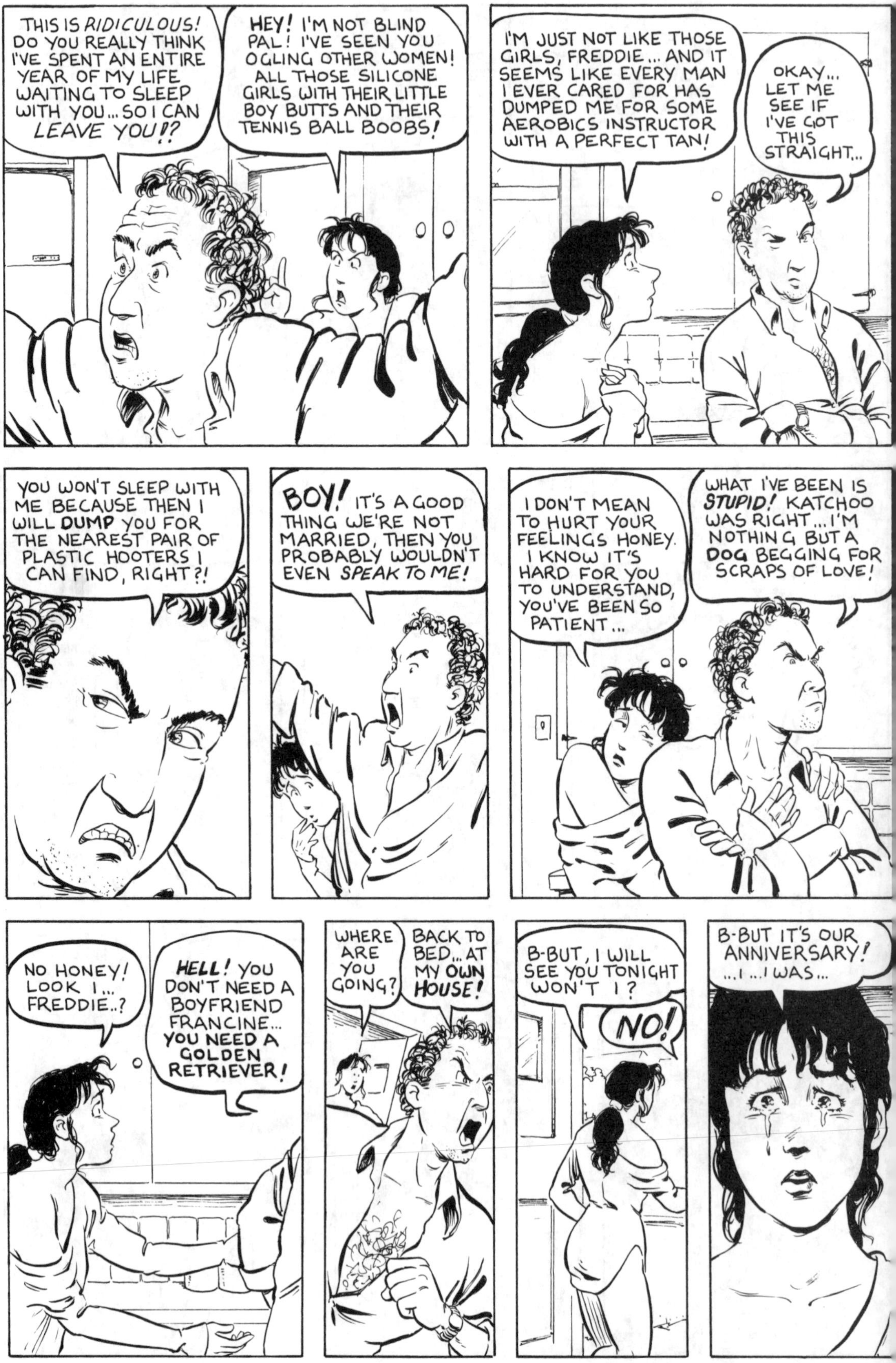
THIS IS RIDICULOUS! DO YOU REALLY THINK I'VE SPENT AN ENTIRE YEAR OF MY LIFE WAITING TO SLEEP WITH YOU... SO I CAN LEAVE YOU!?
HEY! I'M NOT BLIND PAL! I'VE SEEN YOU OGLING OTHER WOMEN! ALL THOSE SILICONE GIRLS WITH THEIR LITTLE BOY BUTTS AND THEIR TENNIS BALL BOOBS!
I'M JUST NOT LIKE THOSE GIRLS, FREDDIE... AND IT SEEMS LIKE EVERY MAN I EVER CARED FOR HAS DUMPED ME FOR SOME AEROBICS INSTRUCTOR WITH A PERFECT TAN!
OKAY... LET ME SEE IF I'VE GOT THIS STRAIGHT...
YOU WON'T SLEEP WITH ME BECAUSE THEN I WILL DUMP YOU FOR THE NEAREST PAIR OF PLASTIC HOOTERS I CAN FIND, RIGHT?!
BOY! IT'S A GOOD THING WE'RE NOT MARRIED, THEN YOU PROBABLY WOULDN'T EVEN SPEAK TO ME!
I DON'T MEAN TO HURT YOUR FEELINGS HONEY. I KNOW IT'S HARD FOR YOU TO UNDERSTAND, YOU'VE BEEN SO PATIENT...
WHAT I'VE BEEN IS STUPID! KATCHOO WAS RIGHT... I'M NOTHING BUT A DOG BEGGING FOR SCRAPS OF LOVE!
NO HONEY! LOOK I... FREDDIE..?
HELL! YOU DON'T NEED A BOYFRIEND FRANCINE... YOU NEED A GOLDEN RETRIEVER!
WHERE ARE YOU GOING?
BACK TO BED... AT MY OWN HOUSE!
B-BUT, I WILL SEE YOU TONIGHT WON'T I?
NO!
B-BUT IT'S OUR ANNIVERSARY! ...I ...I WAS...

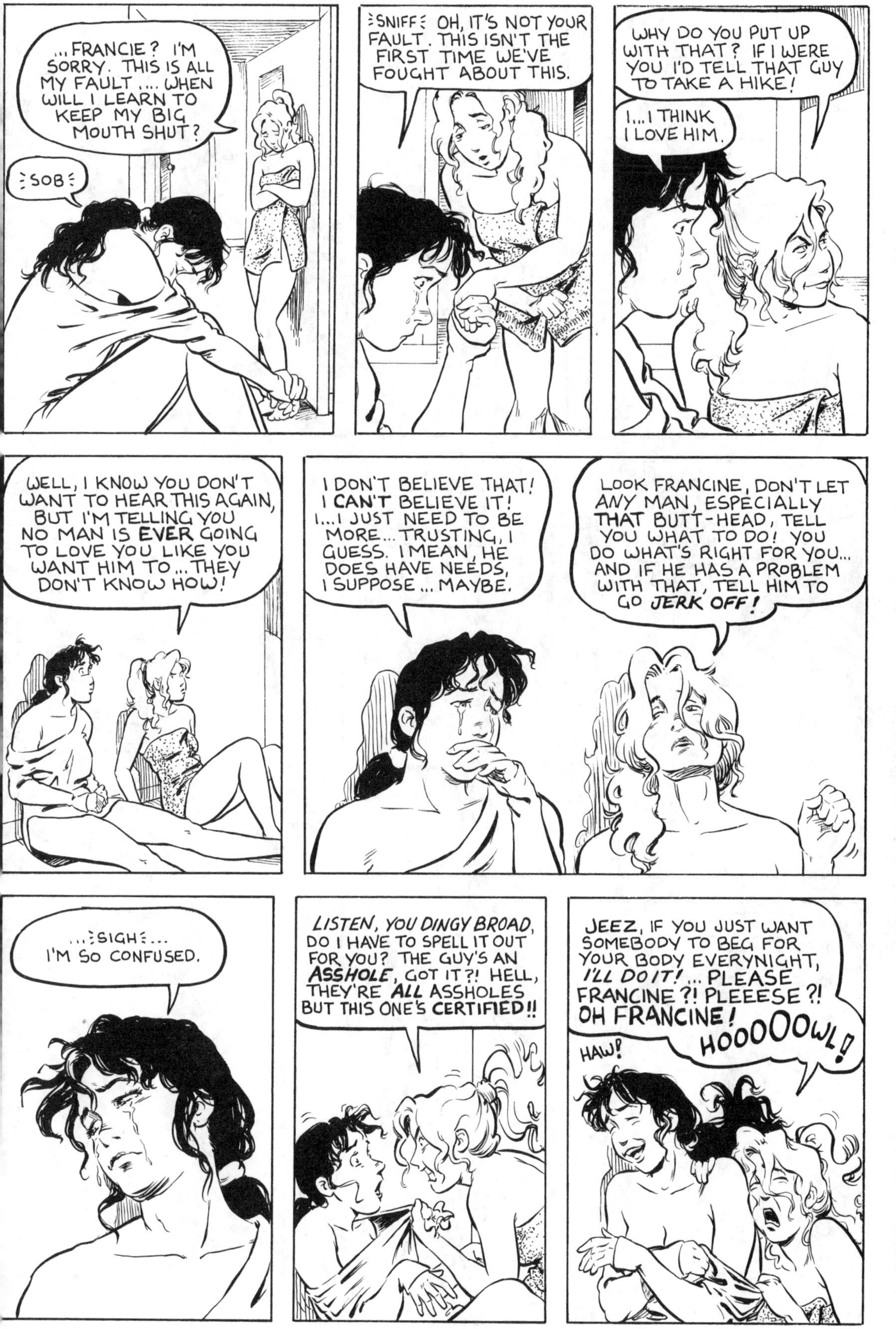
...FRANCIE? I'M SORRY. THIS IS ALL MY FAULT.... WHEN WILL I LEARN TO KEEP MY BIG MOUTH SHUT?
SOB
SNIFF OH, IT'S NOT YOUR FAULT. THIS ISN'T THE FIRST TIME WE'VE FOUGHT ABOUT THIS.
WHY DO YOU PUT UP WITH THAT? IF I WERE YOU I'D TELL THAT GUY TO TAKE A HIKE!
I...I THINK I LOVE HIM.
WELL, I KNOW YOU DON'T WANT TO HEAR THIS AGAIN, BUT I'M TELLING YOU NO MAN IS EVER GOING TO LOVE YOU LIKE YOU WANT HIM TO... THEY DON'T KNOW HOW!
I DON'T BELIEVE THAT! I CAN'T BELIEVE IT! I...I JUST NEED TO BE MORE... TRUSTING, I GUESS. I MEAN, HE DOES HAVE NEEDS, I SUPPOSE... MAYBE.
LOOK FRANCINE, DON'T LET ANY MAN, ESPECIALLY THAT BUTT-HEAD, TELL YOU WHAT TO DO! YOU DO WHAT'S RIGHT FOR YOU... AND IF HE HAS A PROBLEM WITH THAT, TELL HIM TO GO JERK OFF!
...SIGH... I'M SO CONFUSED.
LISTEN, YOU DINGY BROAD, DO I HAVE TO SPELL IT OUT FOR YOU? THE GUY'S AN ASSHOLE, GOT IT?! HELL, THEY'RE ALL ASSHOLES BUT THIS ONE'S CERTIFIED!!
JEEZ, IF YOU JUST WANT SOMEBODY TO BEG FOR YOUR BODY EVERYNIGHT, I'LL DO IT! ... PLEASE FRANCINE?! PLEEESE?! OH FRANCINE! HOOOOOWL!
HAW!

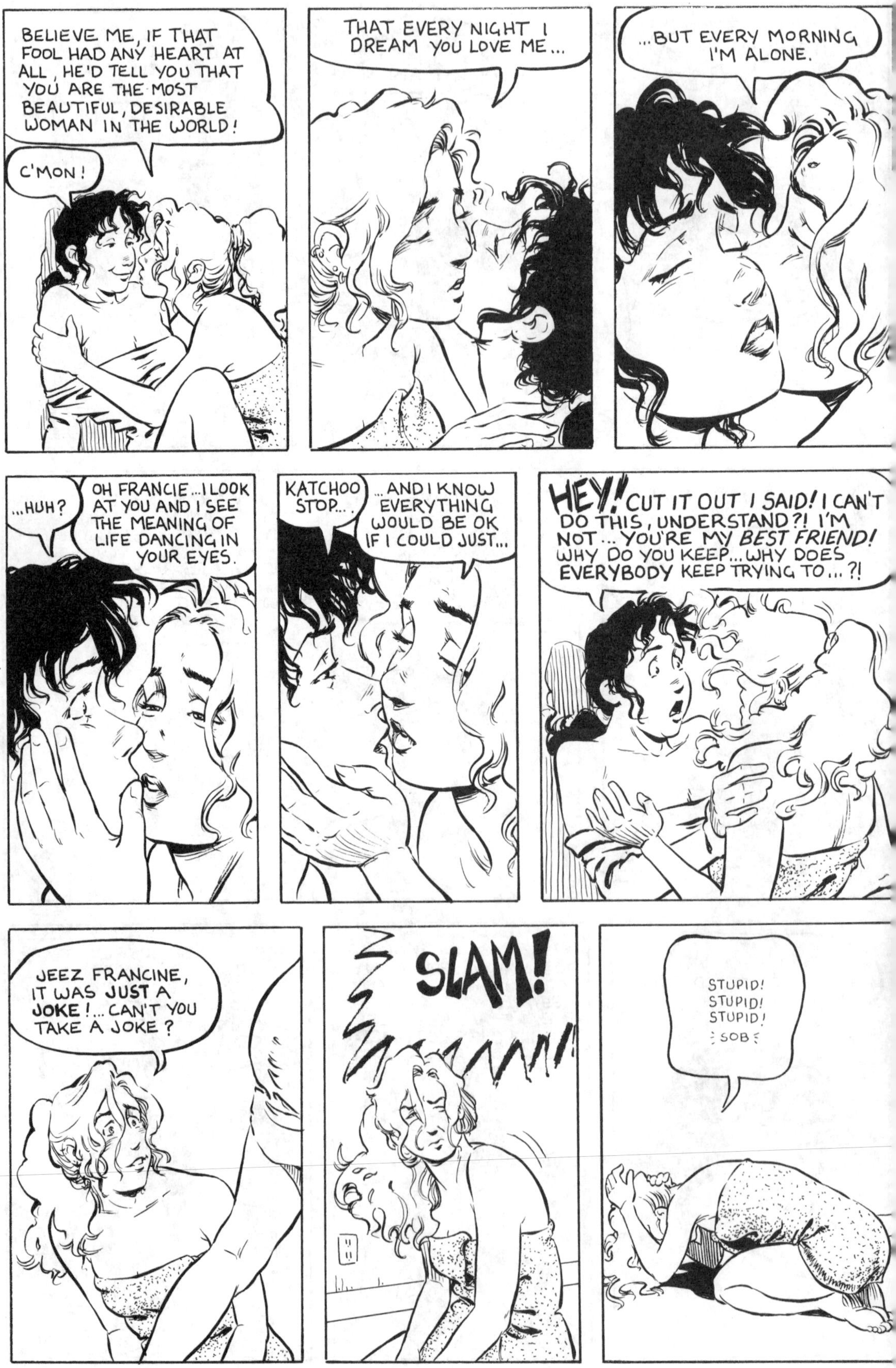
BELIEVE ME, IF THAT FOOL HAD ANY HEART AT ALL, HE'D TELL YOU THAT YOU ARE THE MOST BEAUTIFUL, DESIRABLE WOMAN IN THE WORLD!
C'MON!
THAT EVERY NIGHT I DREAM YOU LOVE ME...
...BUT EVERY MORNING I'M ALONE.
...HUH?
OH FRANCIE...I LOOK AT YOU AND I SEE THE MEANING OF LIFE DANCING IN YOUR EYES.
KATCHOO STOP...
...AND I KNOW EVERYTHING WOULD BE OK IF I COULD JUST...
HEY! CUT IT OUT I SAID! I CAN'T DO THIS, UNDERSTAND?! I'M NOT... YOU'RE MY BEST FRIEND! WHY DO YOU KEEP... WHY DOES EVERYBODY KEEP TRYING TO...?!
JEEZ FRANCINE, IT WAS JUST A JOKE!... CAN'T YOU TAKE A JOKE?
SLAM!
STUPID! STUPID! STUPID!
SOB

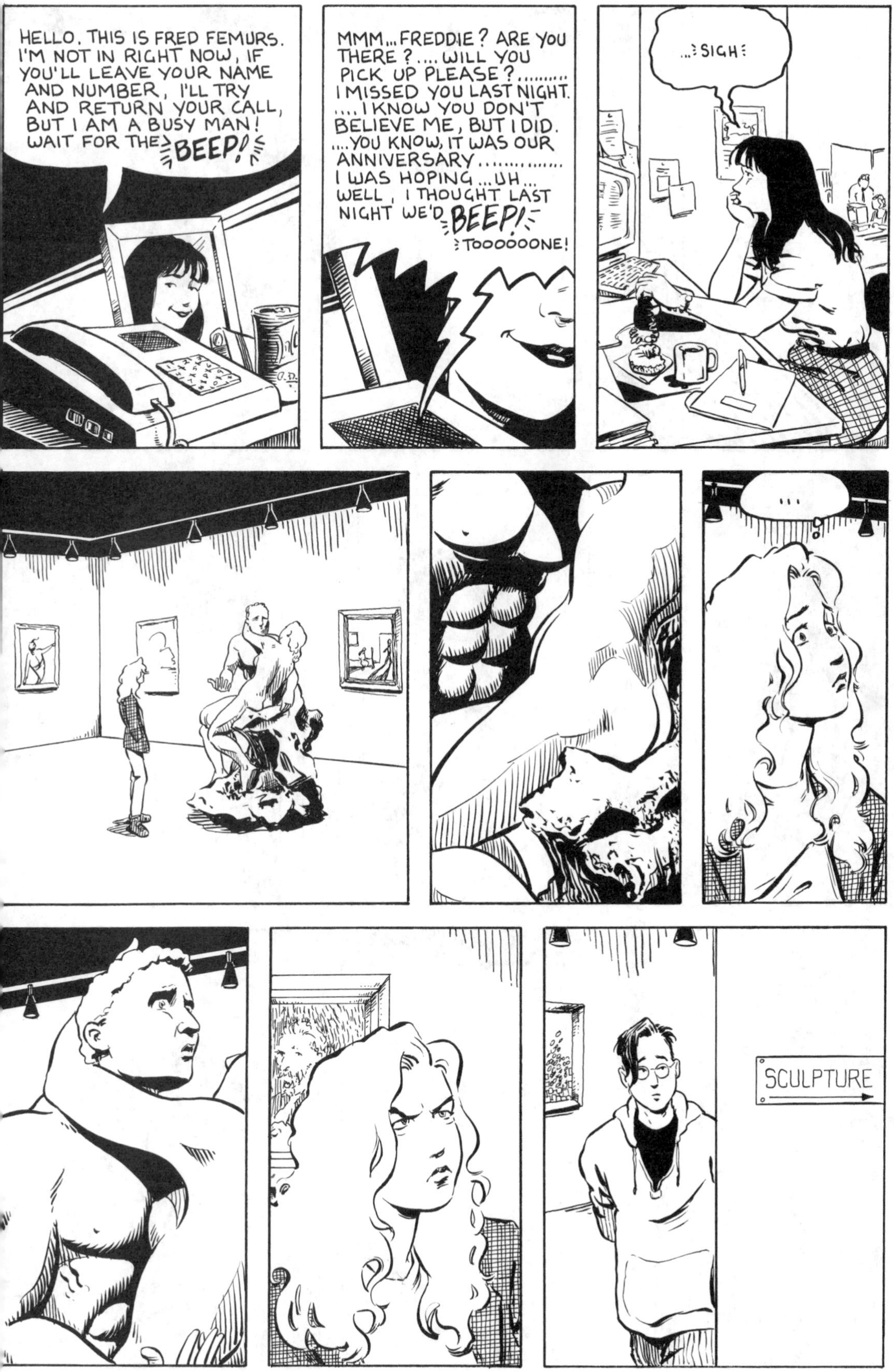
HELLO, THIS IS FRED FEMURS. I'M NOT IN RIGHT NOW, IF YOU'LL LEAVE YOUR NAME AND NUMBER, I'LL TRY AND RETURN YOUR CALL, BUT I AM A BUSY MAN! WAIT FOR THE BEEP!
MMM... FREDDIE? ARE YOU THERE?.... WILL YOU PICK UP PLEASE?.......... I MISSED YOU LAST NIGHT. .... I KNOW YOU DON'T BELIEVE ME, BUT I DID. ....YOU KNOW, IT WAS OUR ANNIVERSARY............... I WAS HOPING ... UH ... WELL, I THOUGHT LAST NIGHT WE'D BEEP!
TOOOOOONE!
...SIGH
...
SCULPTURE

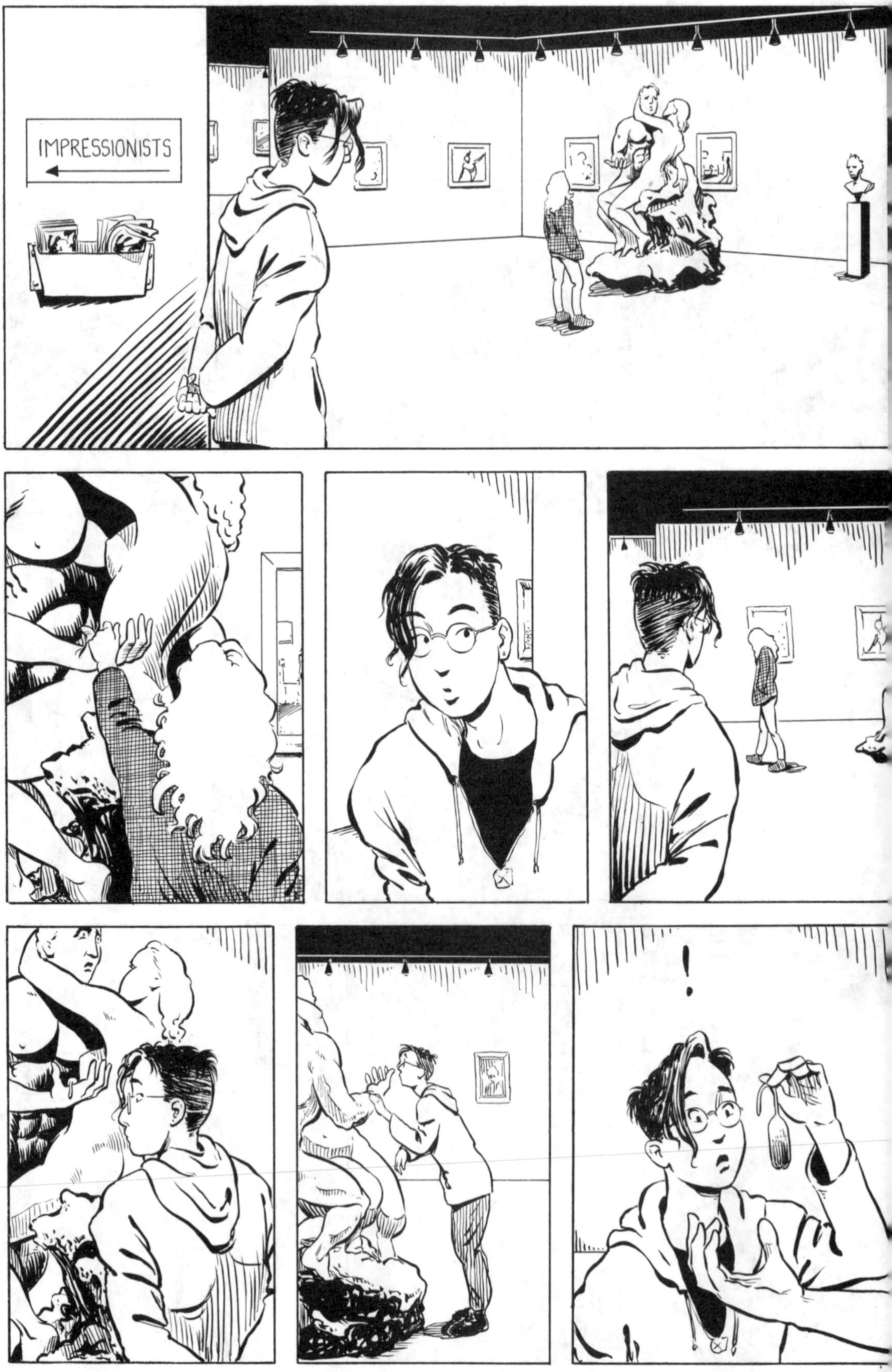
IMPRESSIONISTS
!

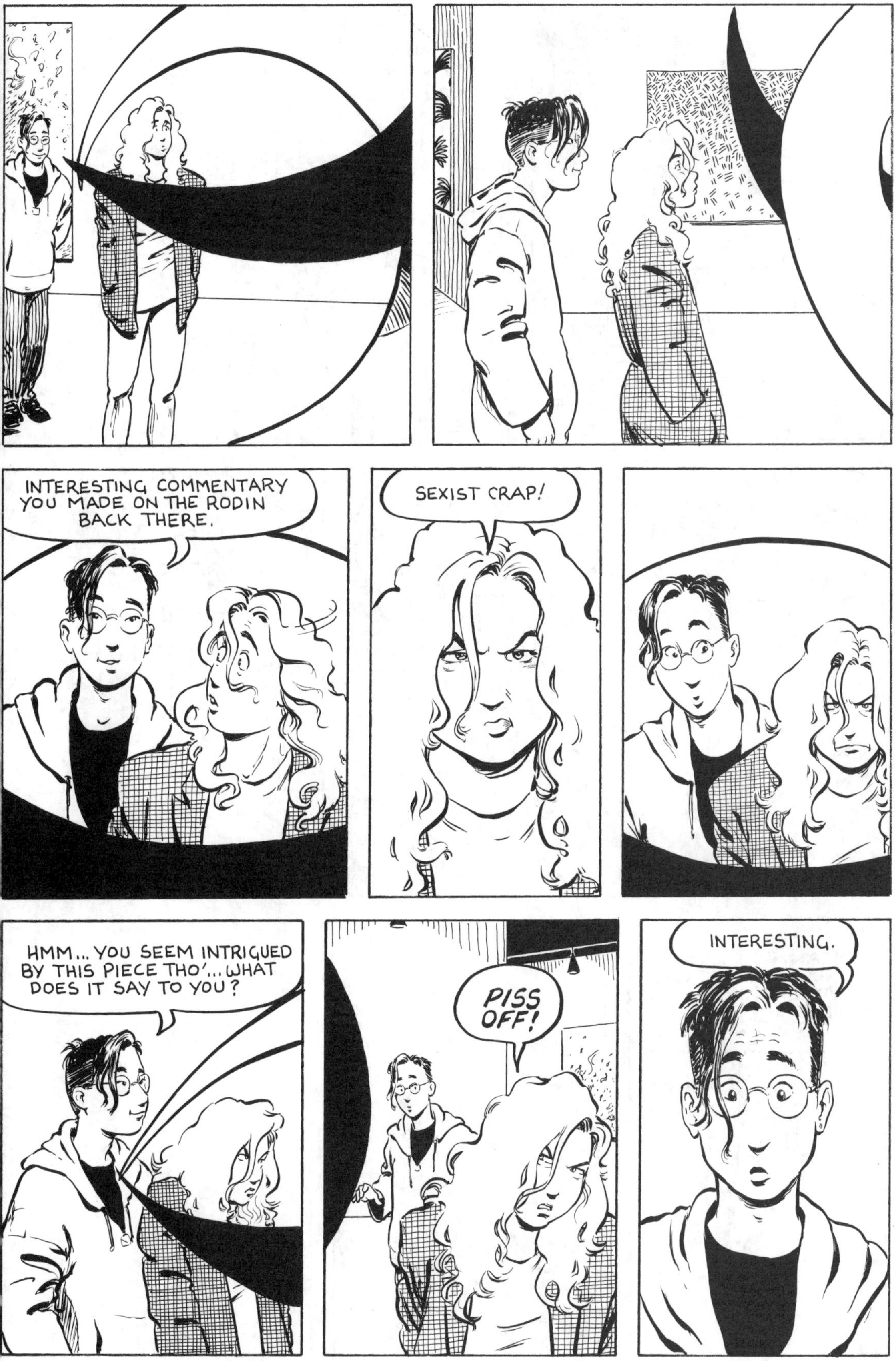
INTERESTING COMMENTARY YOU MADE ON THE RODIN BACK THERE.
SEXIST CRAP!
HMM... YOU SEEM INTRIGUED BY THIS PIECE THO'... WHAT DOES IT SAY TO YOU?
PISS OFF!
INTERESTING.

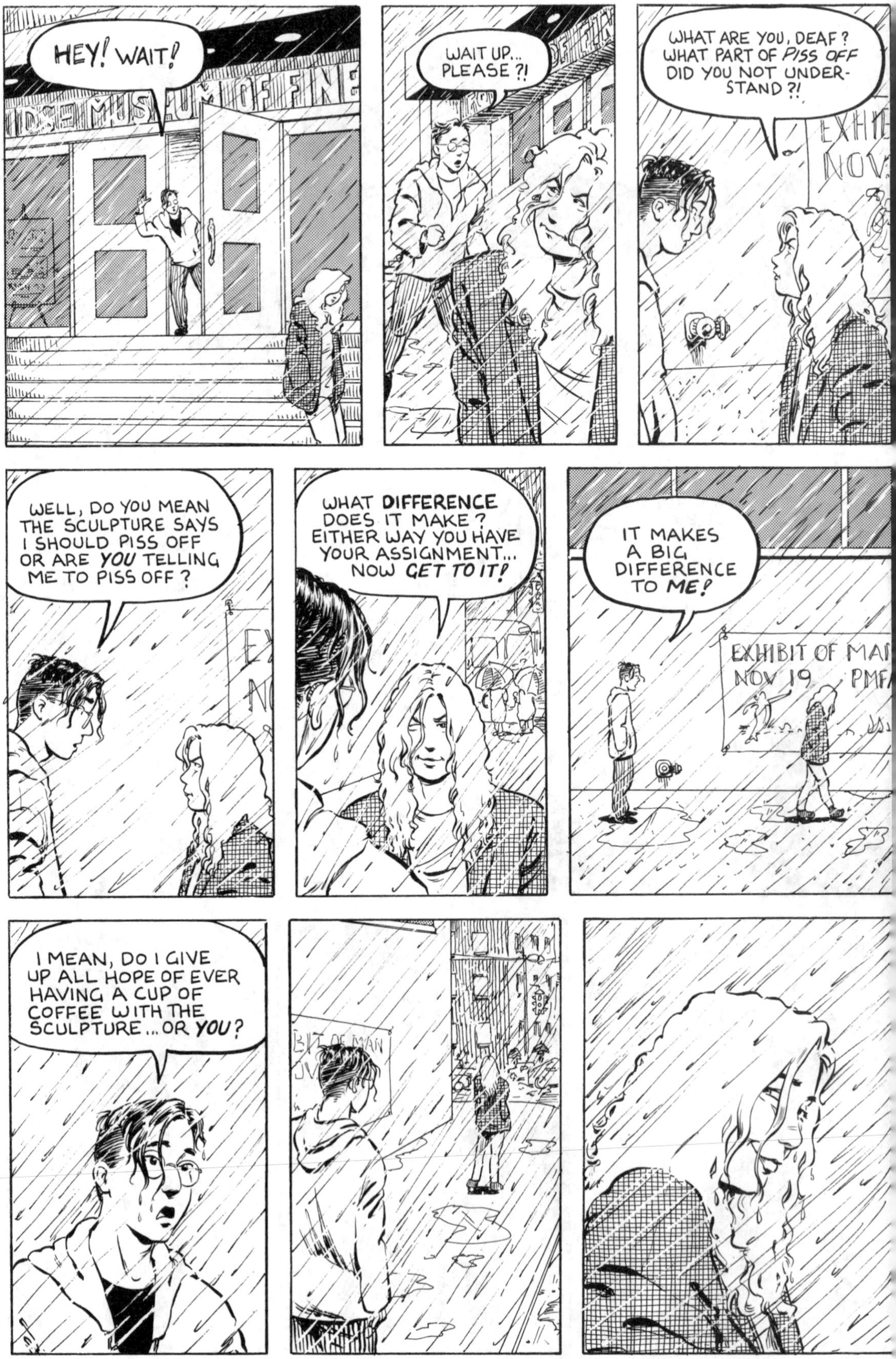
HEY! WAIT!
WAIT UP... PLEASE?!
WHAT ARE YOU, DEAF? WHAT PART OF PISS OFF DID YOU NOT UNDERSTAND?!
WELL, DO YOU MEAN THE SCULPTURE SAYS I SHOULD PISS OFF OR ARE YOU TELLING ME TO PISS OFF?
WHAT DIFFERENCE DOES IT MAKE? EITHER WAY YOU HAVE YOUR ASSIGNMENT... NOW GET TO IT!
IT MAKES A BIG DIFFERENCE TO ME!
EXHIBIT OF MA
NOV 19 PMF
I MEAN, DO I GIVE UP ALL HOPE OF EVER HAVING A CUP OF COFFEE WITH THE SCULPTURE... OR YOU?

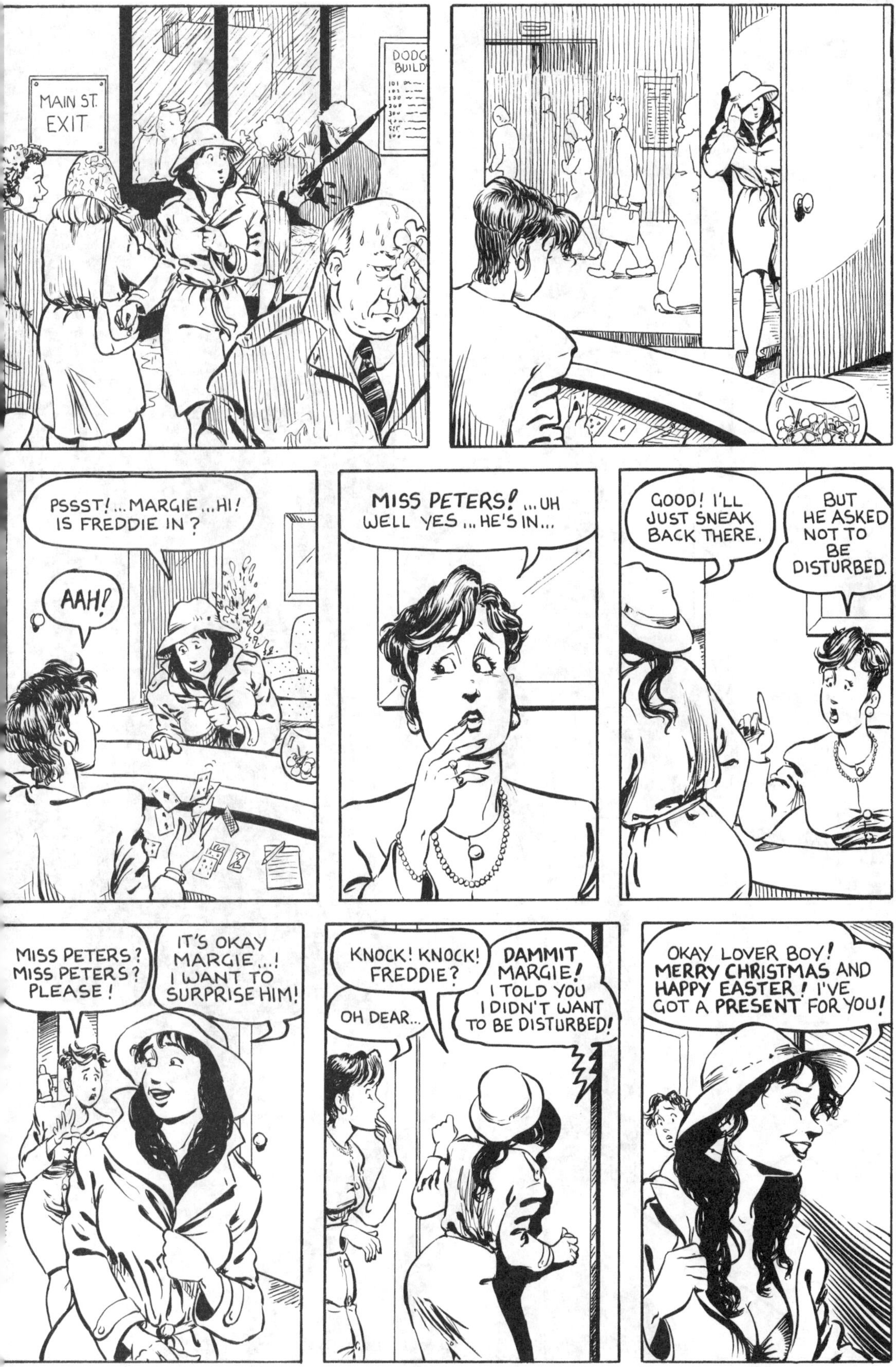
MAIN ST. EXIT
PSSST! ... MARGIE ... HI! IS FREDDIE IN?
AAH!
MISS PETERS! ... UH WELL YES ... HE'S IN...
GOOD! I'LL JUST SNEAK BACK THERE.
BUT HE ASKED NOT TO BE DISTURBED.
MISS PETERS? MISS PETERS? PLEASE!
IT'S OKAY MARGIE...! I WANT TO SURPRISE HIM!
KNOCK! KNOCK! FREDDIE?
OH DEAR...
DAMMIT MARGIE! I TOLD YOU I DIDN'T WANT TO BE DISTURBED!
OKAY LOVER BOY! MERRY CHRISTMAS AND HAPPY EASTER! I'VE GOT A PRESENT FOR YOU!

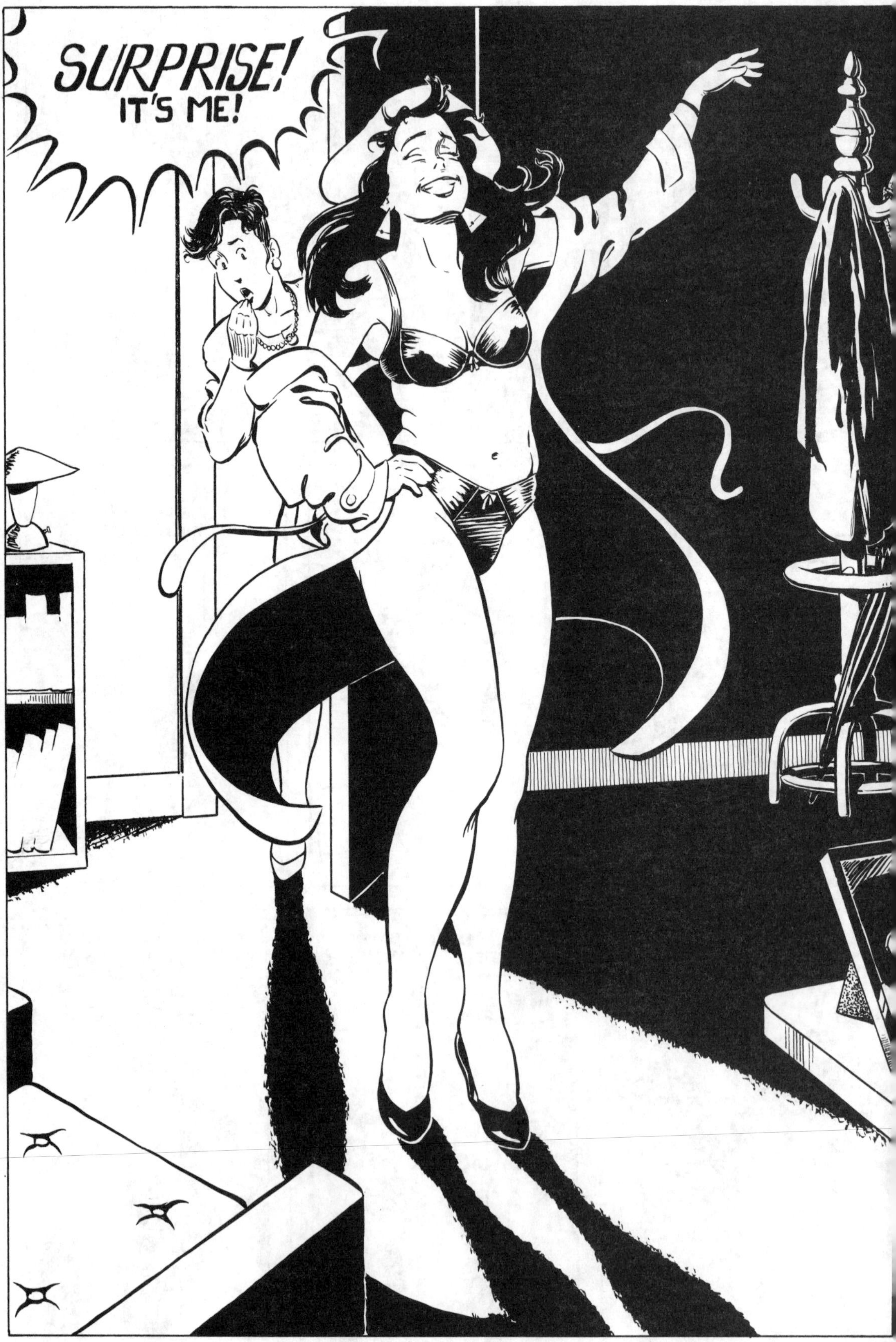
SURPRISE! IT'S ME!

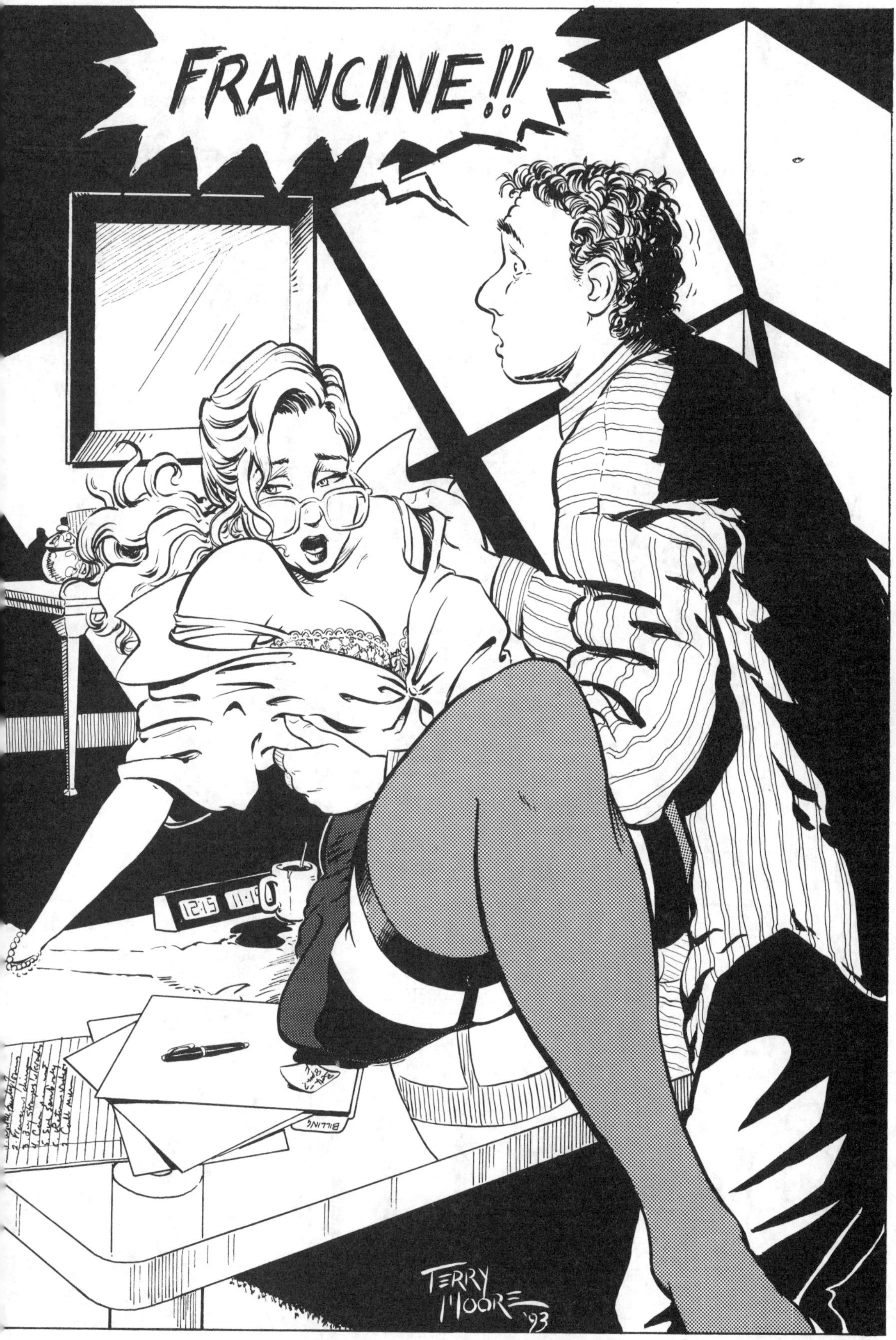
FRANCINE!!
12:15
BILLING
TERRY MOORE '93

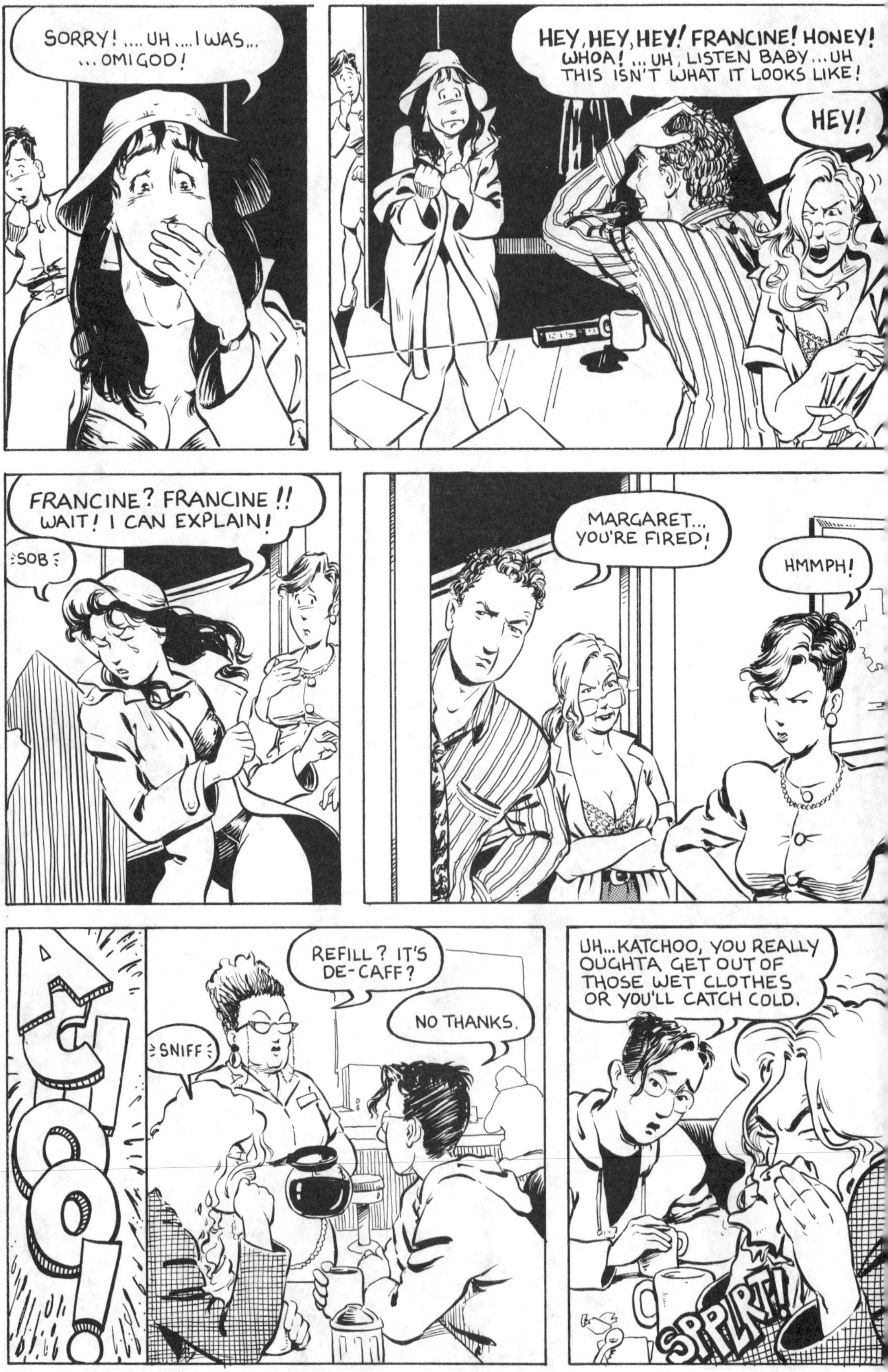
SORRY! .... UH .... I WAS... ... OMIGOD!
HEY, HEY, HEY! FRANCINE! HONEY! WHOA! ... UH, LISTEN BABY ... UH THIS ISN'T WHAT IT LOOKS LIKE!
HEY!
FRANCINE? FRANCINE!! WAIT! I CAN EXPLAIN!
SOB
MARGARET... YOU'RE FIRED!
HMMPH!
ACHOO!
REFILL? IT'S DE-CAFF?
SNIFF
NO THANKS.
UH...KATCHOO, YOU REALLY OUGHTA GET OUT OF THOSE WET CLOTHES OR YOU'LL CATCH COLD.
SPPLRT!

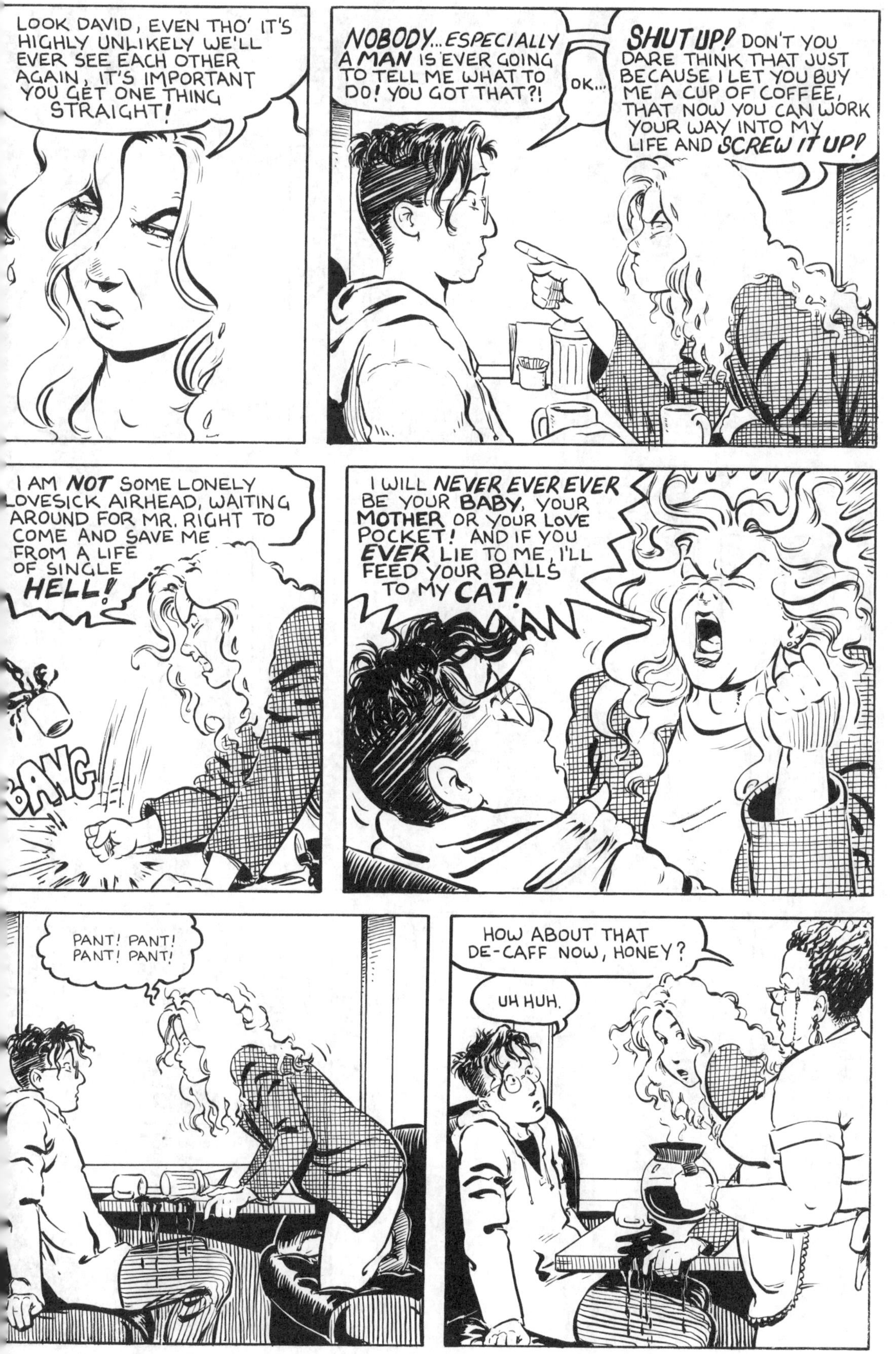
LOOK DAVID, EVEN THO' IT'S HIGHLY UNLIKELY WE'LL EVER SEE EACH OTHER AGAIN, IT'S IMPORTANT YOU GET ONE THING STRAIGHT!
NOBODY...ESPECIALLY A MAN IS EVER GOING TO TELL ME WHAT TO DO! YOU GOT THAT?!
OK...
SHUT UP! DON'T YOU DARE THINK THAT JUST BECAUSE I LET YOU BUY ME A CUP OF COFFEE, THAT NOW YOU CAN WORK YOUR WAY INTO MY LIFE AND SCREW IT UP!
I AM NOT SOME LONELY LOVESICK AIRHEAD, WAITING AROUND FOR MR. RIGHT TO COME AND SAVE ME FROM A LIFE OF SINGLE HELL!
BANG
I WILL NEVER EVER EVER BE YOUR BABY, YOUR MOTHER OR YOUR LOVE POCKET! AND IF YOU EVER LIE TO ME, I'LL FEED YOUR BALLS TO MY CAT!
PANT! PANT! PANT! PANT!
HOW ABOUT THAT DE-CAFF NOW, HONEY?
UH HUH.

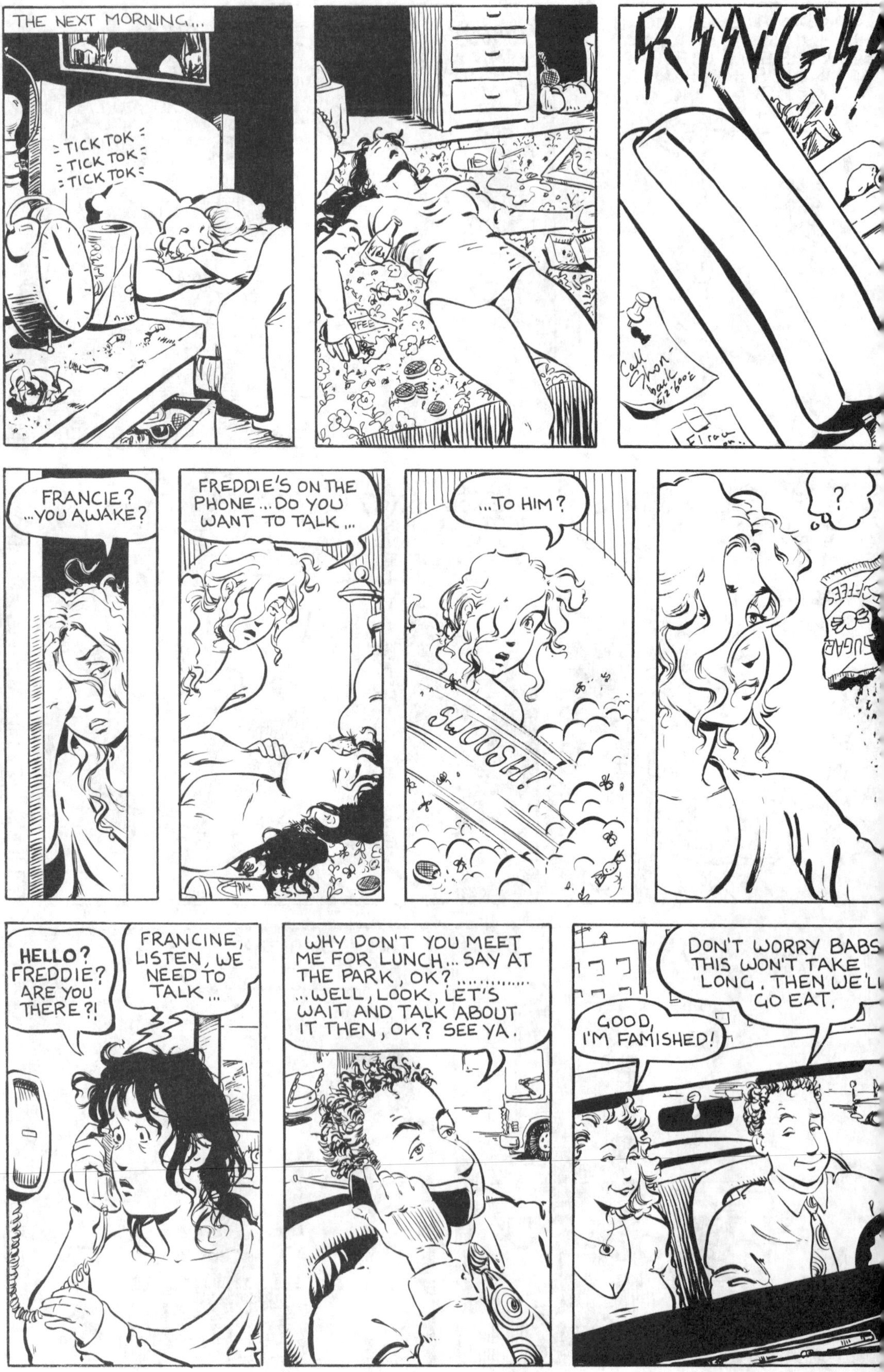

THE NEXT MORNING...
TICK TOK
TICK TOK
TICK TOK
RING!!
FRANCIE? ...YOU AWAKE?
FREDDIE'S ON THE PHONE... DO YOU WANT TO TALK...
...TO HIM?
SWOOSH!
?
SUGAR
HELLO? FREDDIE? ARE YOU THERE?!
FRANCINE, LISTEN, WE NEED TO TALK...
WHY DON'T YOU MEET ME FOR LUNCH... SAY AT THE PARK, OK? ....WELL, LOOK, LET'S WAIT AND TALK ABOUT IT THEN, OK? SEE YA.
DON'T WORRY BABS THIS WON'T TAKE LONG. THEN WE'LL GO EAT.
GOOD, I'M FAMISHED!

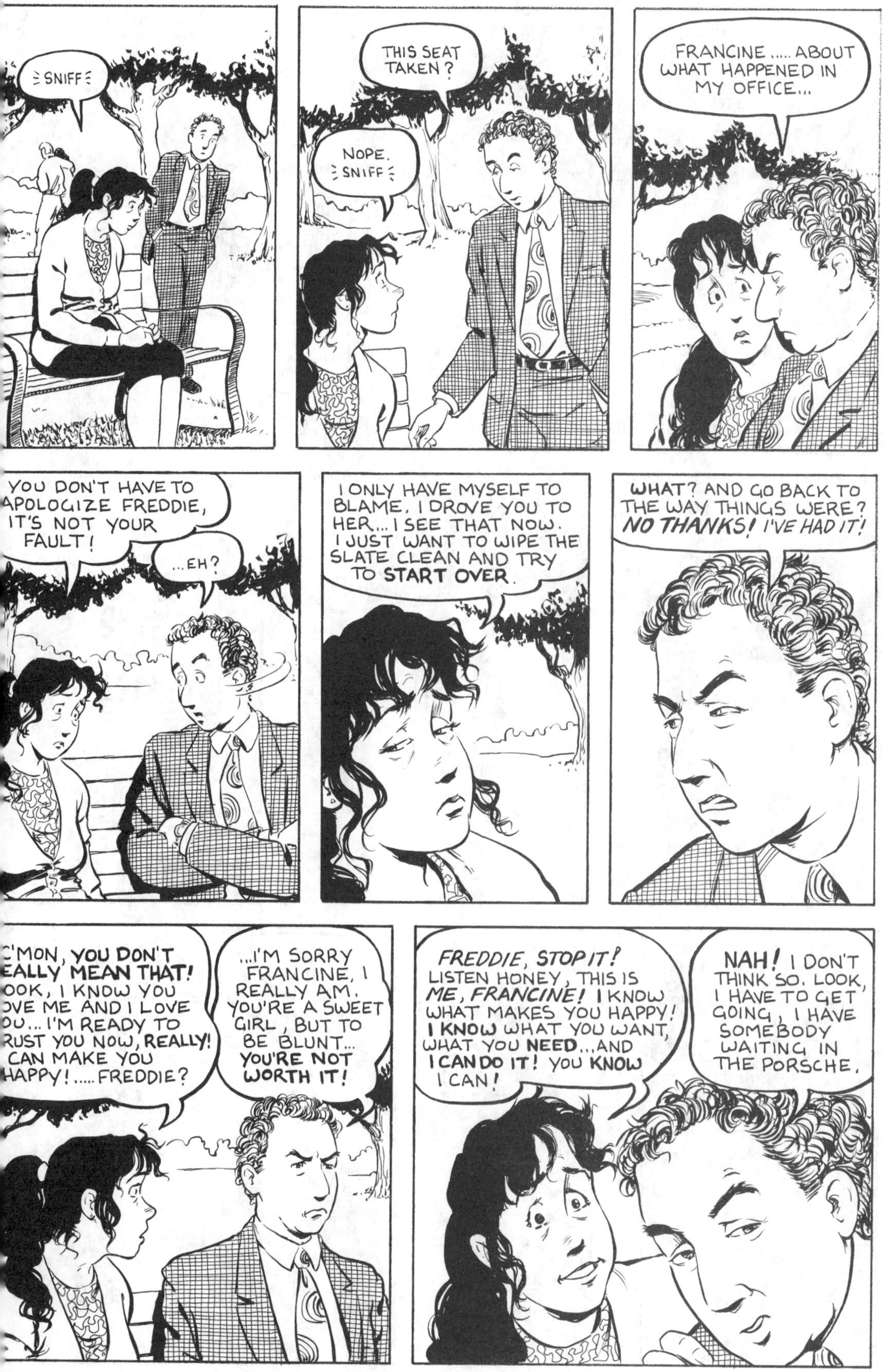
SNIFF
THIS SEAT TAKEN?
NOPE. SNIFF
FRANCINE..... ABOUT WHAT HAPPENED IN MY OFFICE...
YOU DON'T HAVE TO APOLOGIZE FREDDIE, IT'S NOT YOUR FAULT!
...EH?
I ONLY HAVE MYSELF TO BLAME. I DROVE YOU TO HER... I SEE THAT NOW. I JUST WANT TO WIPE THE SLATE CLEAN AND TRY TO START OVER.
WHAT? AND GO BACK TO THE WAY THINGS WERE? NO THANKS! I'VE HAD IT!
C'MON, YOU DON'T REALLY MEAN THAT! LOOK, I KNOW YOU LOVE ME AND I LOVE YOU... I'M READY TO TRUST YOU NOW, REALLY! I CAN MAKE YOU HAPPY!..... FREDDIE?
...I'M SORRY FRANCINE, I REALLY AM. YOU'RE A SWEET GIRL, BUT TO BE BLUNT... YOU'RE NOT WORTH IT!
FREDDIE, STOP IT! LISTEN HONEY, THIS IS ME, FRANCINE! I KNOW WHAT MAKES YOU HAPPY! I KNOW WHAT YOU WANT, WHAT YOU NEED... AND I CAN DO IT! YOU KNOW I CAN!
NAH! I DON'T THINK SO. LOOK, I HAVE TO GET GOING, I HAVE SOMEBODY WAITING IN THE PORSCHE.

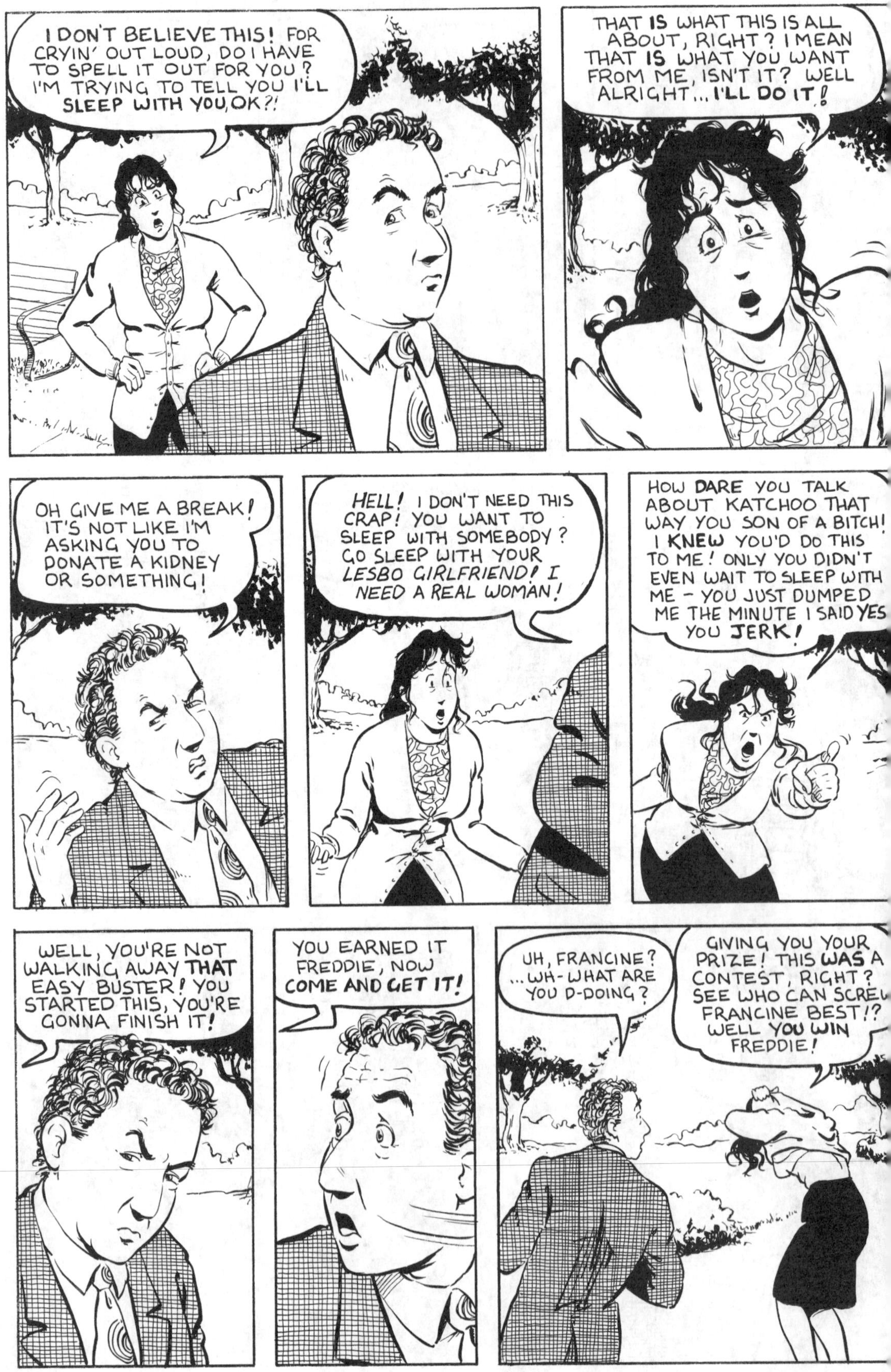
I DON'T BELIEVE THIS! FOR CRYIN' OUT LOUD, DO I HAVE TO SPELL IT OUT FOR YOU? I'M TRYING TO TELL YOU I'LL SLEEP WITH YOU, OK?!
THAT IS WHAT THIS IS ALL ABOUT, RIGHT? I MEAN THAT IS WHAT YOU WANT FROM ME, ISN'T IT? WELL ALRIGHT... I'LL DO IT!
OH GIVE ME A BREAK! IT'S NOT LIKE I'M ASKING YOU TO DONATE A KIDNEY OR SOMETHING!
HELL! I DON'T NEED THIS CRAP! YOU WANT TO SLEEP WITH SOMEBODY? GO SLEEP WITH YOUR LESBO GIRLFRIEND! I NEED A REAL WOMAN!
HOW DARE YOU TALK ABOUT KATCHOO THAT WAY YOU SON OF A BITCH! I KNEW YOU'D DO THIS TO ME! ONLY YOU DIDN'T EVEN WAIT TO SLEEP WITH ME - YOU JUST DUMPED ME THE MINUTE I SAID YES YOU JERK!
WELL, YOU'RE NOT WALKING AWAY THAT EASY BUSTER! YOU STARTED THIS, YOU'RE GONNA FINISH IT!
YOU EARNED IT FREDDIE, NOW COME AND GET IT!
UH, FRANCINE? ...WH-WHAT ARE YOU D-DOING?
GIVING YOU YOUR PRIZE! THIS WAS A CONTEST, RIGHT? SEE WHO CAN SCREW FRANCINE BEST!? WELL YOU WIN FREDDIE!

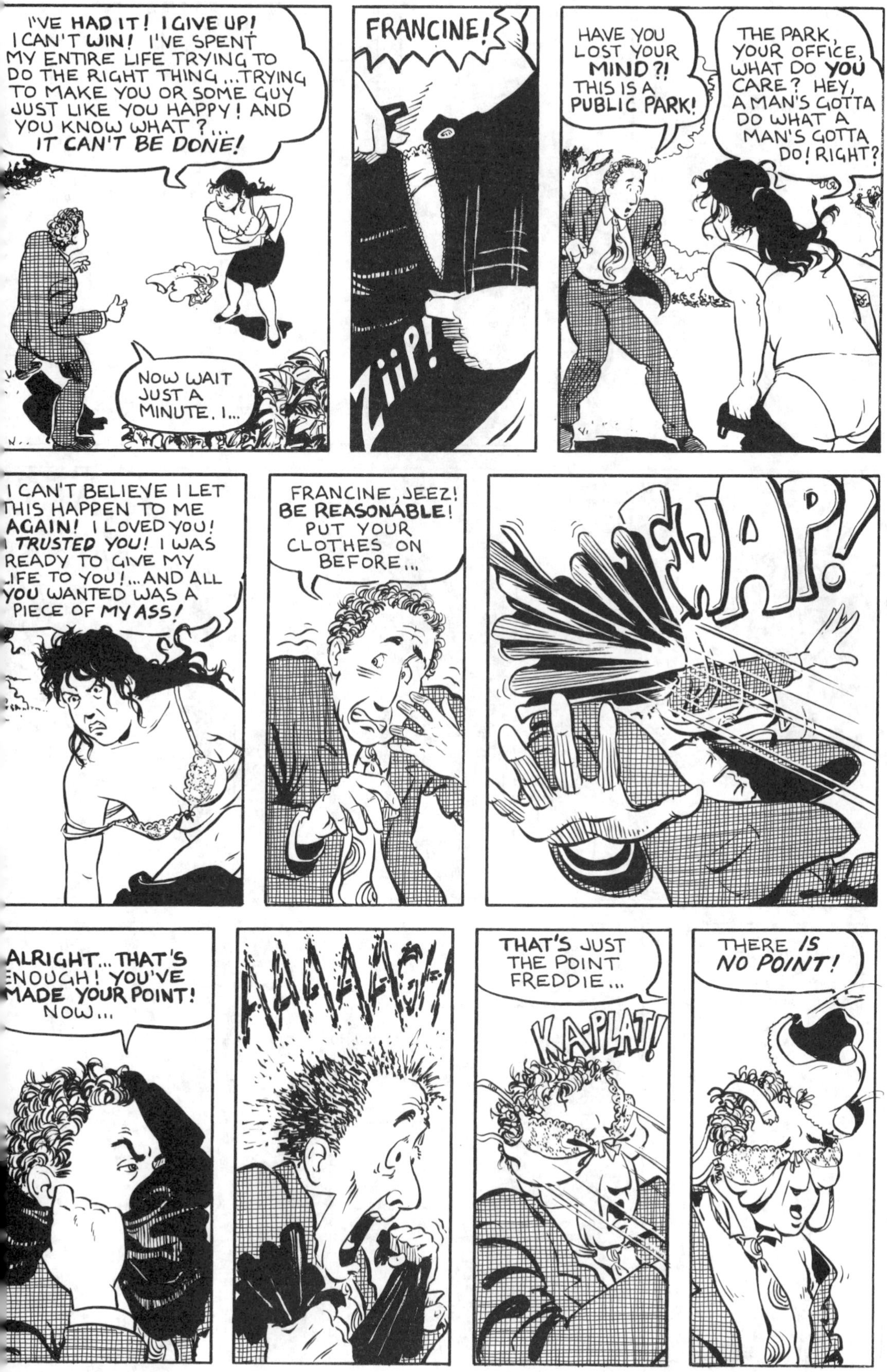
I'VE HAD IT! I GIVE UP! I CAN'T WIN! I'VE SPENT MY ENTIRE LIFE TRYING TO DO THE RIGHT THING...TRYING TO MAKE YOU OR SOME GUY JUST LIKE YOU HAPPY! AND YOU KNOW WHAT?... IT CAN'T BE DONE!
NOW WAIT JUST A MINUTE. I...
FRANCINE!
ZIIP!
HAVE YOU LOST YOUR MIND?! THIS IS A PUBLIC PARK!
THE PARK, YOUR OFFICE, WHAT DO YOU CARE? HEY, A MAN'S GOTTA DO WHAT A MAN'S GOTTA DO! RIGHT?
I CAN'T BELIEVE I LET THIS HAPPEN TO ME AGAIN! I LOVED YOU! I TRUSTED YOU! I WAS READY TO GIVE MY LIFE TO YOU!...AND ALL YOU WANTED WAS A PIECE OF MY ASS!
FRANCINE, JEEZ! BE REASONABLE! PUT YOUR CLOTHES ON BEFORE...
SWAP!
ALRIGHT...THAT'S ENOUGH! YOU'VE MADE YOUR POINT! NOW...
AAAAAGH
THAT'S JUST THE POINT FREDDIE...
KA-PLAT!
THERE IS NO POINT!

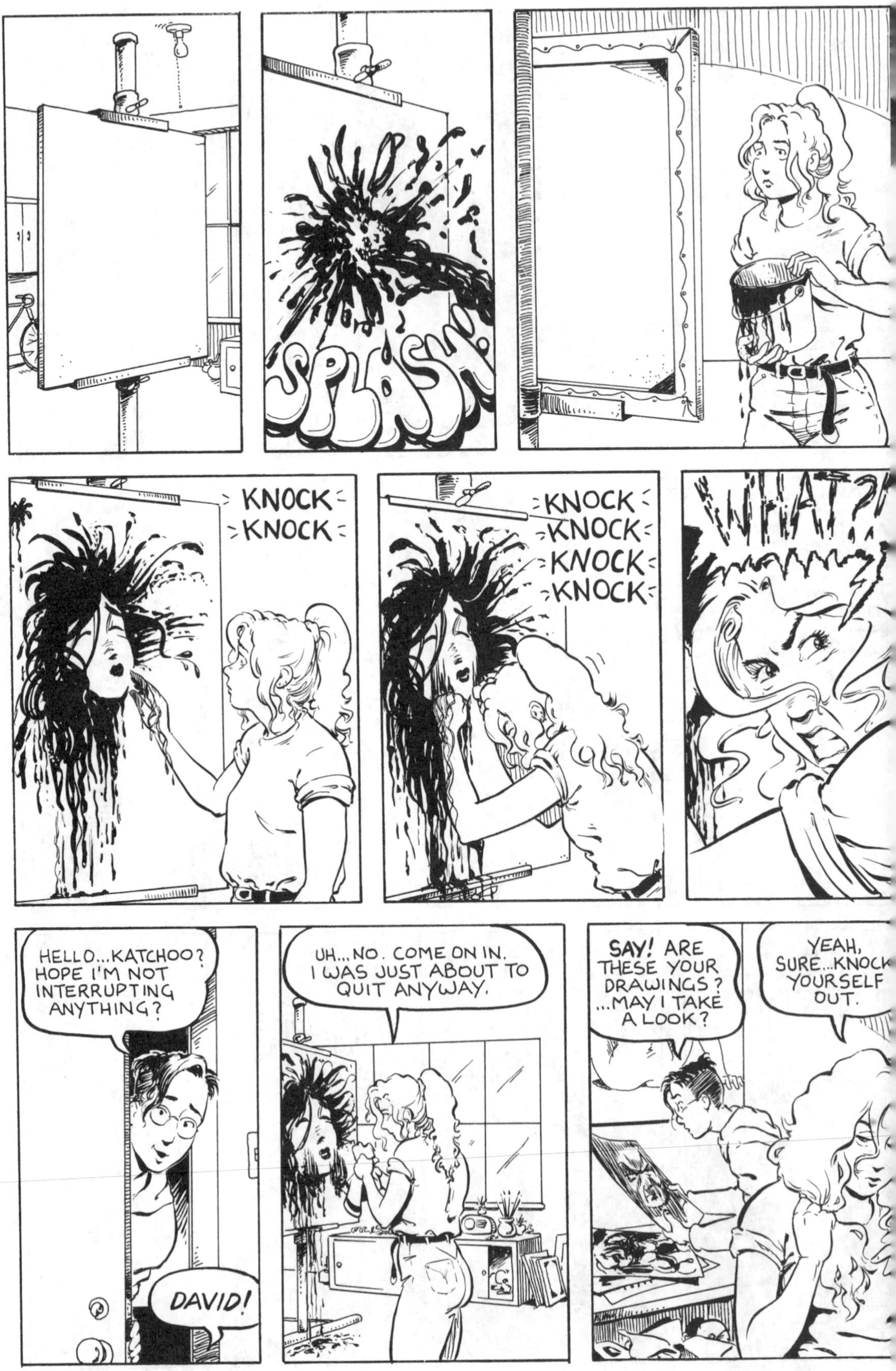
SPLASH
KNOCK KNOCK
KNOCK KNOCK KNOCK KNOCK
WHAT?!
HELLO...KATCHOO? HOPE I'M NOT INTERRUPTING ANYTHING?
DAVID!
UH...NO. COME ON IN. I WAS JUST ABOUT TO QUIT ANYWAY.
SAY! ARE THESE YOUR DRAWINGS? ...MAY I TAKE A LOOK?
YEAH, SURE...KNOCK YOURSELF OUT.

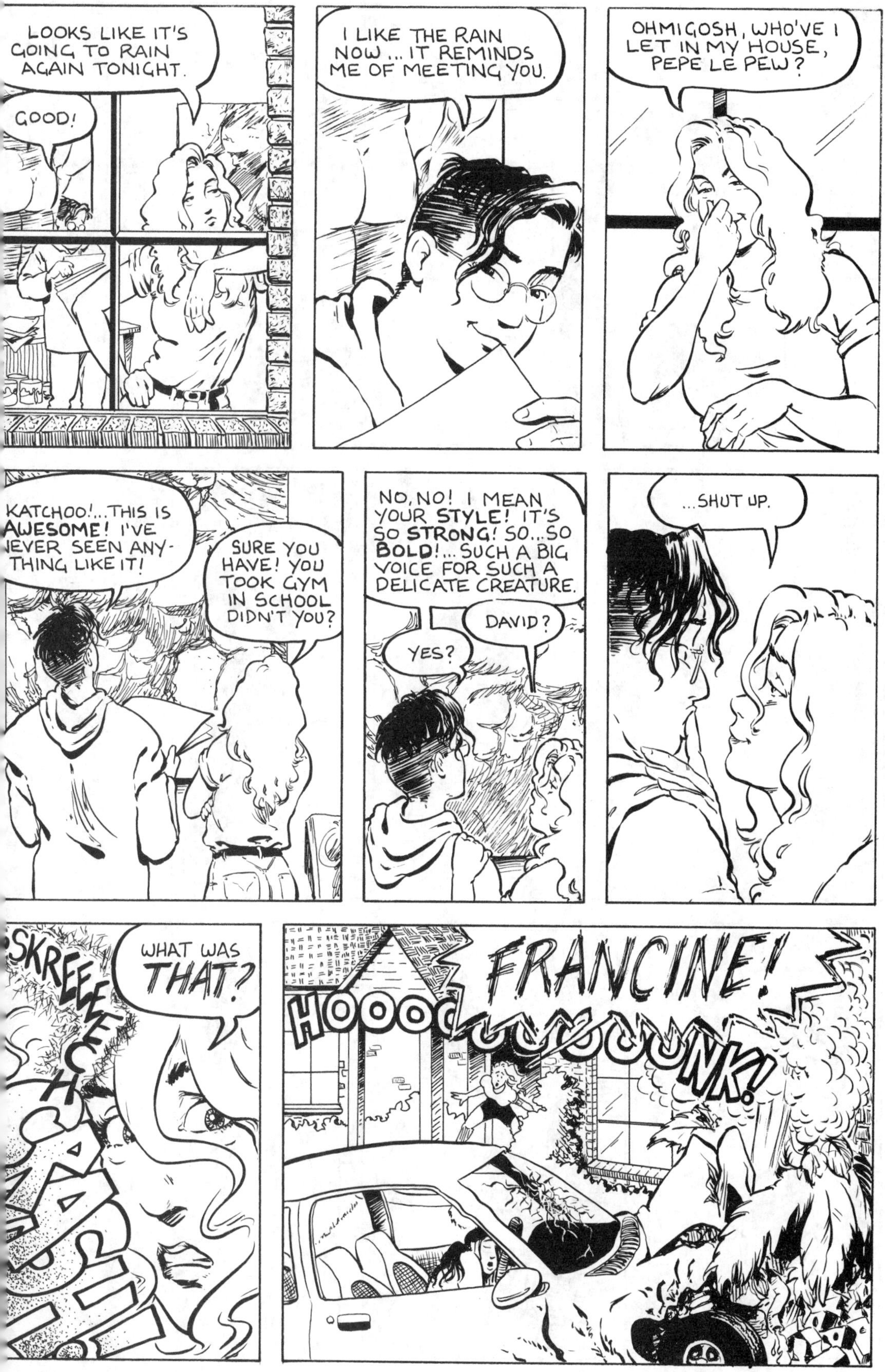

LOOKS LIKE IT'S GOING TO RAIN AGAIN TONIGHT.
GOOD!
I LIKE THE RAIN NOW... IT REMINDS ME OF MEETING YOU.
OHMIGOSH, WHO'VE I LET IN MY HOUSE, PEPE LE PEW?
KATCHOO!... THIS IS AWESOME! I'VE NEVER SEEN ANYTHING LIKE IT!
SURE YOU HAVE! YOU TOOK GYM IN SCHOOL DIDN'T YOU?
NO, NO! I MEAN YOUR STYLE! IT'S SO STRONG! SO...SO BOLD!... SUCH A BIG VOICE FOR SUCH A DELICATE CREATURE.
DAVID?
YES?
...SHUT UP.
SKREEEEECH
WHAT WAS THAT?
FRANCINE!
HOOOOUUUUUUNK!

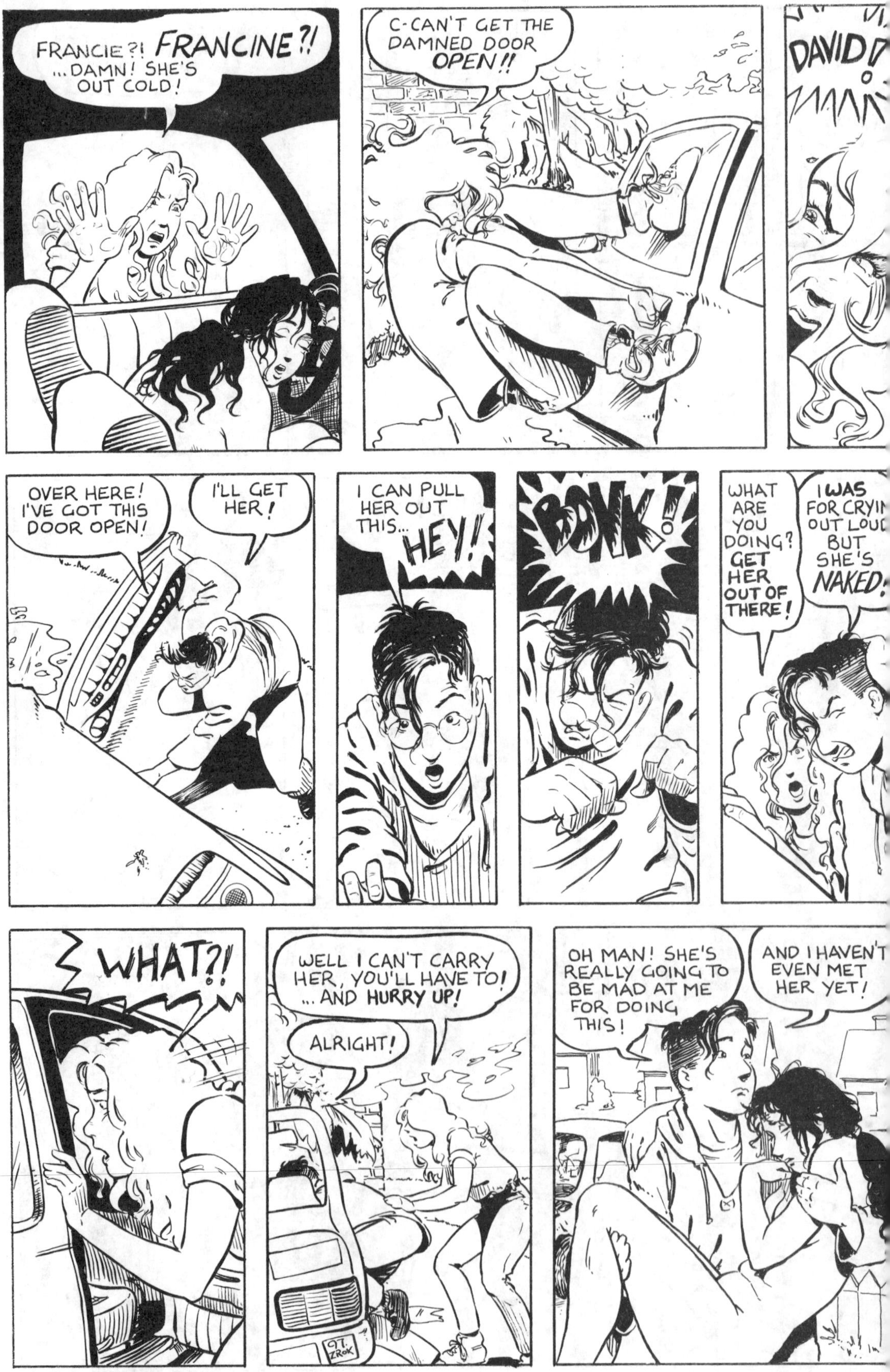

FRANCIE?! FRANCINE?! ...DAMN! SHE'S OUT COLD!
C-CAN'T GET THE DAMNED DOOR OPEN!!
DAVID?!
OVER HERE! I'VE GOT THIS DOOR OPEN!
I'LL GET HER!
I CAN PULL HER OUT THIS... HEY!
BONK!
WHAT ARE YOU DOING? GET HER OUT OF THERE!
I WAS FOR CRYIN OUT LOUD BUT SHE'S NAKED!
WHAT?!
WELL I CAN'T CARRY HER, YOU'LL HAVE TO! ...AND HURRY UP!
ALRIGHT!
OH MAN! SHE'S REALLY GOING TO BE MAD AT ME FOR DOING THIS!
AND I HAVEN'T EVEN MET HER YET!

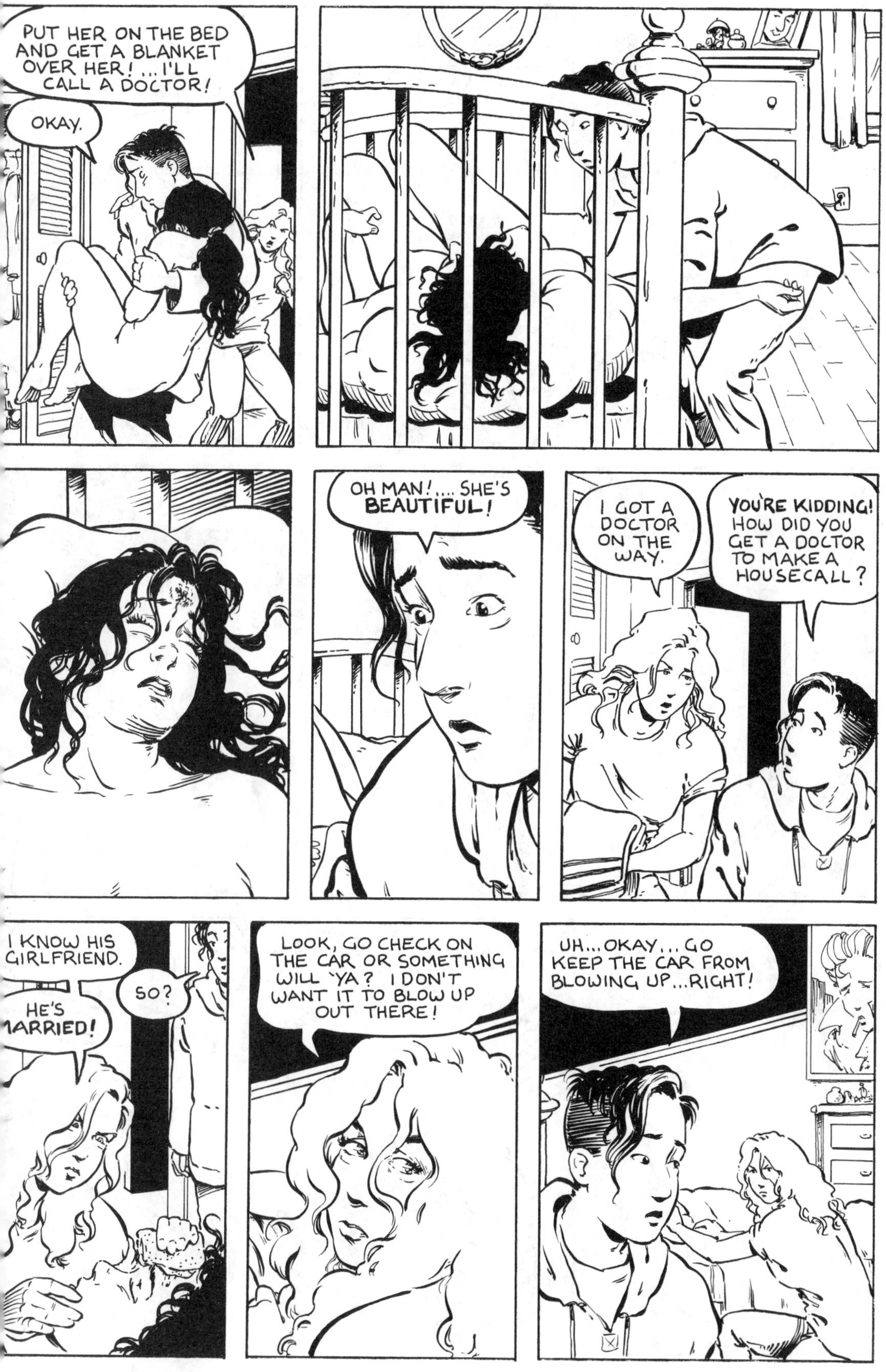
PUT HER ON THE BED AND GET A BLANKET OVER HER! ...I'LL CALL A DOCTOR!
OKAY.
OH MAN!.... SHE'S **BEAUTIFUL**!
I GOT A DOCTOR ON THE WAY.
YOU'RE KIDDING! HOW DID YOU GET A DOCTOR TO MAKE A HOUSECALL?
I KNOW HIS GIRLFRIEND.
SO?
HE'S MARRIED!
LOOK, GO CHECK ON THE CAR OR SOMETHING WILL 'YA? I DON'T WANT IT TO BLOW UP OUT THERE!
UH...OKAY...GO KEEP THE CAR FROM BLOWING UP...RIGHT!

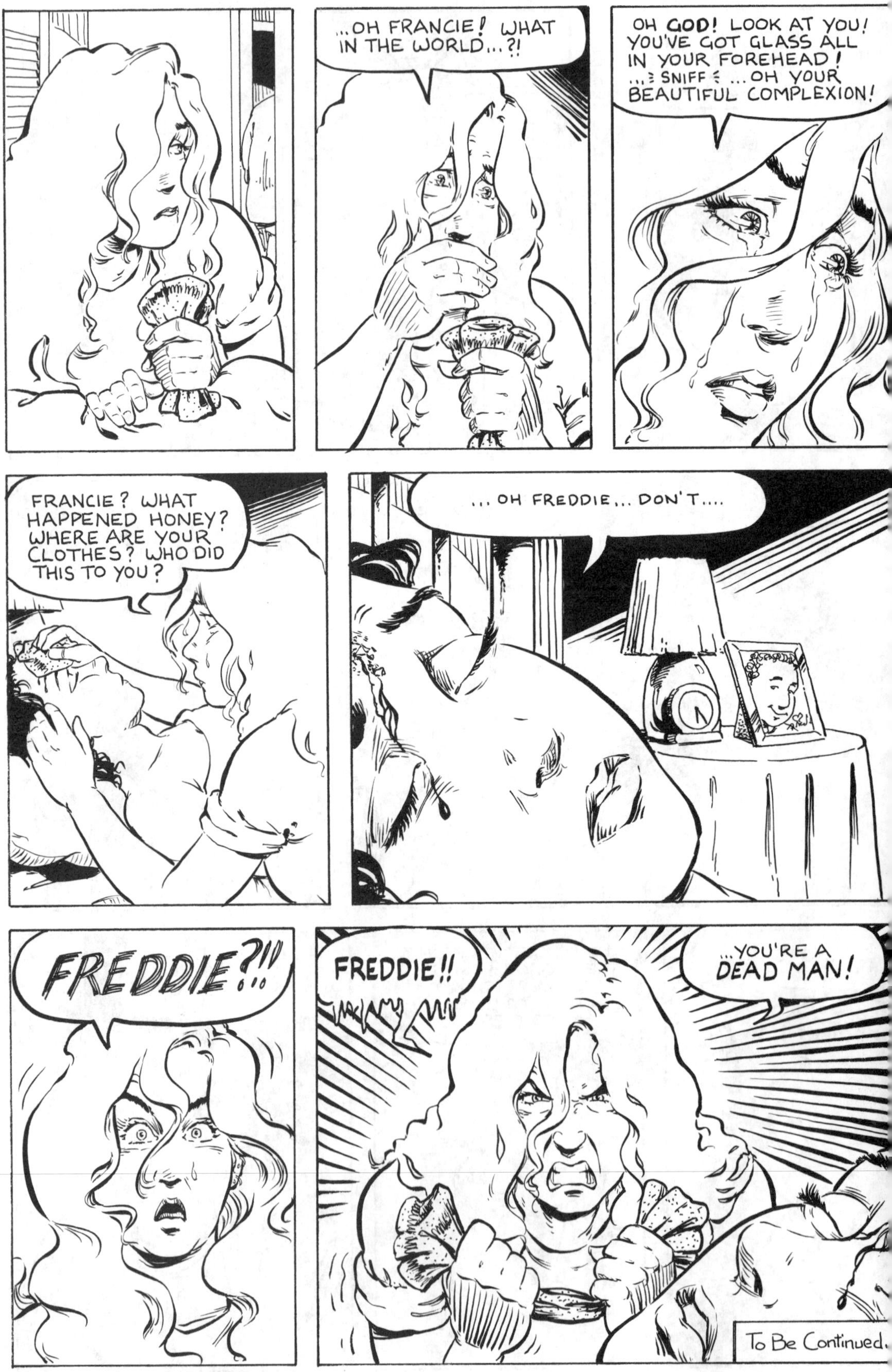
...OH FRANCIE! WHAT IN THE WORLD...?!
OH GOD! LOOK AT YOU! YOU'VE GOT GLASS ALL IN YOUR FOREHEAD! ...≷SNIFF≶ ...OH YOUR BEAUTIFUL COMPLEXION!
FRANCIE? WHAT HAPPENED HONEY? WHERE ARE YOUR CLOTHES? WHO DID THIS TO YOU?
...OH FREDDIE... DON'T....
FREDDIE?!!
FREDDIE!!
...YOU'RE A DEAD MAN!
To Be Continued.

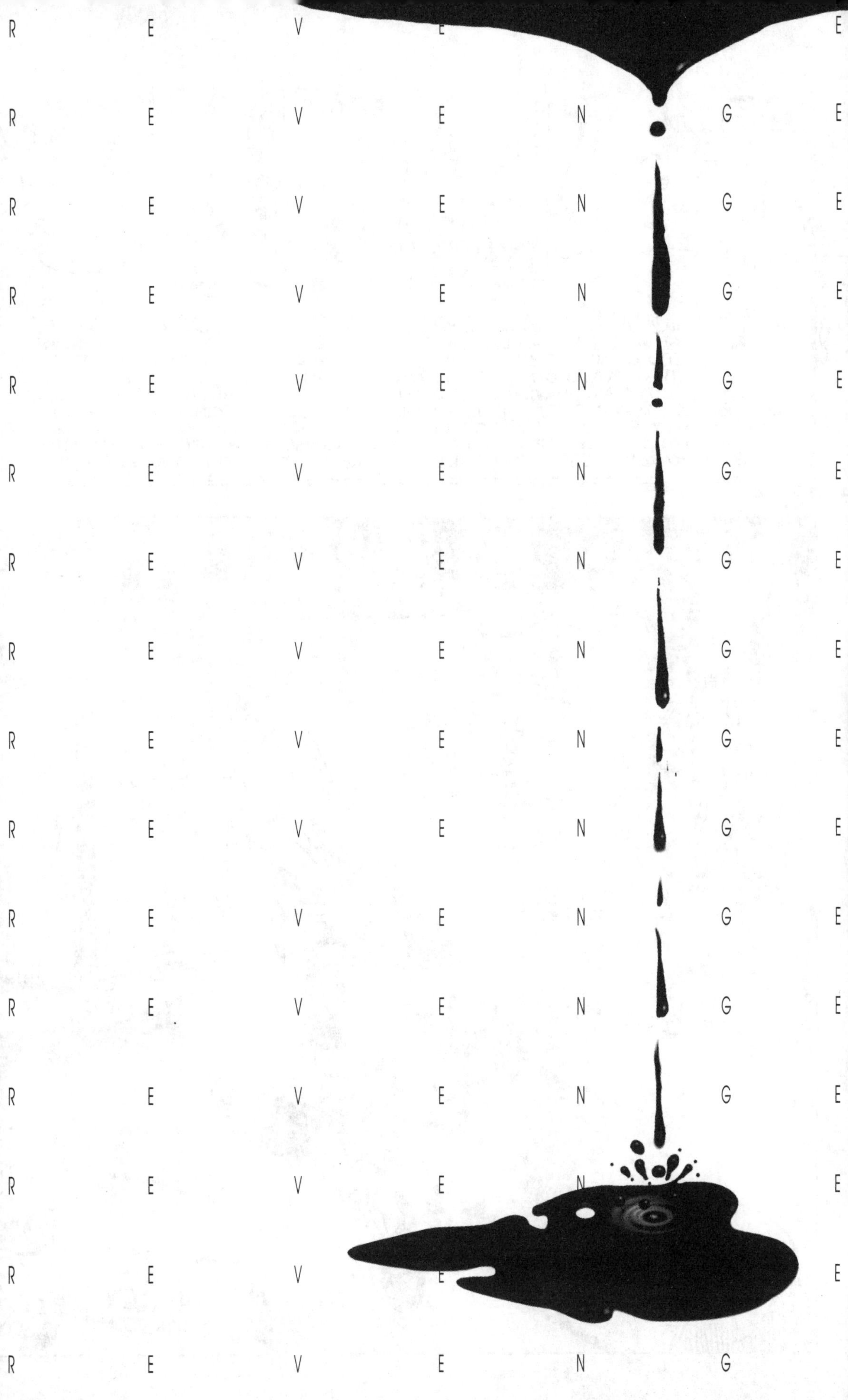
R E V E E
R E V E N G E
R E V E N G E
R E V E N G E
R E V E N G E
R E V E N G E
R E V E N G E
R E V E N G E
R E V E N G E
R E V E N G E
R E V E N G E
R E V E N G E
R E V E N G E
R E V E N E
R E V E E
R E V E N G

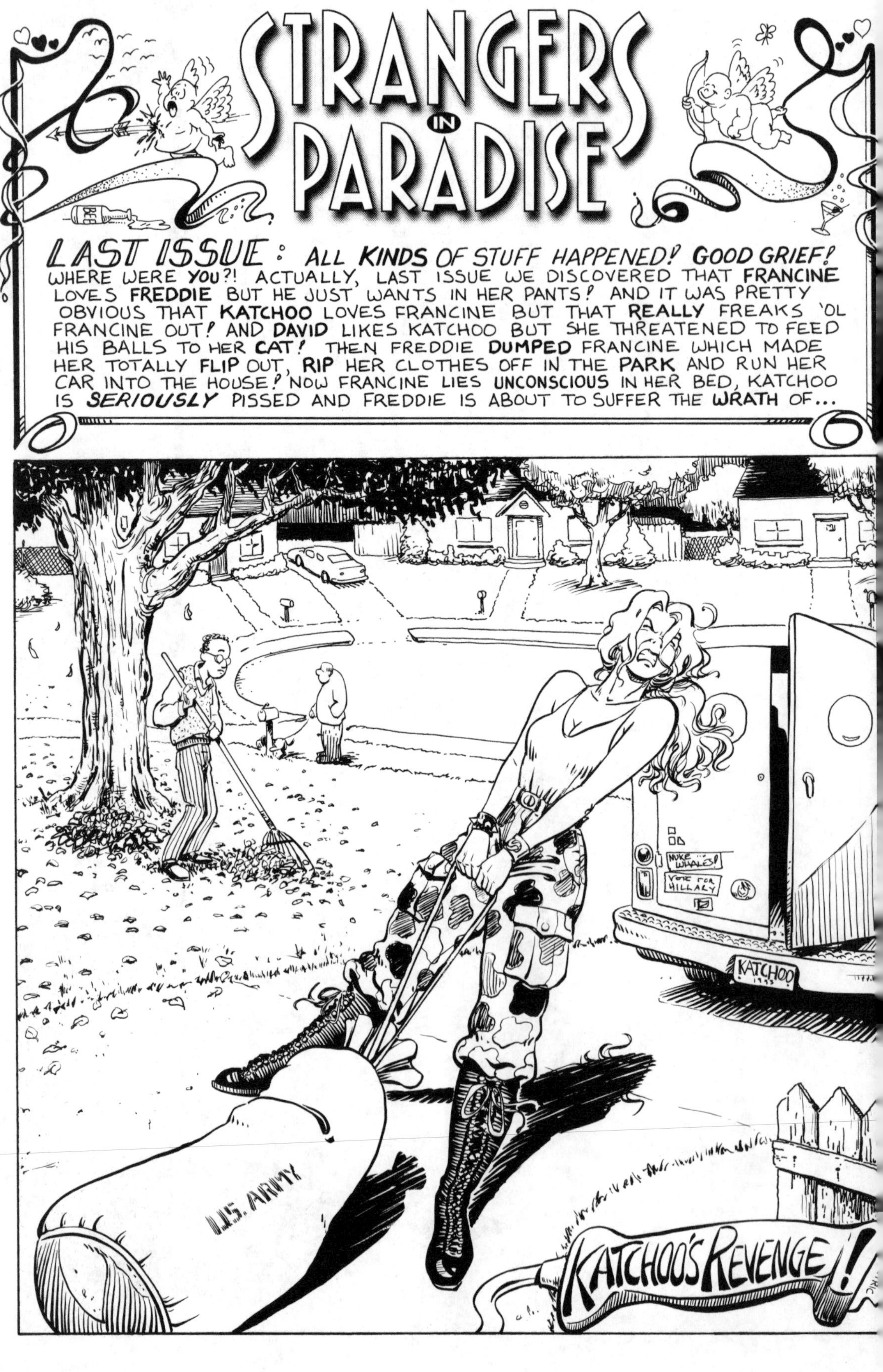
STRANGERS IN PARADISE
LAST ISSUE: ALL KINDS OF STUFF HAPPENED! GOOD GRIEF! WHERE WERE YOU?! ACTUALLY, LAST ISSUE WE DISCOVERED THAT FRANCINE LOVES FREDDIE BUT HE JUST WANTS IN HER PANTS! AND IT WAS PRETTY OBVIOUS THAT KATCHOO LOVES FRANCINE BUT THAT REALLY FREAKS 'OL FRANCINE OUT! AND DAVID LIKES KATCHOO BUT SHE THREATENED TO FEED HIS BALLS TO HER CAT! THEN FREDDIE DUMPED FRANCINE WHICH MADE HER TOTALLY FLIP OUT, RIP HER CLOTHES OFF IN THE PARK AND RUN HER CAR INTO THE HOUSE! NOW FRANCINE LIES UNCONSCIOUS IN HER BED, KATCHOO IS SERIOUSLY PISSED AND FREDDIE IS ABOUT TO SUFFER THE WRATH OF...
NUKE WHALES!
VOTE FOR HILLARY
KATCHOO
U.S. ARMY
KATCHOO'S REVENGE!

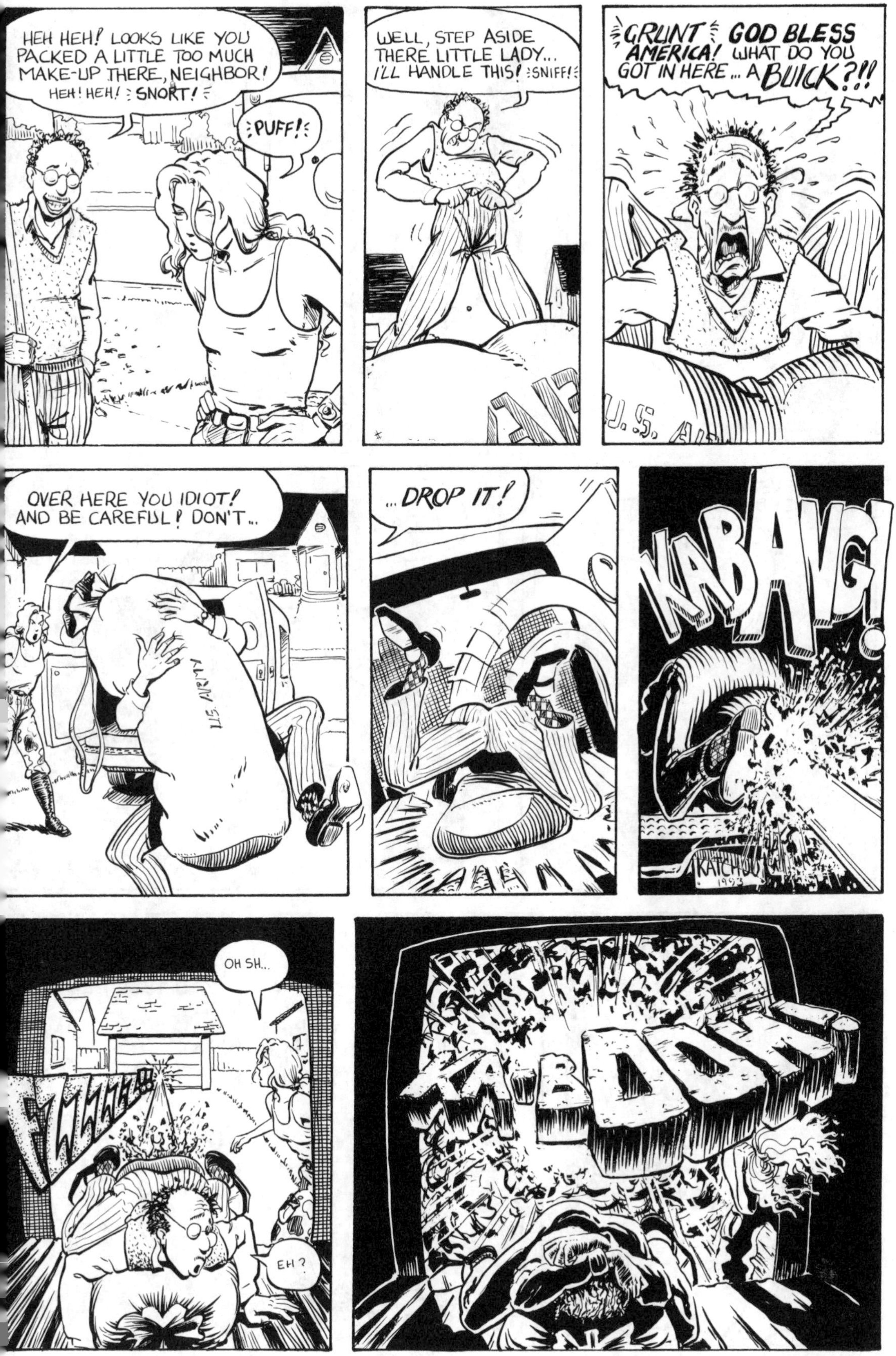
HEH HEH! LOOKS LIKE YOU PACKED A LITTLE TOO MUCH MAKE-UP THERE, NEIGHBOR! HEH! HEH! SNORT!
PUFF!
WELL, STEP ASIDE THERE LITTLE LADY... I'LL HANDLE THIS! SNIFF!
GRUNT GOD BLESS AMERICA! WHAT DO YOU GOT IN HERE... A BUICK?!!
U.S.
OVER HERE YOU IDIOT! AND BE CAREFUL! DON'T...
U.S. ARMY
...DROP IT!
KABANG!
KATCHOR 1993
OH SH...
FWWWW!!!
EH?
KA-BOOM

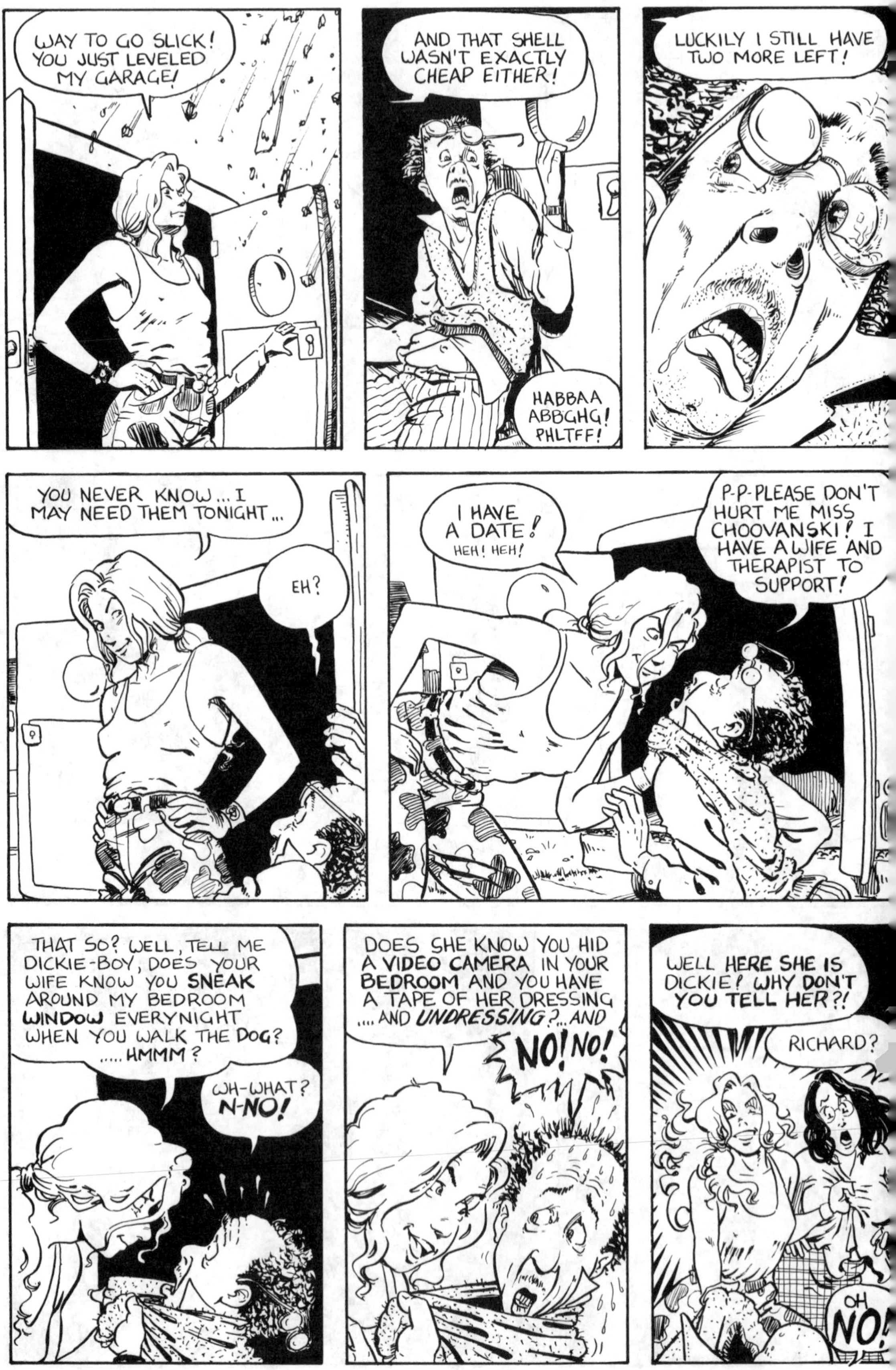

WAY TO GO SLICK! YOU JUST LEVELED MY GARAGE!
AND THAT SHELL WASN'T EXACTLY CHEAP EITHER!
HABBAA ABBGHG! PHLTFF!
LUCKILY I STILL HAVE TWO MORE LEFT!
YOU NEVER KNOW... I MAY NEED THEM TONIGHT...
EH?
I HAVE A DATE! HEH! HEH!
P-P-PLEASE DON'T HURT ME MISS CHOOVANSKI! I HAVE A WIFE AND THERAPIST TO SUPPORT!
THAT SO? WELL, TELL ME DICKIE-BOY, DOES YOUR WIFE KNOW YOU SNEAK AROUND MY BEDROOM WINDOW EVERYNIGHT WHEN YOU WALK THE DOG? .....HMMM?
WH-WHAT? N-NO!
DOES SHE KNOW YOU HID A VIDEO CAMERA IN YOUR BEDROOM AND YOU HAVE A TAPE OF HER DRESSING ....AND UNDRESSING?...AND
NO! NO!
WELL HERE SHE IS DICKIE! WHY DON'T YOU TELL HER?!
RICHARD?
OH NO!

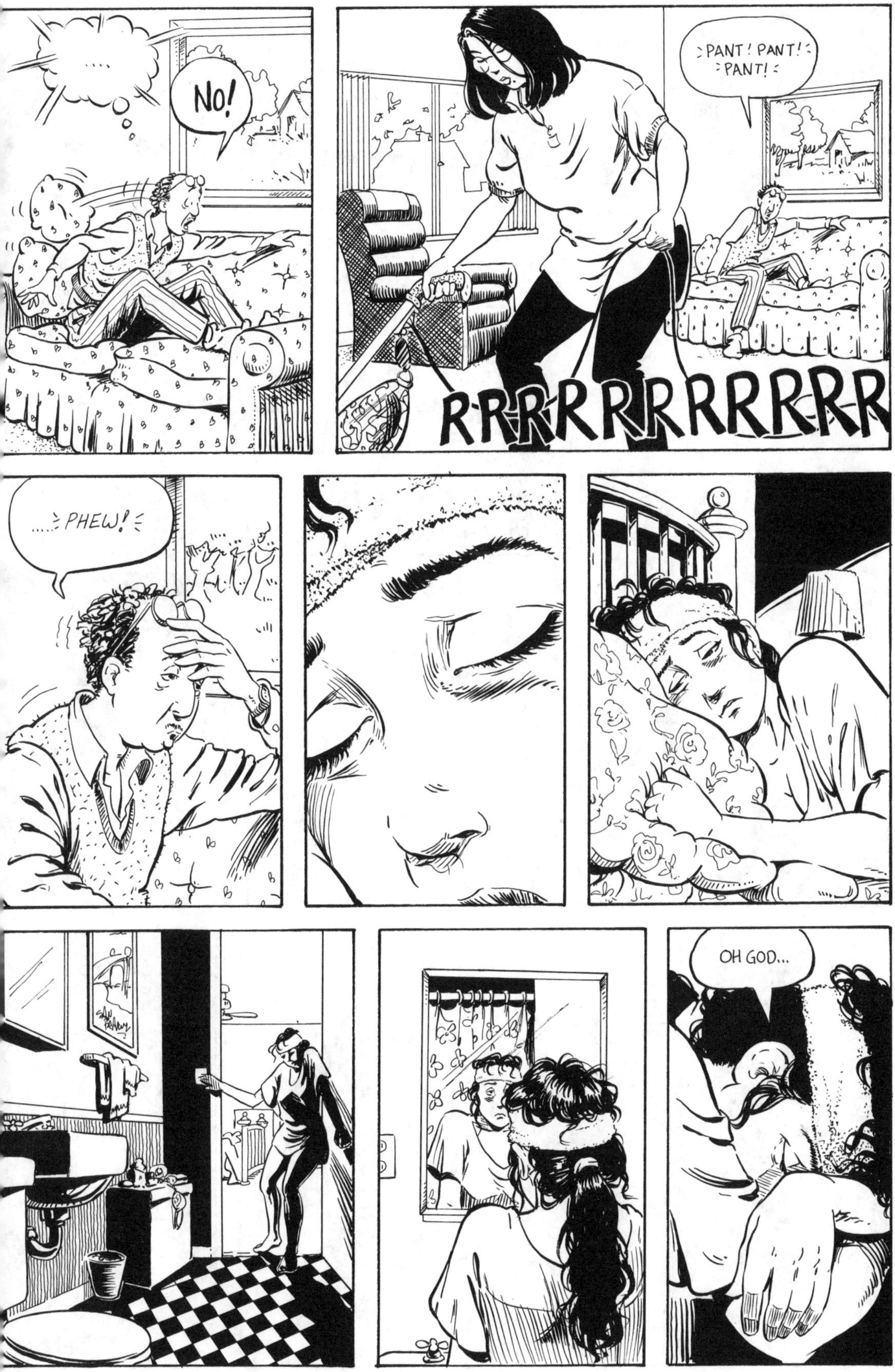
No!
PANT! PANT! PANT!
RRRRRRRRRRR
.....PHEW!
OH GOD...

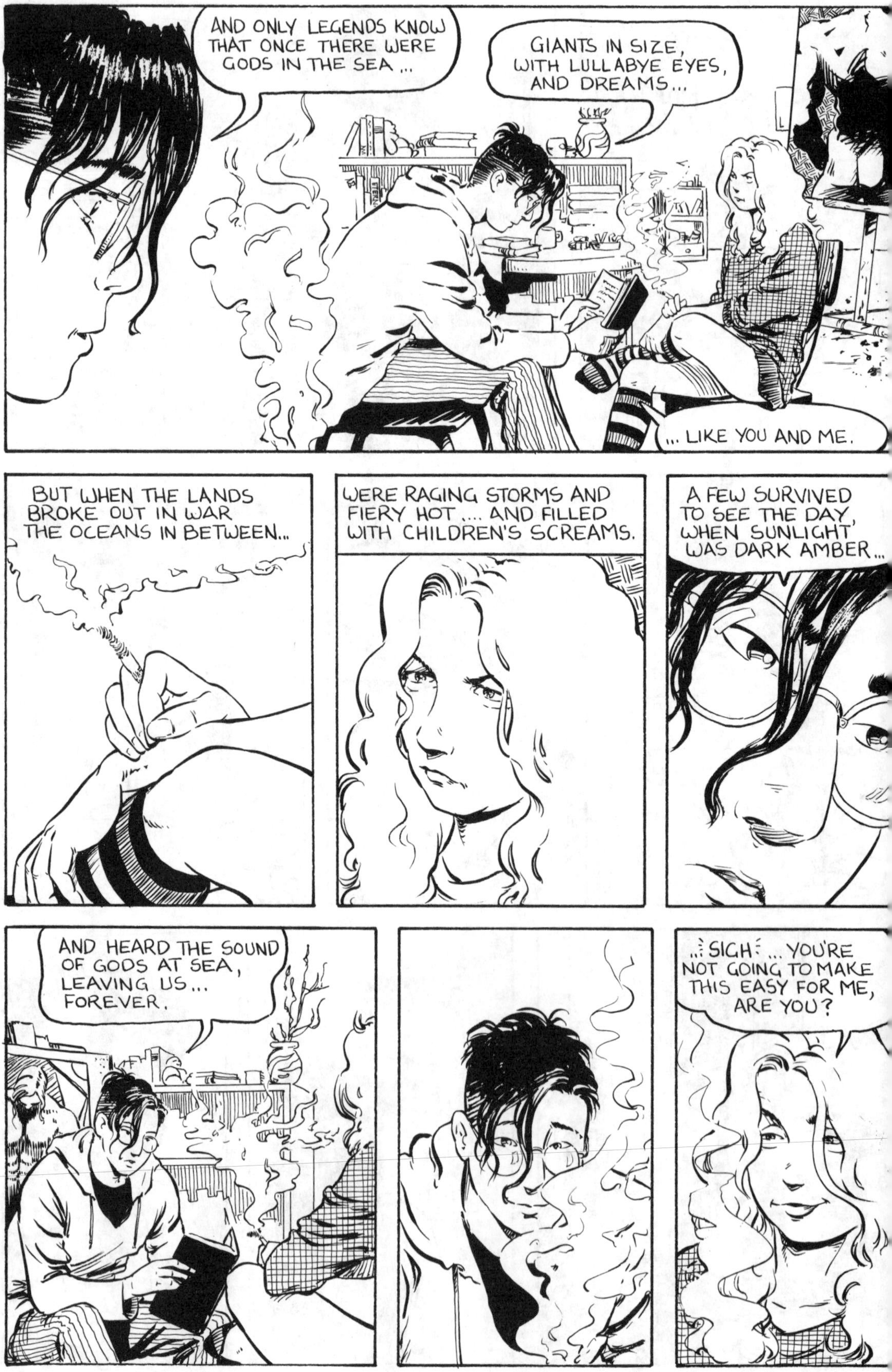
AND ONLY LEGENDS KNOW THAT ONCE THERE WERE GODS IN THE SEA...
GIANTS IN SIZE, WITH LULLABYE EYES, AND DREAMS...
... LIKE YOU AND ME.
BUT WHEN THE LANDS BROKE OUT IN WAR THE OCEANS IN BETWEEN...
WERE RAGING STORMS AND FIERY HOT.... AND FILLED WITH CHILDREN'S SCREAMS.
A FEW SURVIVED TO SEE THE DAY, WHEN SUNLIGHT WAS DARK AMBER...
AND HEARD THE SOUND OF GODS AT SEA, LEAVING US... FOREVER.
...SIGH... YOU'RE NOT GOING TO MAKE THIS EASY FOR ME, ARE YOU?

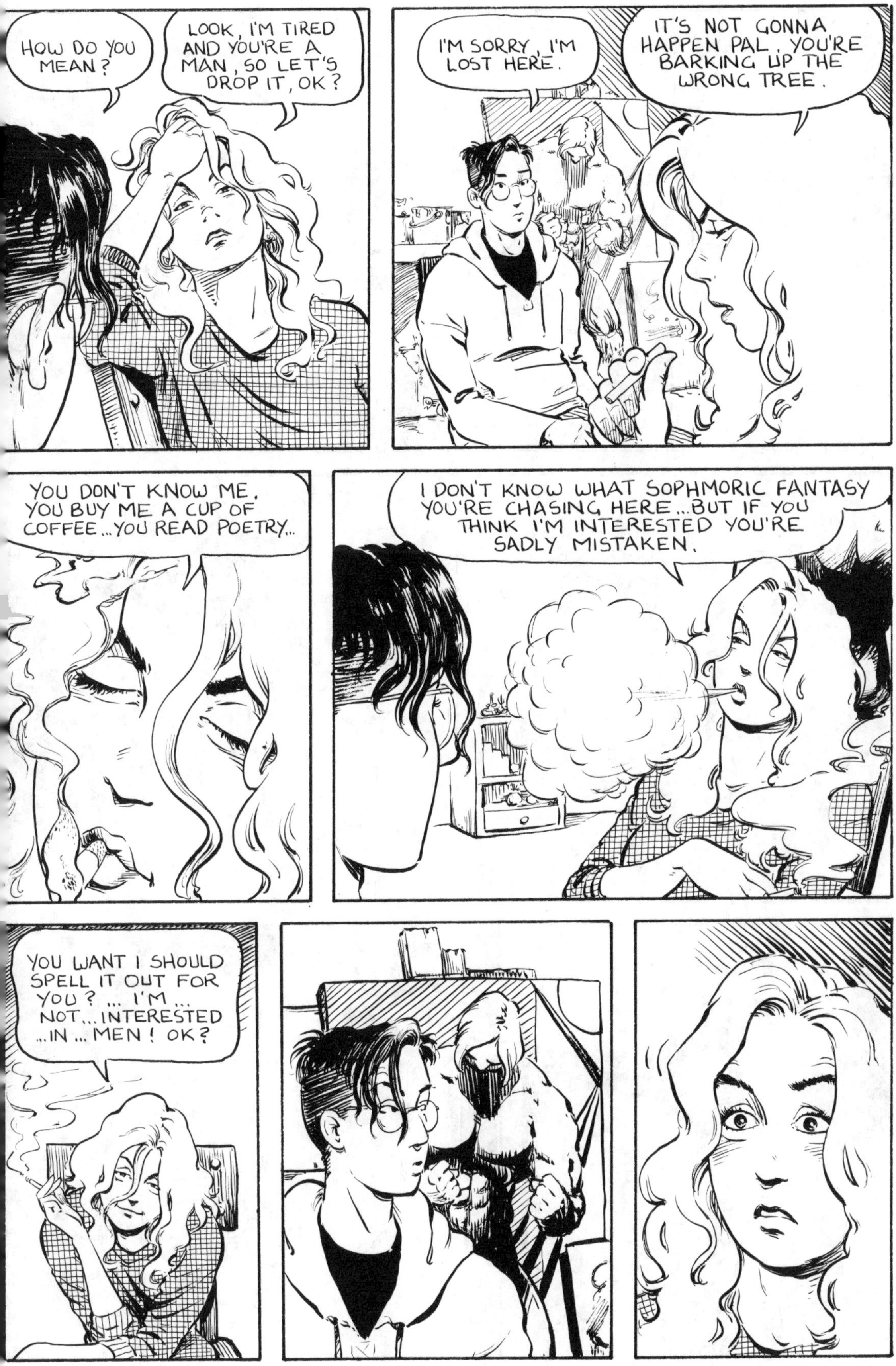
HOW DO YOU MEAN?
LOOK, I'M TIRED AND YOU'RE A MAN, SO LET'S DROP IT, OK?
I'M SORRY, I'M LOST HERE.
IT'S NOT GONNA HAPPEN PAL, YOU'RE BARKING UP THE WRONG TREE.
YOU DON'T KNOW ME, YOU BUY ME A CUP OF COFFEE... YOU READ POETRY...
I DON'T KNOW WHAT SOPHMORIC FANTASY YOU'RE CHASING HERE... BUT IF YOU THINK I'M INTERESTED YOU'RE SADLY MISTAKEN.
YOU WANT I SHOULD SPELL IT OUT FOR YOU? ... I'M ... NOT... INTERESTED ...IN ... MEN! OK?

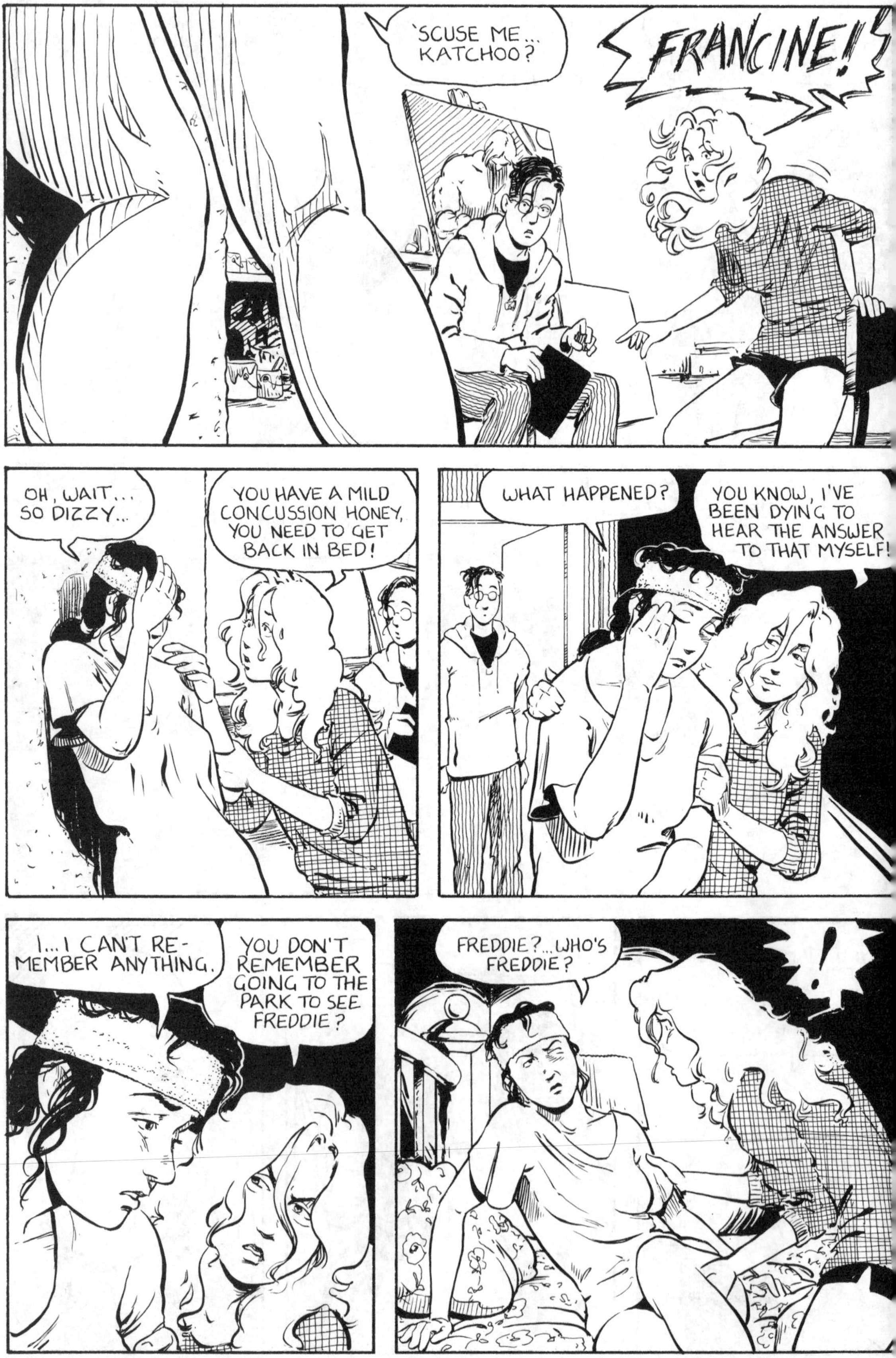
`SCUSE ME... KATCHOO?
FRANCINE!
OH, WAIT... SO DIZZY...
YOU HAVE A MILD CONCUSSION HONEY, YOU NEED TO GET BACK IN BED!
WHAT HAPPENED?
YOU KNOW, I'VE BEEN DYING TO HEAR THE ANSWER TO THAT MYSELF!
I... I CAN'T RE- MEMBER ANYTHING.
YOU DON'T REMEMBER GOING TO THE PARK TO SEE FREDDIE?
FREDDIE?... WHO'S FREDDIE?
!

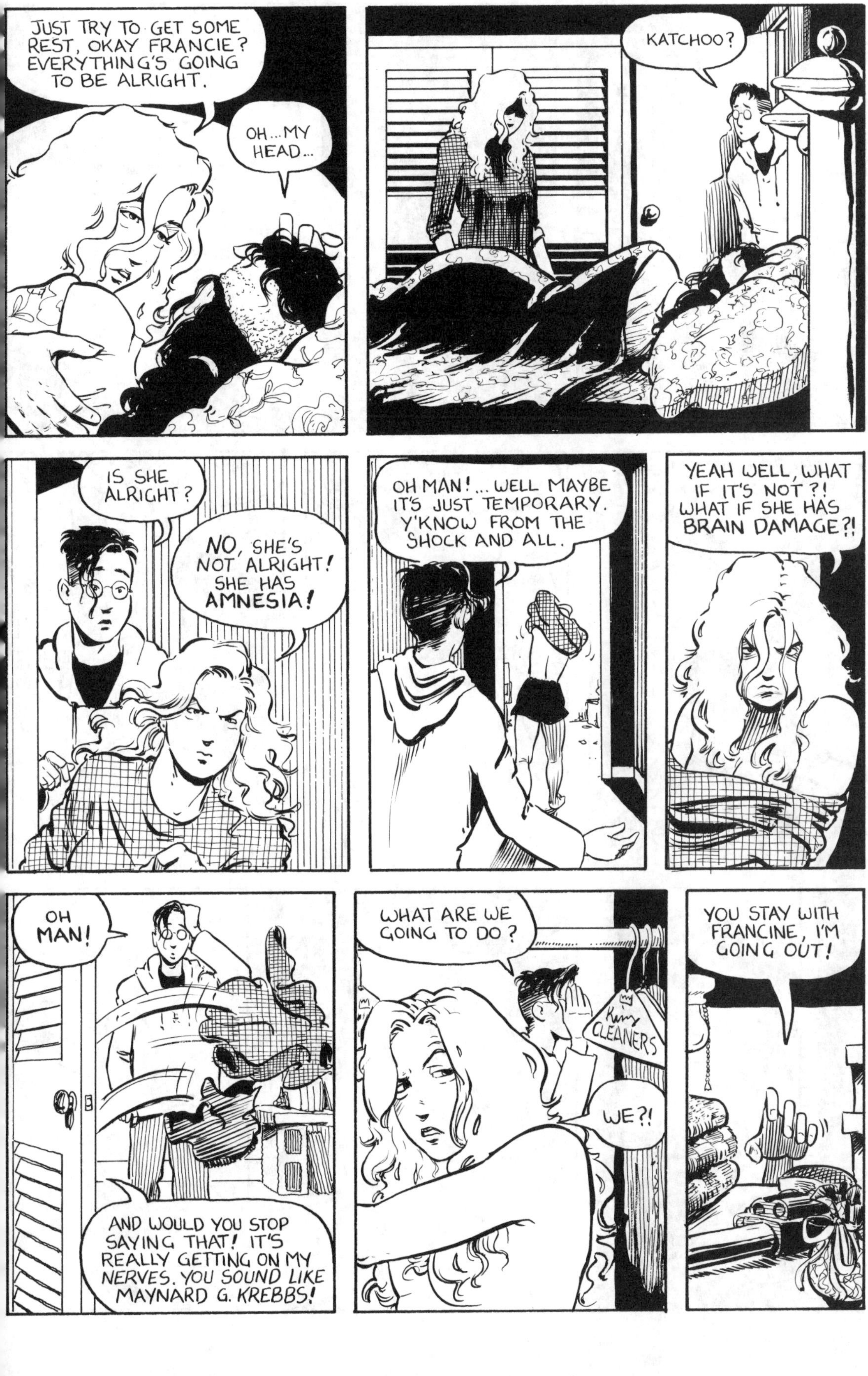
JUST TRY TO GET SOME REST, OKAY FRANCIE? EVERYTHING'S GOING TO BE ALRIGHT.
OH...MY HEAD...
KATCHOO?
IS SHE ALRIGHT?
NO, SHE'S NOT ALRIGHT! SHE HAS AMNESIA!
OH MAN!... WELL MAYBE IT'S JUST TEMPORARY. Y'KNOW FROM THE SHOCK AND ALL.
YEAH WELL, WHAT IF IT'S NOT?! WHAT IF SHE HAS BRAIN DAMAGE?!
OH MAN!
AND WOULD YOU STOP SAYING THAT! IT'S REALLY GETTING ON MY NERVES. YOU SOUND LIKE MAYNARD G. KREBBS!
WHAT ARE WE GOING TO DO?
CLEANERS
WE?!
YOU STAY WITH FRANCINE, I'M GOING OUT!

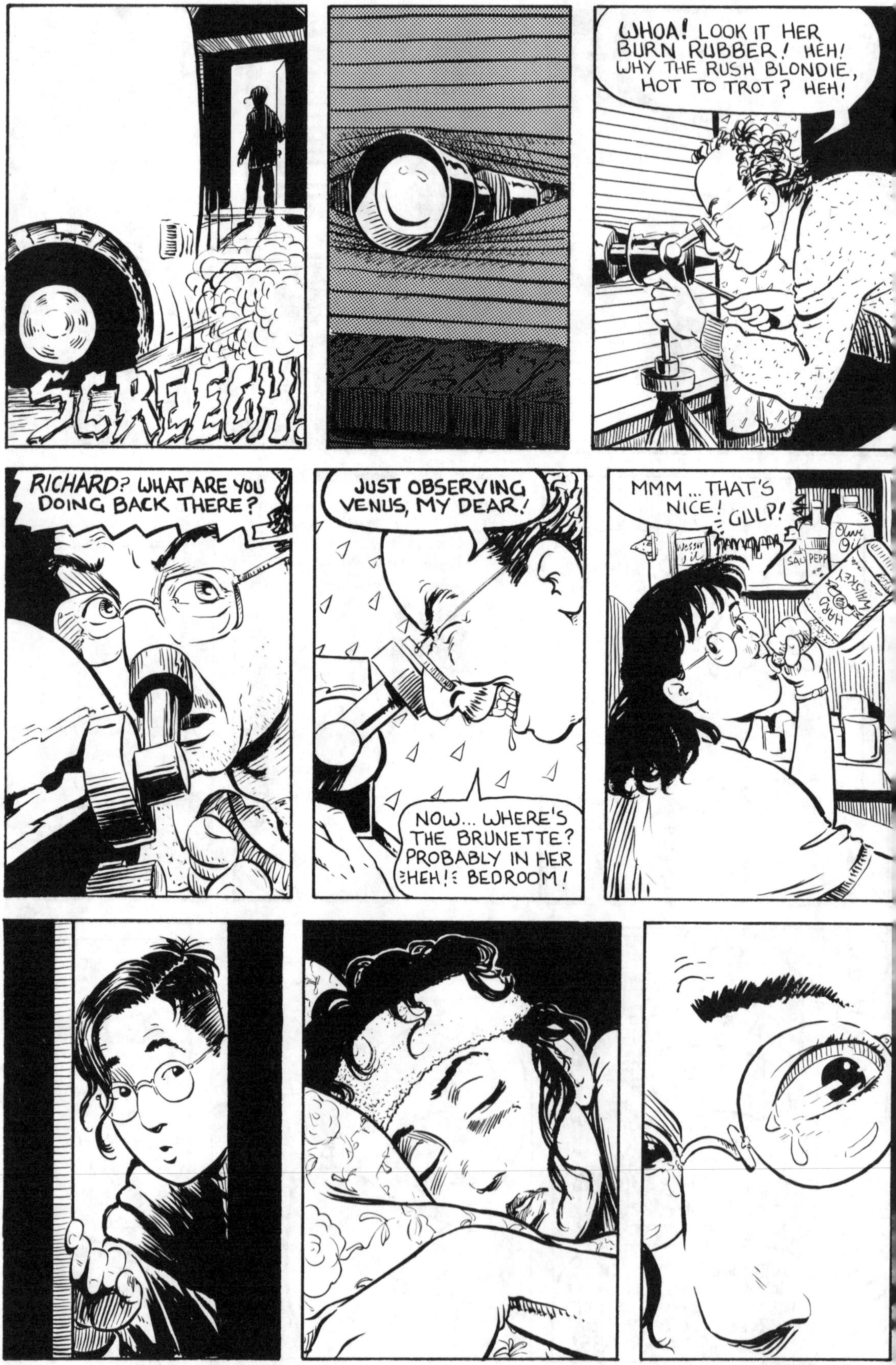
SCREECH!
WHOA! LOOK IT HER BURN RUBBER! HEH! WHY THE RUSH BLONDIE, HOT TO TROT? HEH!
RICHARD? WHAT ARE YOU DOING BACK THERE?
JUST OBSERVING VENUS, MY DEAR!
NOW... WHERE'S THE BRUNETTE? PROBABLY IN HER HEH! BEDROOM!
MMM... THAT'S NICE!
GULP!
HARD WHISKEY
Olive Oil

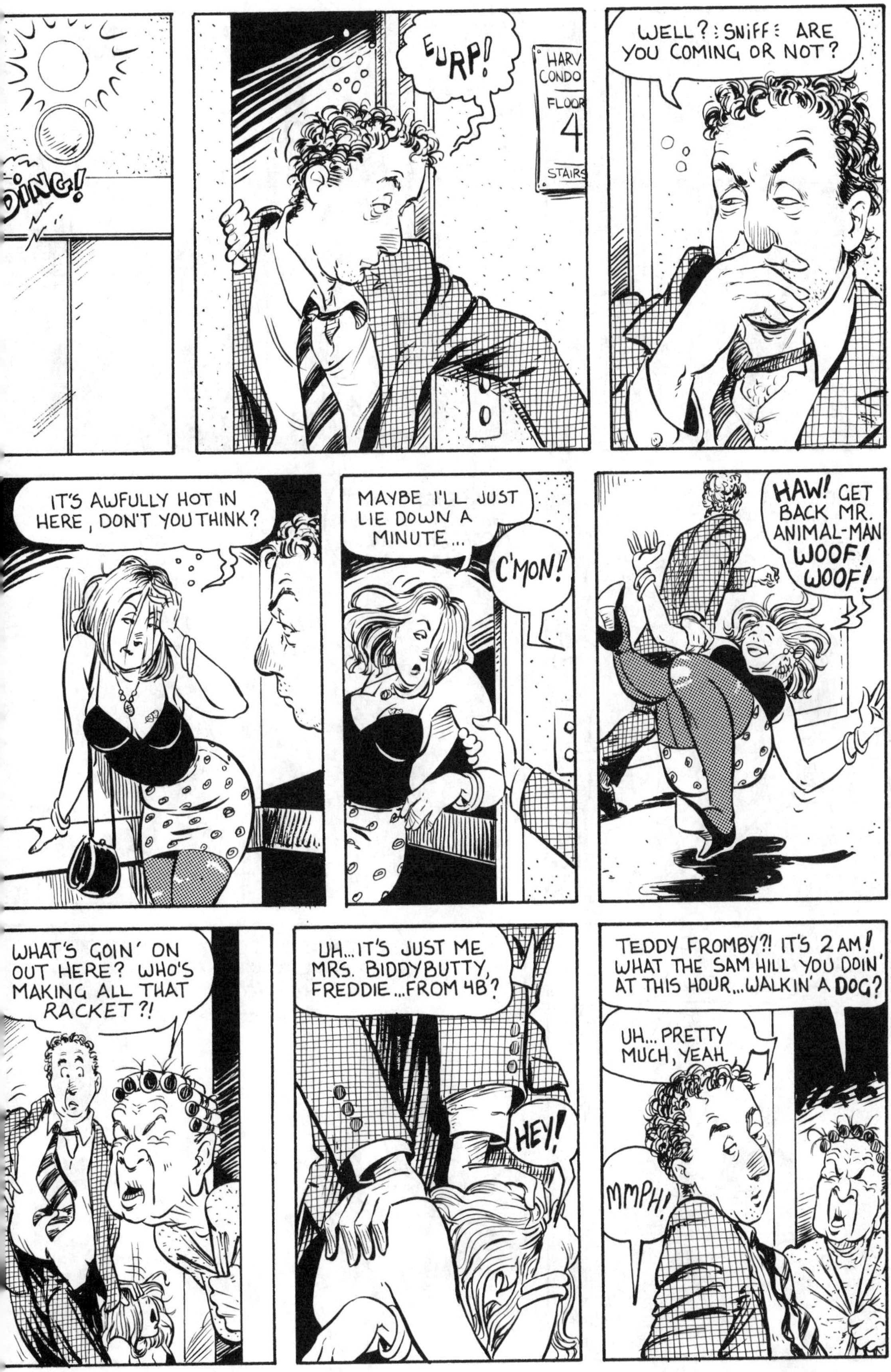
DING!
EURP!
HARV CONDO
FLOOR 4
STAIRS
WELL? :SNIFF: ARE YOU COMING OR NOT?
IT'S AWFULLY HOT IN HERE, DON'T YOU THINK?
MAYBE I'LL JUST LIE DOWN A MINUTE...
C'MON!
HAW! GET BACK MR. ANIMAL-MAN
WOOF! WOOF!
WHAT'S GOIN' ON OUT HERE? WHO'S MAKING ALL THAT RACKET?!
UH... IT'S JUST ME MRS. BIDDYBUTTY, FREDDIE... FROM 4B?
HEY!
TEDDY FROMBY?! IT'S 2 AM! WHAT THE SAM HILL YOU DOIN' AT THIS HOUR... WALKIN' A DOG?
UH... PRETTY MUCH, YEAH.
MMPH!

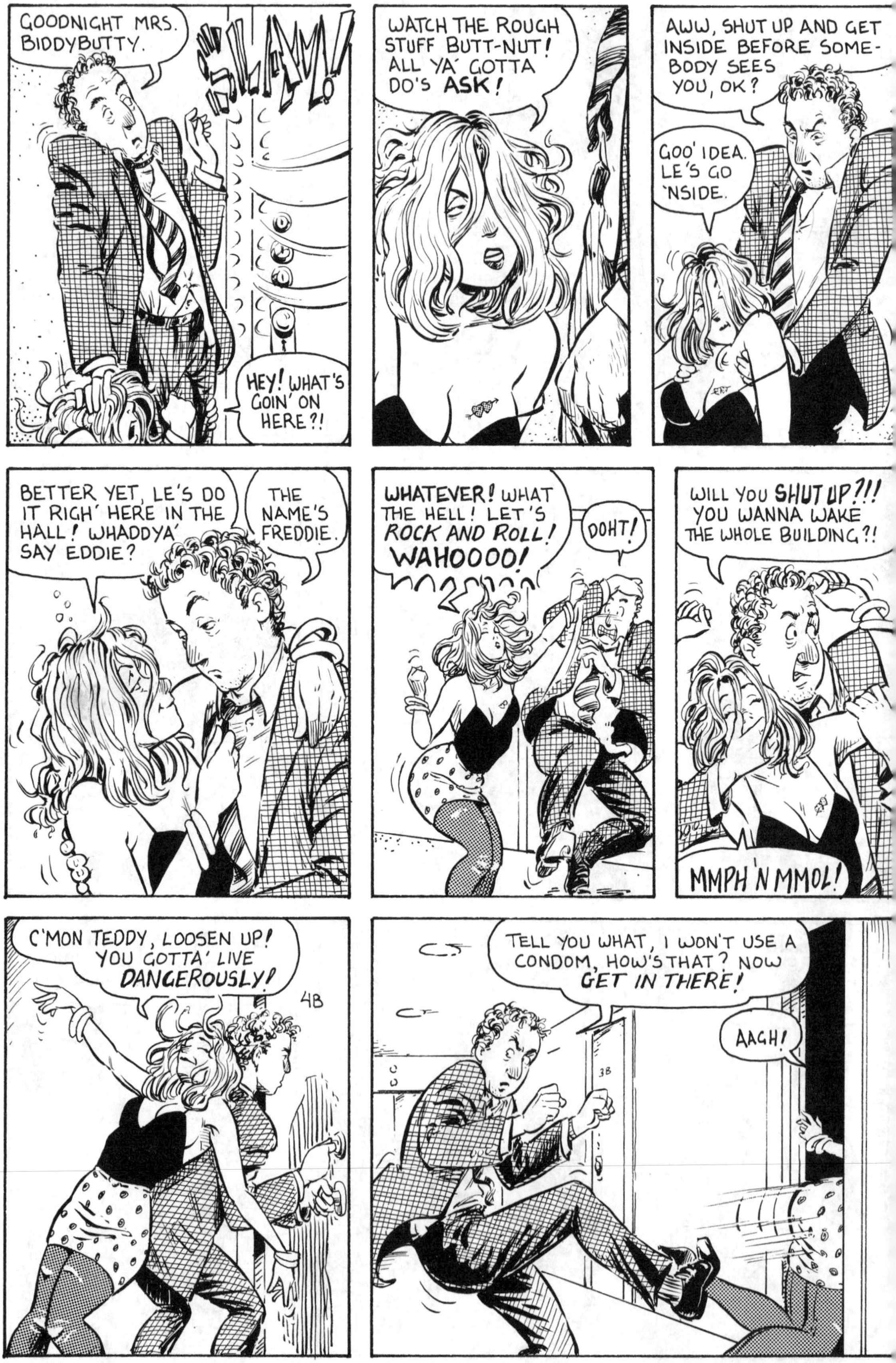

GOODNIGHT MRS. BIDDYBUTTY.
SLAM!
HEY! WHAT'S GOIN' ON HERE?!
WATCH THE ROUGH STUFF BUTT-NUT! ALL YA' GOTTA DO'S ASK!
AWW, SHUT UP AND GET INSIDE BEFORE SOMEBODY SEES YOU, OK?
GOO' IDEA. LE'S GO 'NSIDE.
BETTER YET, LE'S DO IT RIGH' HERE IN THE HALL! WHADDYA' SAY EDDIE?
THE NAME'S FREDDIE.
WHATEVER! WHAT THE HELL! LET'S ROCK AND ROLL! WAHOOOO!
DOHT!
WILL YOU SHUT UP?!! YOU WANNA WAKE THE WHOLE BUILDING?!
MMPH 'N MMOL!
C'MON TEDDY, LOOSEN UP! YOU GOTTA' LIVE DANGEROUSLY!
4B
TELL YOU WHAT, I WON'T USE A CONDOM, HOW'S THAT? NOW GET IN THERE!
AAGH!
3B

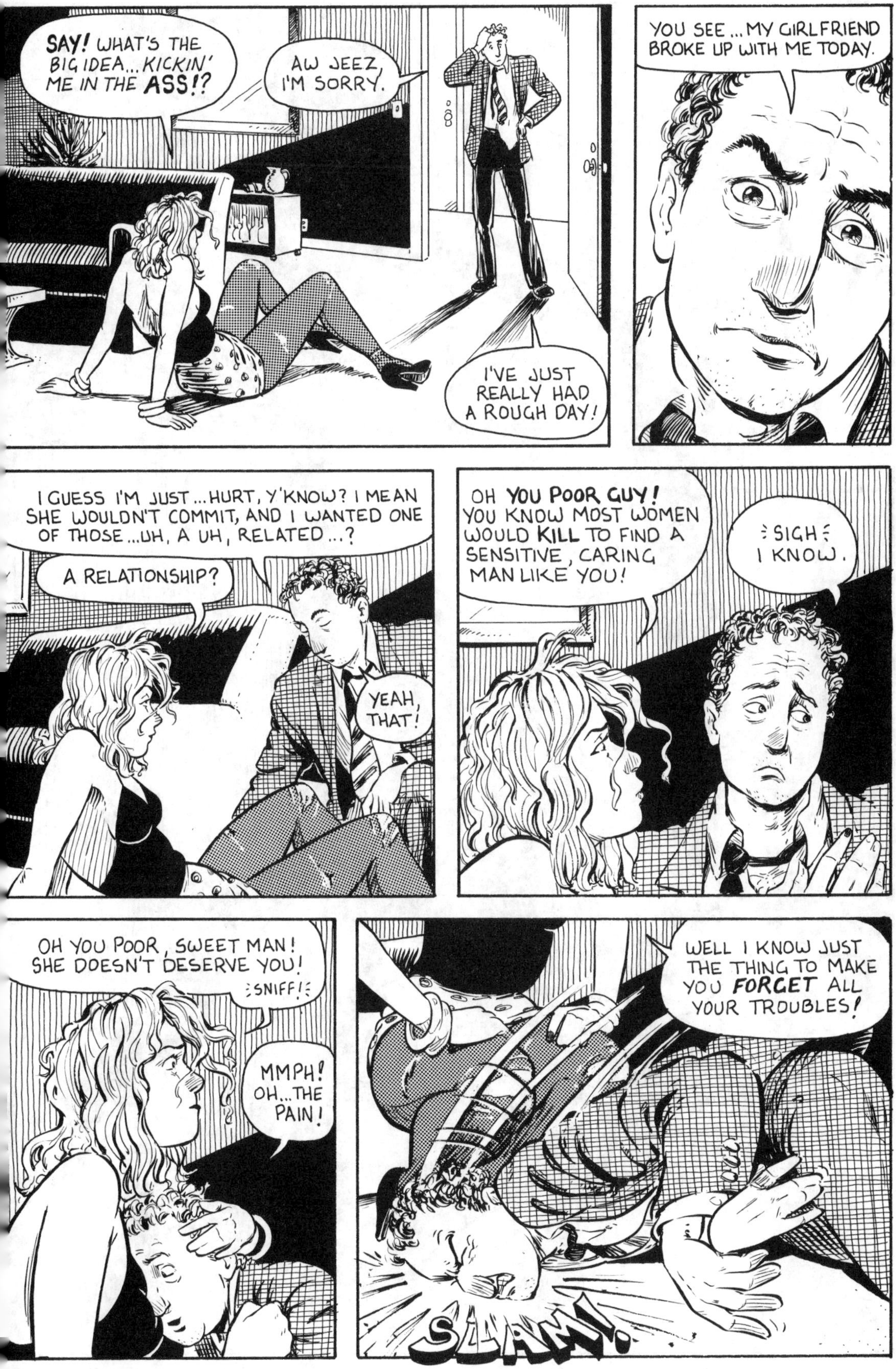
SAY! WHAT'S THE BIG IDEA... KICKIN' ME IN THE ASS!?
AW JEEZ, I'M SORRY.
I'VE JUST REALLY HAD A ROUGH DAY!
YOU SEE... MY GIRLFRIEND BROKE UP WITH ME TODAY.
I GUESS I'M JUST... HURT, Y'KNOW? I MEAN SHE WOULDN'T COMMIT, AND I WANTED ONE OF THOSE... UH, A UH, RELATED...?
A RELATIONSHIP?
YEAH, THAT!
OH YOU POOR GUY! YOU KNOW MOST WOMEN WOULD KILL TO FIND A SENSITIVE, CARING MAN LIKE YOU!
SIGH I KNOW.
OH YOU POOR, SWEET MAN! SHE DOESN'T DESERVE YOU!
SNIFF!
MMPH! OH... THE PAIN!
WELL I KNOW JUST THE THING TO MAKE YOU FORGET ALL YOUR TROUBLES!
SLAM!

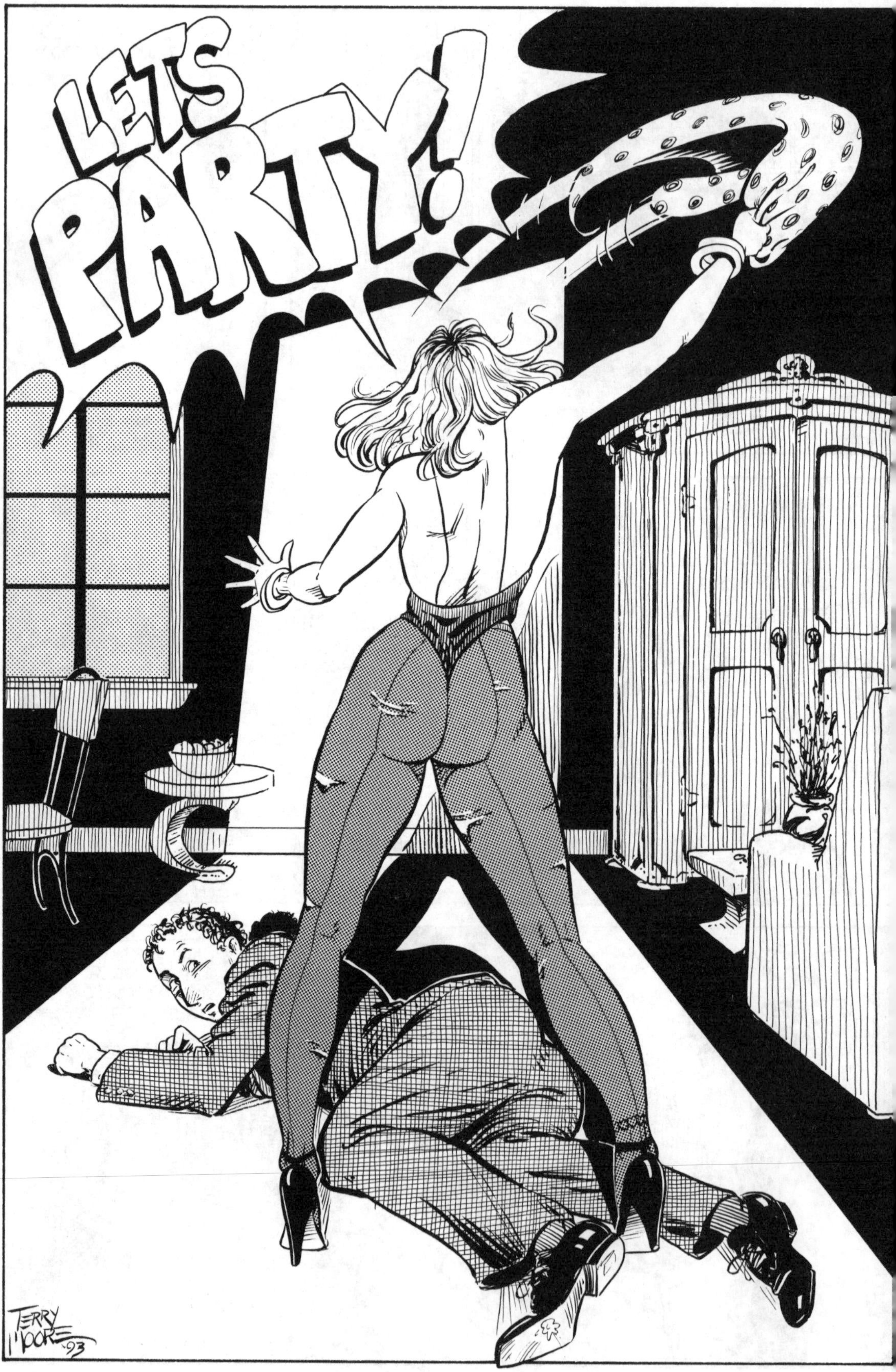
LETS PARTY!
TERRY MOORE '93

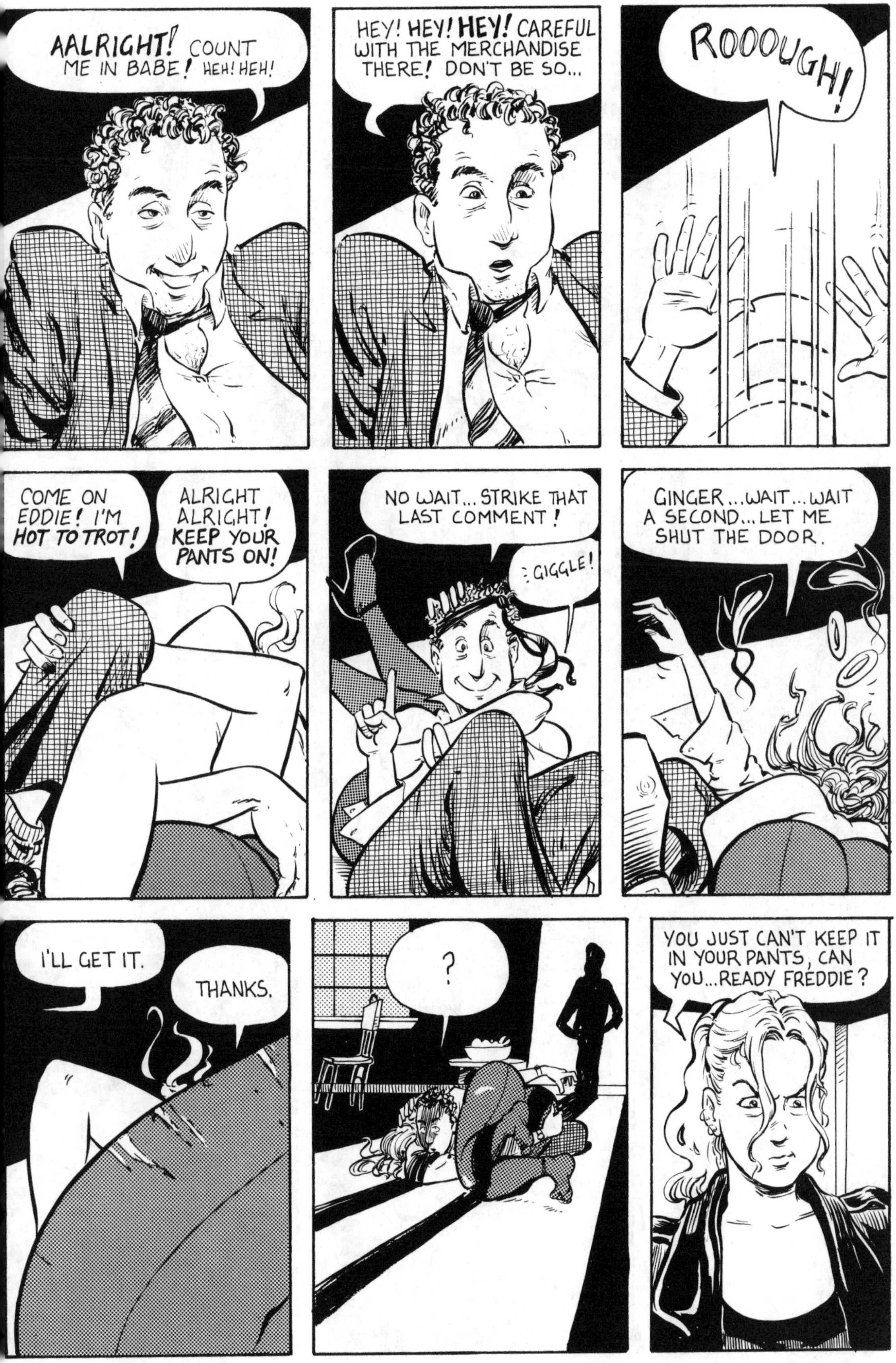
AALRIGHT! COUNT ME IN BABE! HEH! HEH!
HEY! HEY! HEY! CAREFUL WITH THE MERCHANDISE THERE! DON'T BE SO...
ROOOUGH!
COME ON EDDIE! I'M HOT TO TROT!
ALRIGHT ALRIGHT! KEEP YOUR PANTS ON!
NO WAIT... STRIKE THAT LAST COMMENT!
GIGGLE!
GINGER... WAIT... WAIT A SECOND... LET ME SHUT THE DOOR.
I'LL GET IT.
THANKS.
?
YOU JUST CAN'T KEEP IT IN YOUR PANTS, CAN YOU... READY FREDDIE?

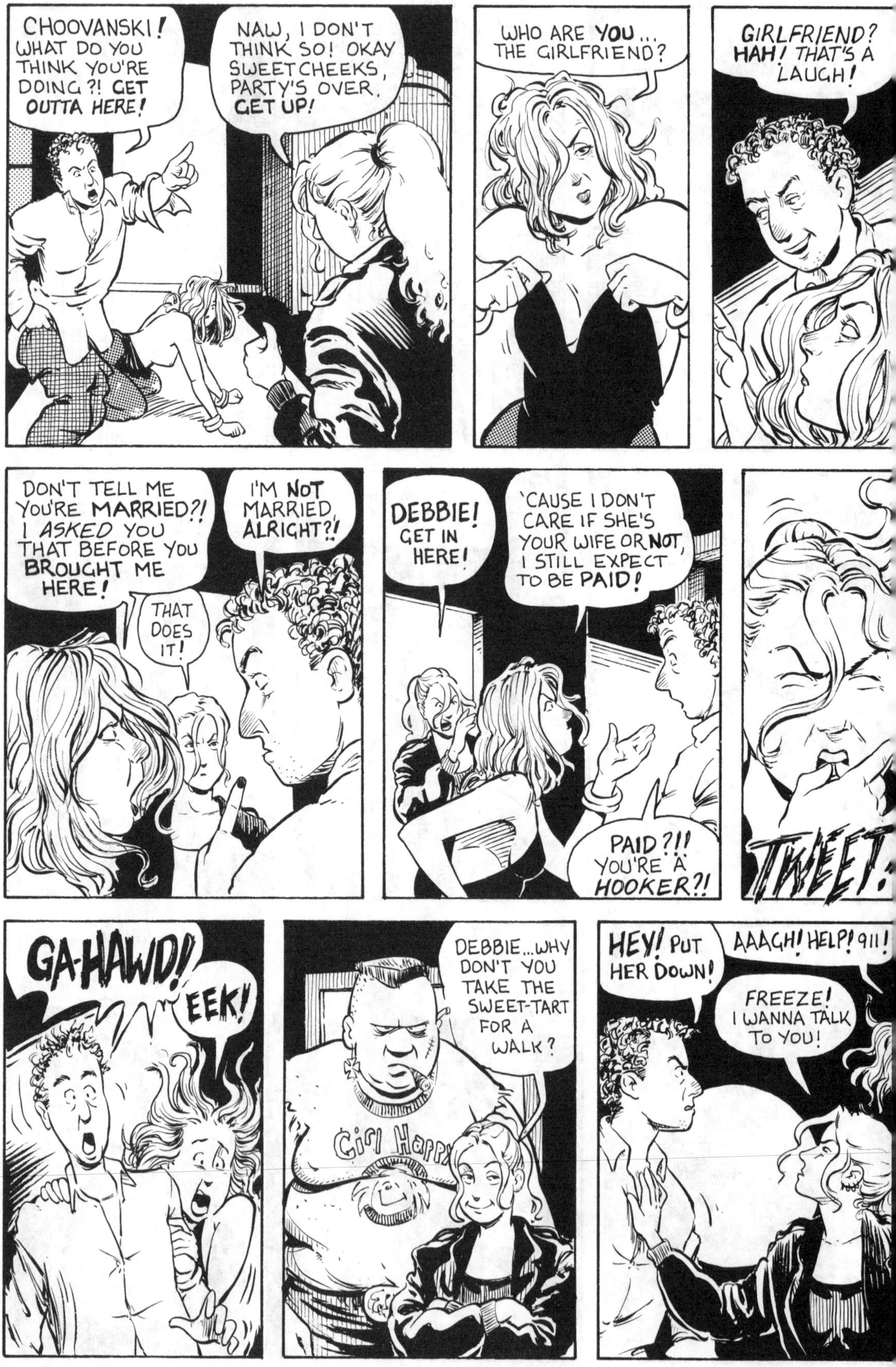

CHOOVANSKI! WHAT DO YOU THINK YOU'RE DOING?! GET OUTTA HERE!
NAW, I DON'T THINK SO! OKAY SWEETCHEEKS, PARTY'S OVER. GET UP!
WHO ARE YOU... THE GIRLFRIEND?
GIRLFRIEND? HAH! THAT'S A LAUGH!
DON'T TELL ME YOU'RE MARRIED?! I ASKED YOU THAT BEFORE YOU BROUGHT ME HERE!
I'M NOT MARRIED, ALRIGHT?!
THAT DOES IT!
DEBBIE! GET IN HERE!
'CAUSE I DON'T CARE IF SHE'S YOUR WIFE OR NOT, I STILL EXPECT TO BE PAID!
PAID?!! YOU'RE A HOOKER?!
TWEET!
GA-HAWD!
EEK!
Girl Happy
DEBBIE... WHY DON'T YOU TAKE THE SWEET-TART FOR A WALK?
HEY! PUT HER DOWN!
AAAGH! HELP! 911!
FREEZE! I WANNA TALK TO YOU!

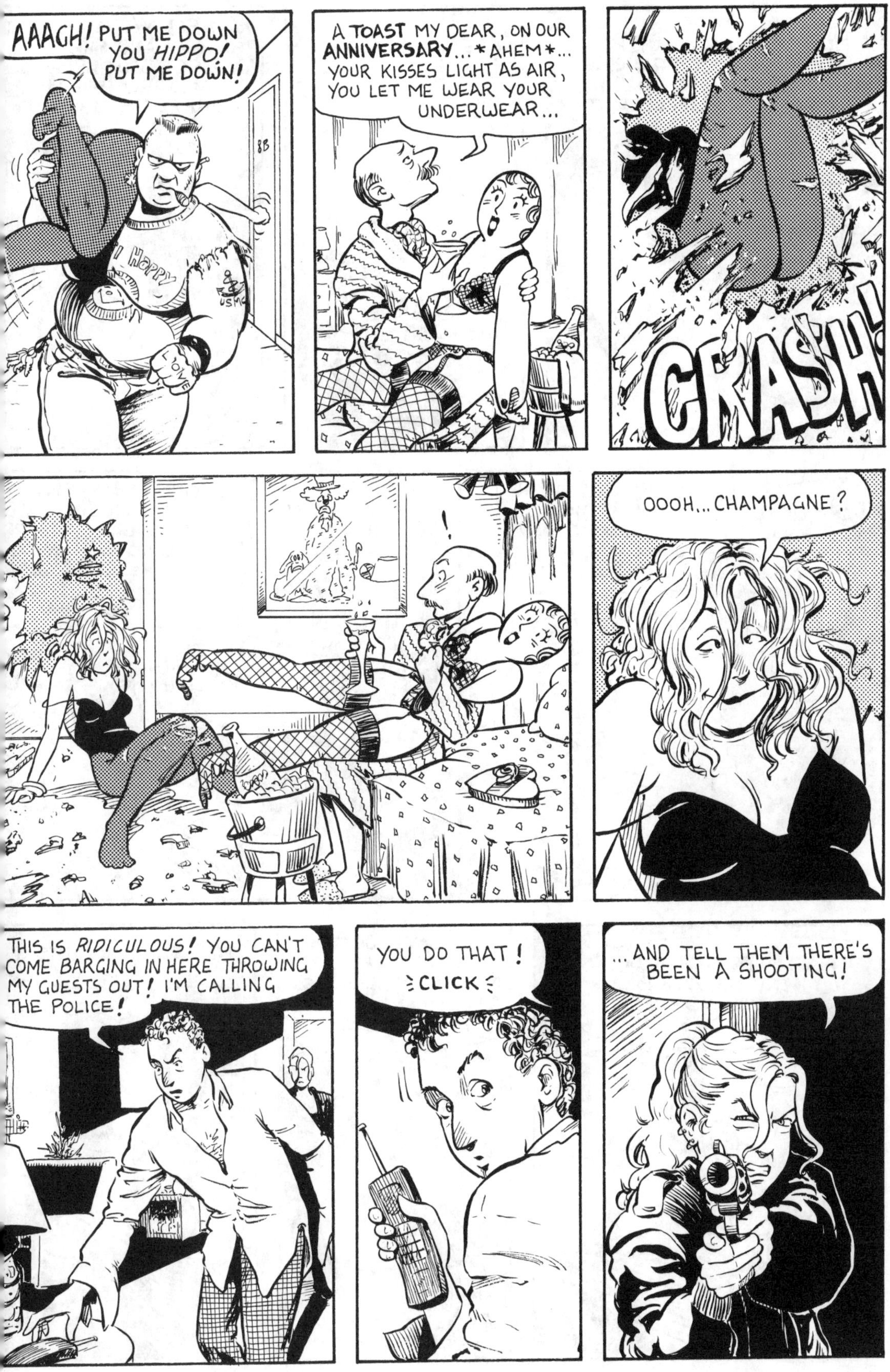
AAAGH! PUT ME DOWN YOU HIPPO! PUT ME DOWN!
A TOAST MY DEAR, ON OUR ANNIVERSARY... *AHEM*... YOUR KISSES LIGHT AS AIR, YOU LET ME WEAR YOUR UNDERWEAR...
CRASH!
OOOH... CHAMPAGNE?
THIS IS RIDICULOUS! YOU CAN'T COME BARGING IN HERE THROWING MY GUESTS OUT! I'M CALLING THE POLICE!
YOU DO THAT!
CLICK
... AND TELL THEM THERE'S BEEN A SHOOTING!

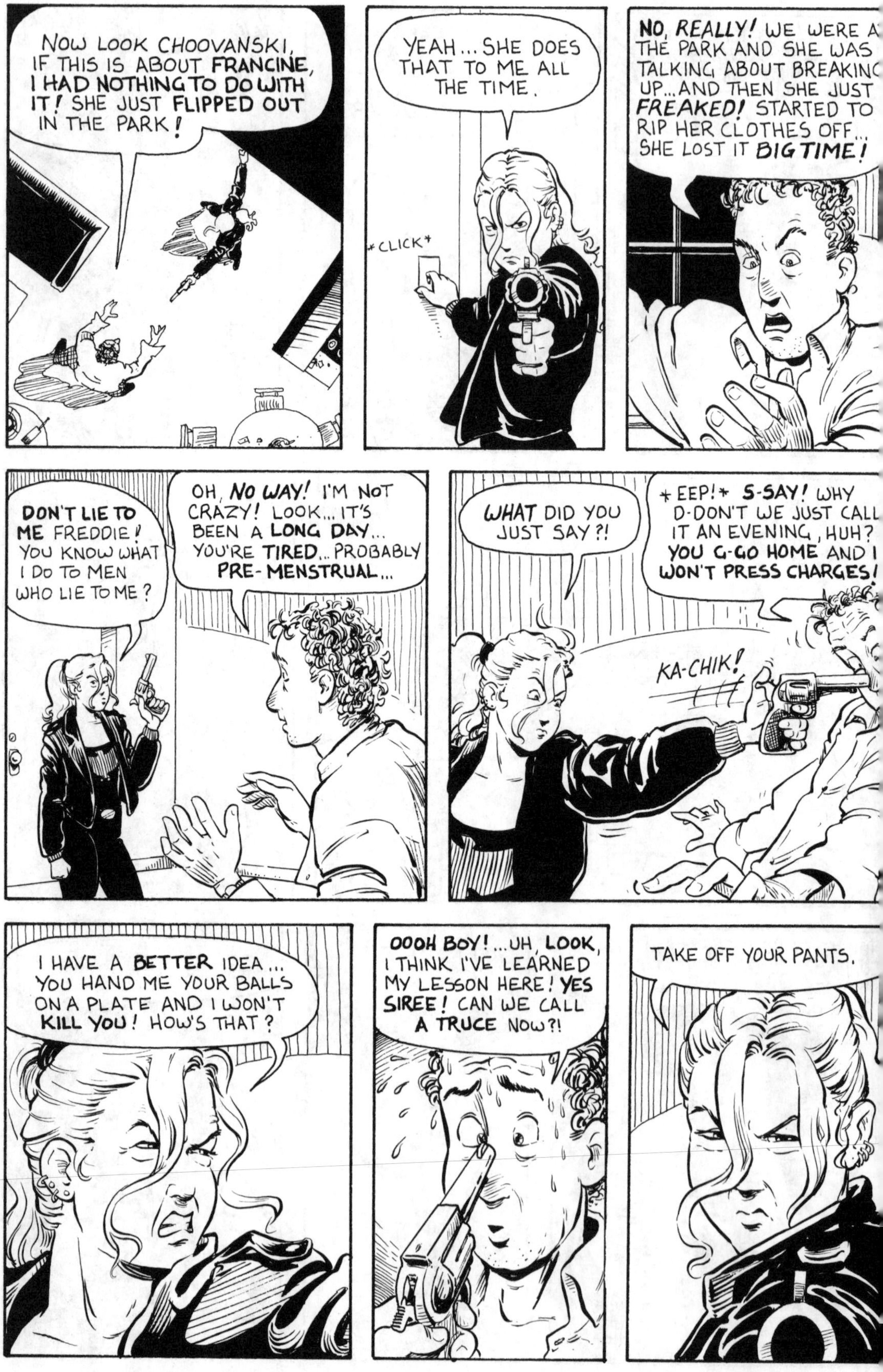
NOW LOOK CHOOVANSKI, IF THIS IS ABOUT FRANCINE, I HAD NOTHING TO DO WITH IT! SHE JUST FLIPPED OUT IN THE PARK!
YEAH... SHE DOES THAT TO ME ALL THE TIME.
CLICK
NO, REALLY! WE WERE A THE PARK AND SHE WAS TALKING ABOUT BREAKIN UP... AND THEN SHE JUST FREAKED! STARTED TO RIP HER CLOTHES OFF... SHE LOST IT BIG TIME!
DON'T LIE TO ME FREDDIE! YOU KNOW WHAT I DO TO MEN WHO LIE TO ME?
OH, NO WAY! I'M NOT CRAZY! LOOK... IT'S BEEN A LONG DAY... YOU'RE TIRED... PROBABLY PRE-MENSTRUAL...
WHAT DID YOU JUST SAY?!
EEP! S-SAY! WHY D-DON'T WE JUST CALL IT AN EVENING, HUH? YOU G-GO HOME AND I WON'T PRESS CHARGES!
KA-CHIK!
I HAVE A BETTER IDEA... YOU HAND ME YOUR BALLS ON A PLATE AND I WON'T KILL YOU! HOW'S THAT?
OOOH BOY! ...UH, LOOK, I THINK I'VE LEARNED MY LESSON HERE! YES SIREE! CAN WE CALL A TRUCE NOW?!
TAKE OFF YOUR PANTS.

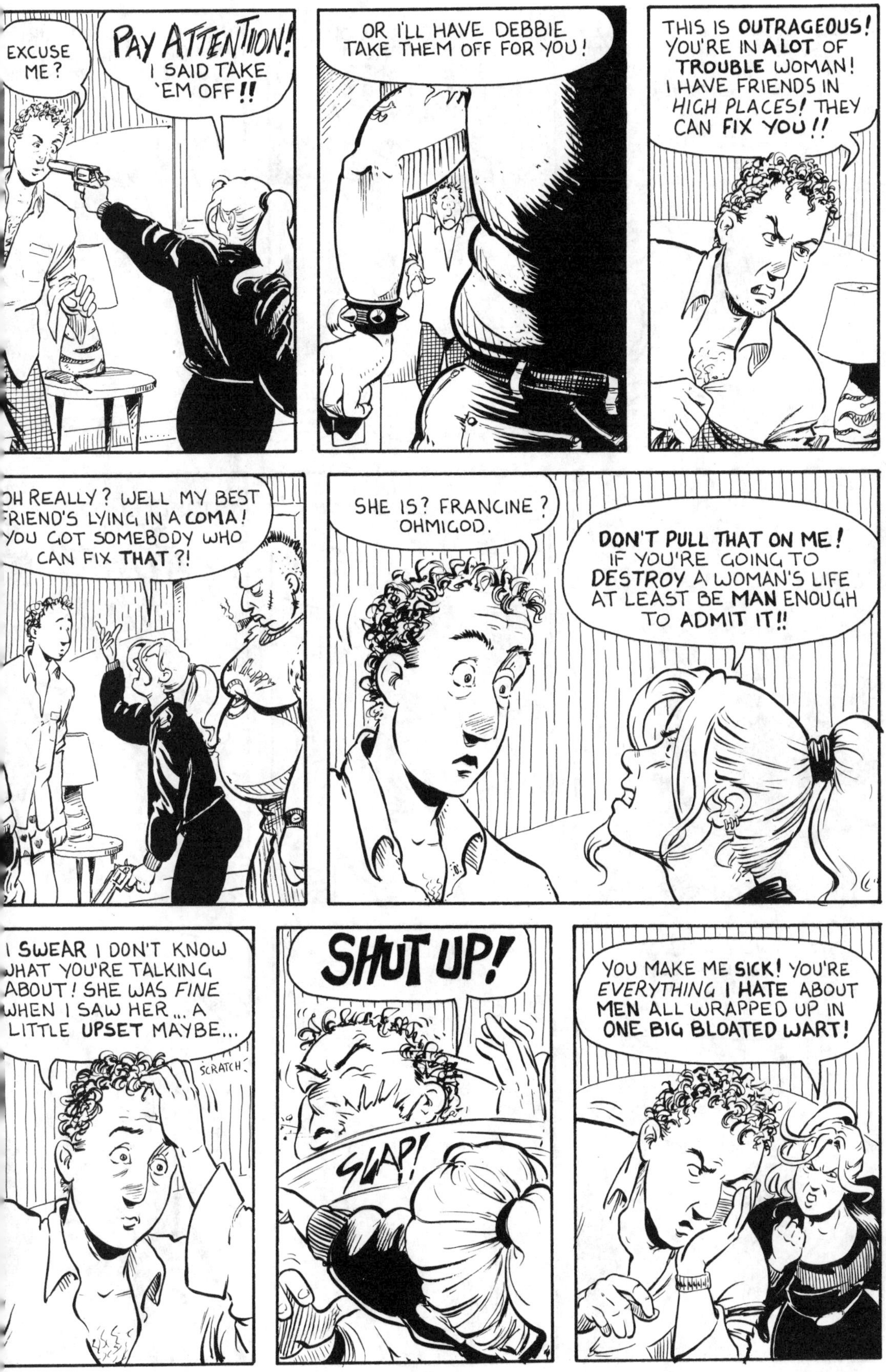
EXCUSE ME?
PAY ATTENTION! I SAID TAKE 'EM OFF!!
OR I'LL HAVE DEBBIE TAKE THEM OFF FOR YOU!
THIS IS OUTRAGEOUS! YOU'RE IN A LOT OF TROUBLE WOMAN! I HAVE FRIENDS IN HIGH PLACES! THEY CAN FIX YOU!!
OH REALLY? WELL MY BEST FRIEND'S LYING IN A COMA! YOU GOT SOMEBODY WHO CAN FIX THAT?!
SHE IS? FRANCINE? OHMIGOD.
DON'T PULL THAT ON ME! IF YOU'RE GOING TO DESTROY A WOMAN'S LIFE AT LEAST BE MAN ENOUGH TO ADMIT IT!!
I SWEAR I DON'T KNOW WHAT YOU'RE TALKING ABOUT! SHE WAS FINE WHEN I SAW HER... A LITTLE UPSET MAYBE...
SCRATCH
SHUT UP!
SLAP!
YOU MAKE ME SICK! YOU'RE EVERYTHING I HATE ABOUT MEN ALL WRAPPED UP IN ONE BIG BLOATED WART!

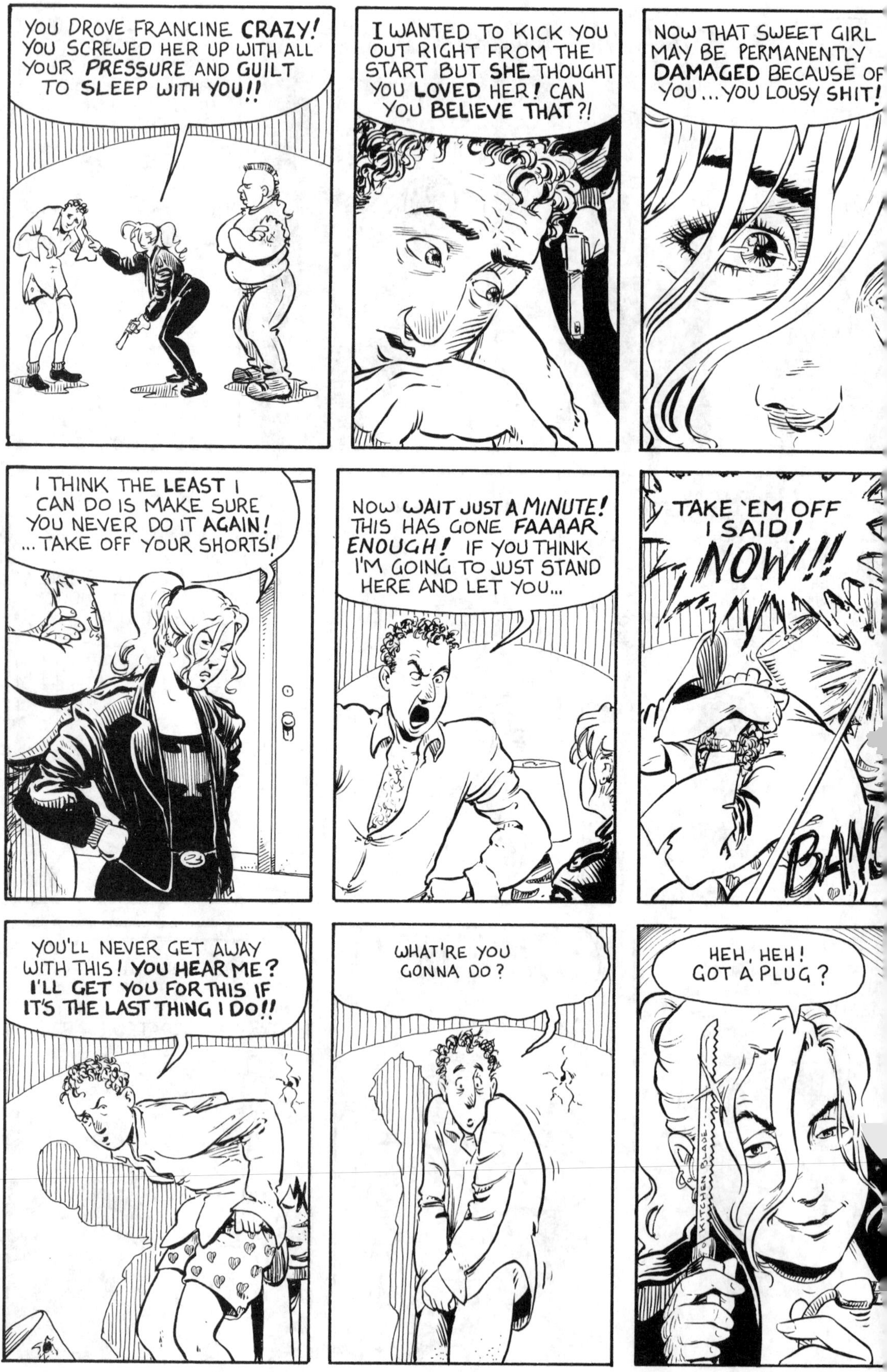
YOU DROVE FRANCINE CRAZY! YOU SCREWED HER UP WITH ALL YOUR PRESSURE AND GUILT TO SLEEP WITH YOU!!
I WANTED TO KICK YOU OUT RIGHT FROM THE START BUT SHE THOUGHT YOU LOVED HER! CAN YOU BELIEVE THAT?!
NOW THAT SWEET GIRL MAY BE PERMANENTLY DAMAGED BECAUSE OF YOU... YOU LOUSY SHIT!
I THINK THE LEAST I CAN DO IS MAKE SURE YOU NEVER DO IT AGAIN! ...TAKE OFF YOUR SHORTS!
NOW WAIT JUST A MINUTE! THIS HAS GONE FAAAAR ENOUGH! IF YOU THINK I'M GOING TO JUST STAND HERE AND LET YOU...
TAKE 'EM OFF I SAID! NOW!!
YOU'LL NEVER GET AWAY WITH THIS! YOU HEAR ME? I'LL GET YOU FOR THIS IF IT'S THE LAST THING I DO!!
WHAT'RE YOU GONNA DO?
HEH, HEH! GOT A PLUG?
KITCHEN BLADE

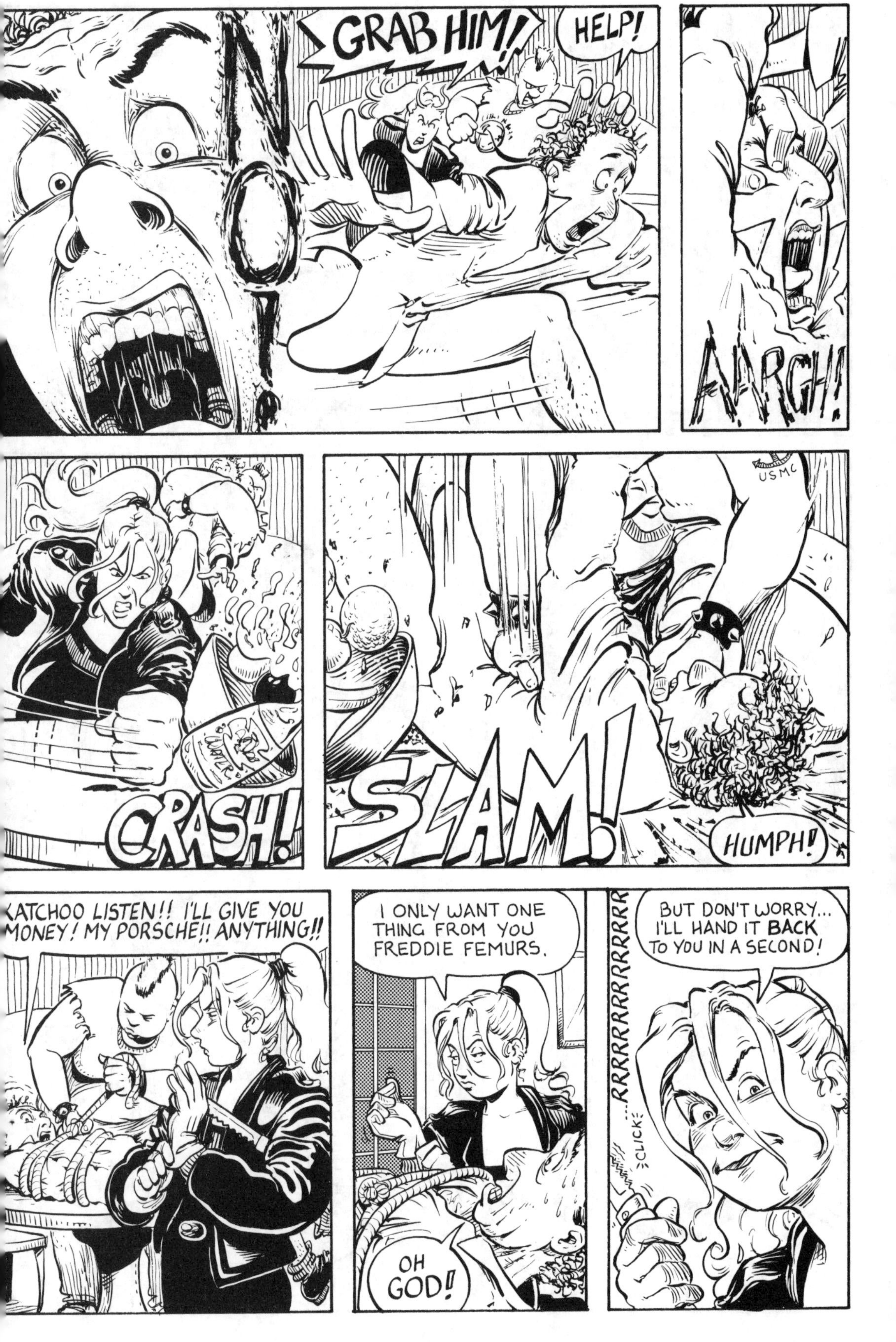
NO!
GRAB HIM!
HELP!
AARGH!
CRASH!
SLAM!
HUMPH!
KATCHOO LISTEN!! I'LL GIVE YOU MONEY! MY PORSCHE!! ANYTHING!!
I ONLY WANT ONE THING FROM YOU FREDDIE FEMURS.
OH GOD!
CLICK!...RRRRRRRRRRRRRRR
BUT DON'T WORRY... I'LL HAND IT BACK TO YOU IN A SECOND!

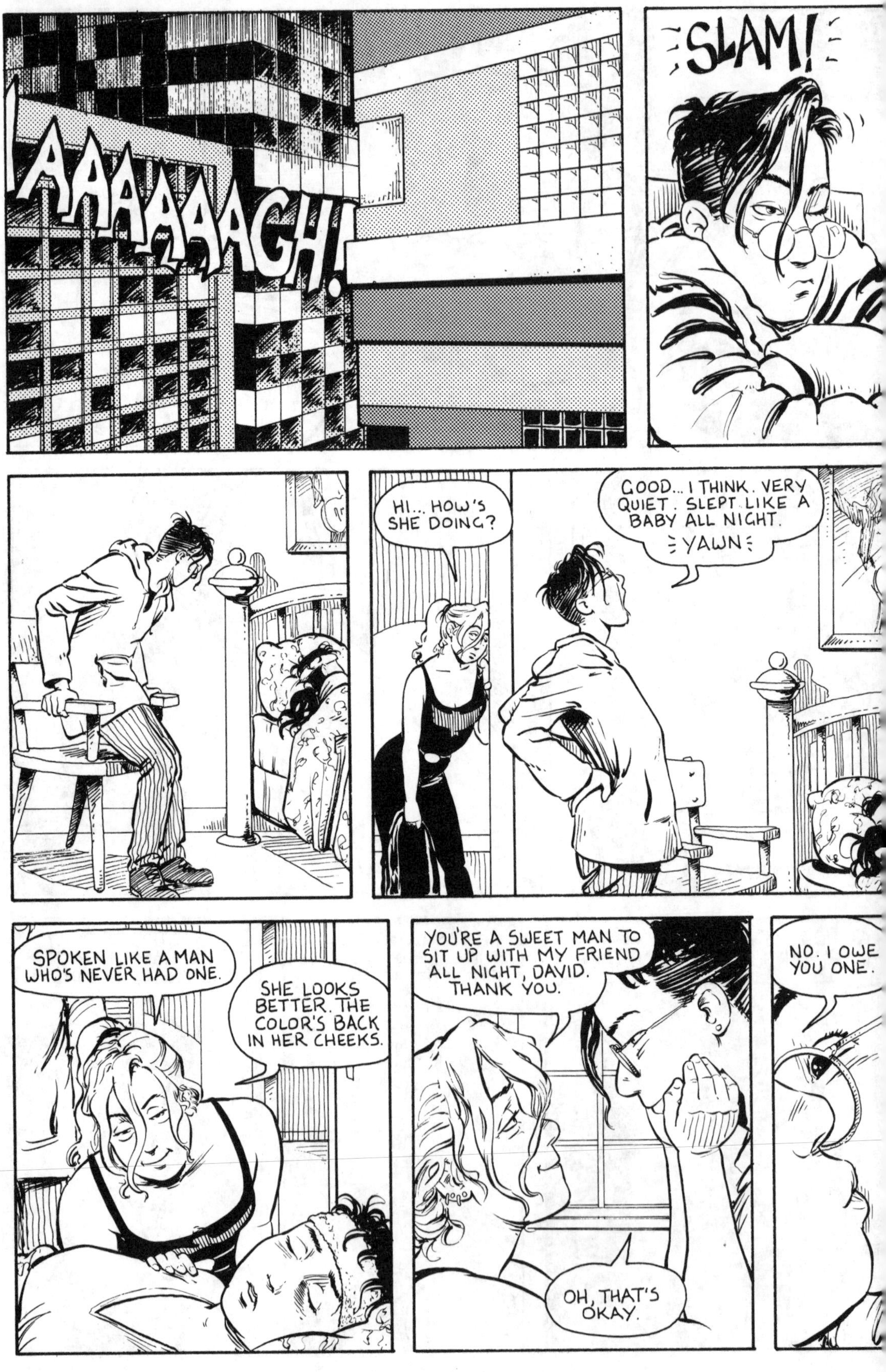
AAAAAAAGH!
SLAM!
HI... HOW'S SHE DOING?
GOOD... I THINK. VERY QUIET. SLEPT LIKE A BABY ALL NIGHT.
YAWN
SPOKEN LIKE A MAN WHO'S NEVER HAD ONE.
SHE LOOKS BETTER. THE COLOR'S BACK IN HER CHEEKS.
YOU'RE A SWEET MAN TO SIT UP WITH MY FRIEND ALL NIGHT, DAVID. THANK YOU.
OH, THAT'S OKAY.
NO. I OWE YOU ONE.

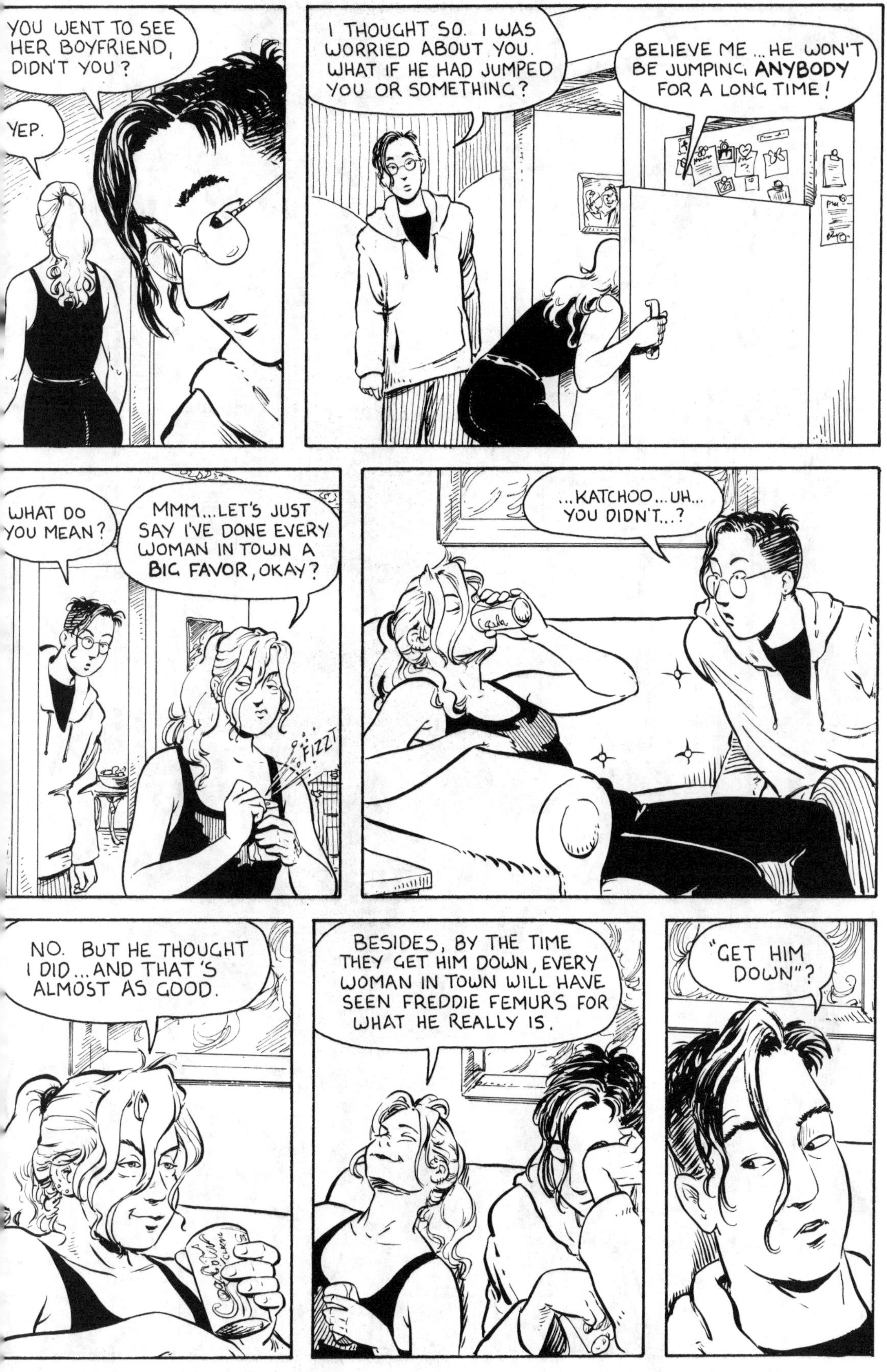
YOU WENT TO SEE HER BOYFRIEND, DIDN'T YOU?
YEP.
I THOUGHT SO. I WAS WORRIED ABOUT YOU. WHAT IF HE HAD JUMPED YOU OR SOMETHING?
BELIEVE ME ... HE WON'T BE JUMPING ANYBODY FOR A LONG TIME!
WHAT DO YOU MEAN?
MMM... LET'S JUST SAY I'VE DONE EVERY WOMAN IN TOWN A BIG FAVOR, OKAY?
FIZZT
...KATCHOO... UH... YOU DIDN'T...?
NO. BUT HE THOUGHT I DID... AND THAT'S ALMOST AS GOOD.
BESIDES, BY THE TIME THEY GET HIM DOWN, EVERY WOMAN IN TOWN WILL HAVE SEEN FREDDIE FEMURS FOR WHAT HE REALLY IS.
"GET HIM DOWN"?

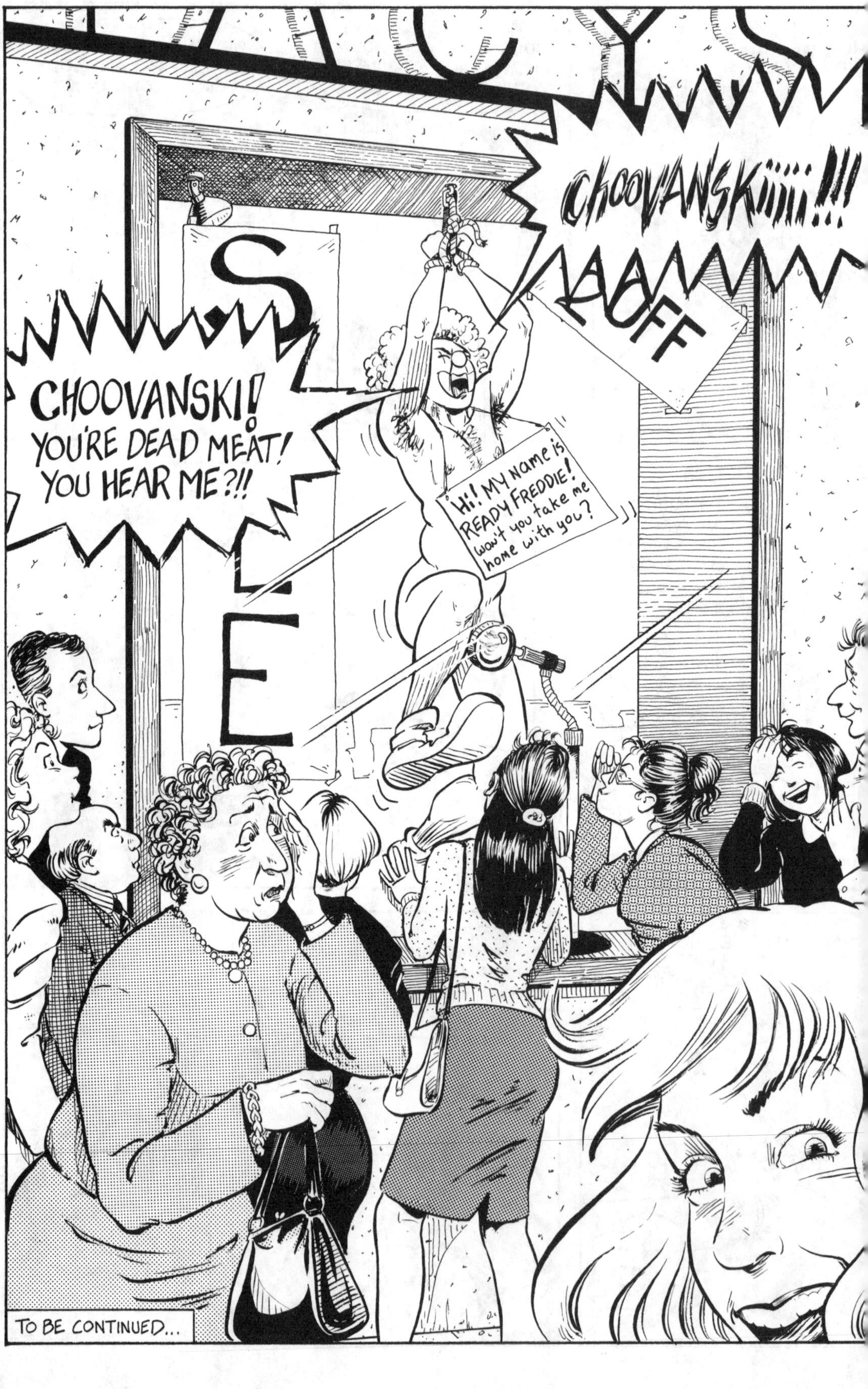
CHOOVANSKIIIII!!!
AAAUFF
CHOOVANSKI! YOU'RE DEAD MEAT! YOU HEAR ME?!!
Hi! MY Name is READY FREDDIE! Won't you take me home with you?
TO BE CONTINUED...

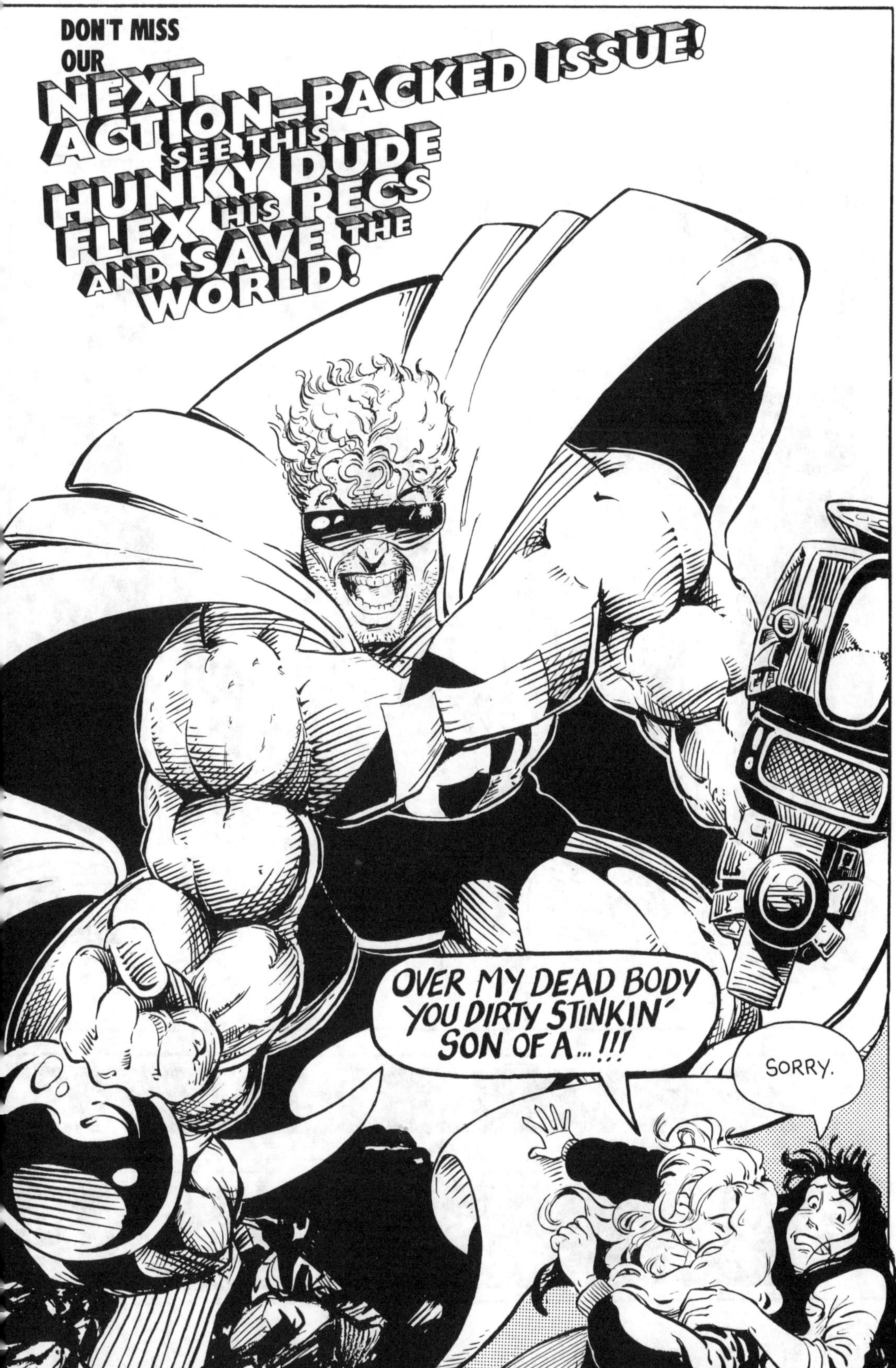
DON'T MISS OUR NEXT ACTION-PACKED ISSUE!
SEE THIS HUNKY DUDE FLEX HIS PECS AND SAVE THE WORLD!
OVER MY DEAD BODY YOU DIRTY STINKIN' SON OF A...!!!
SORRY.

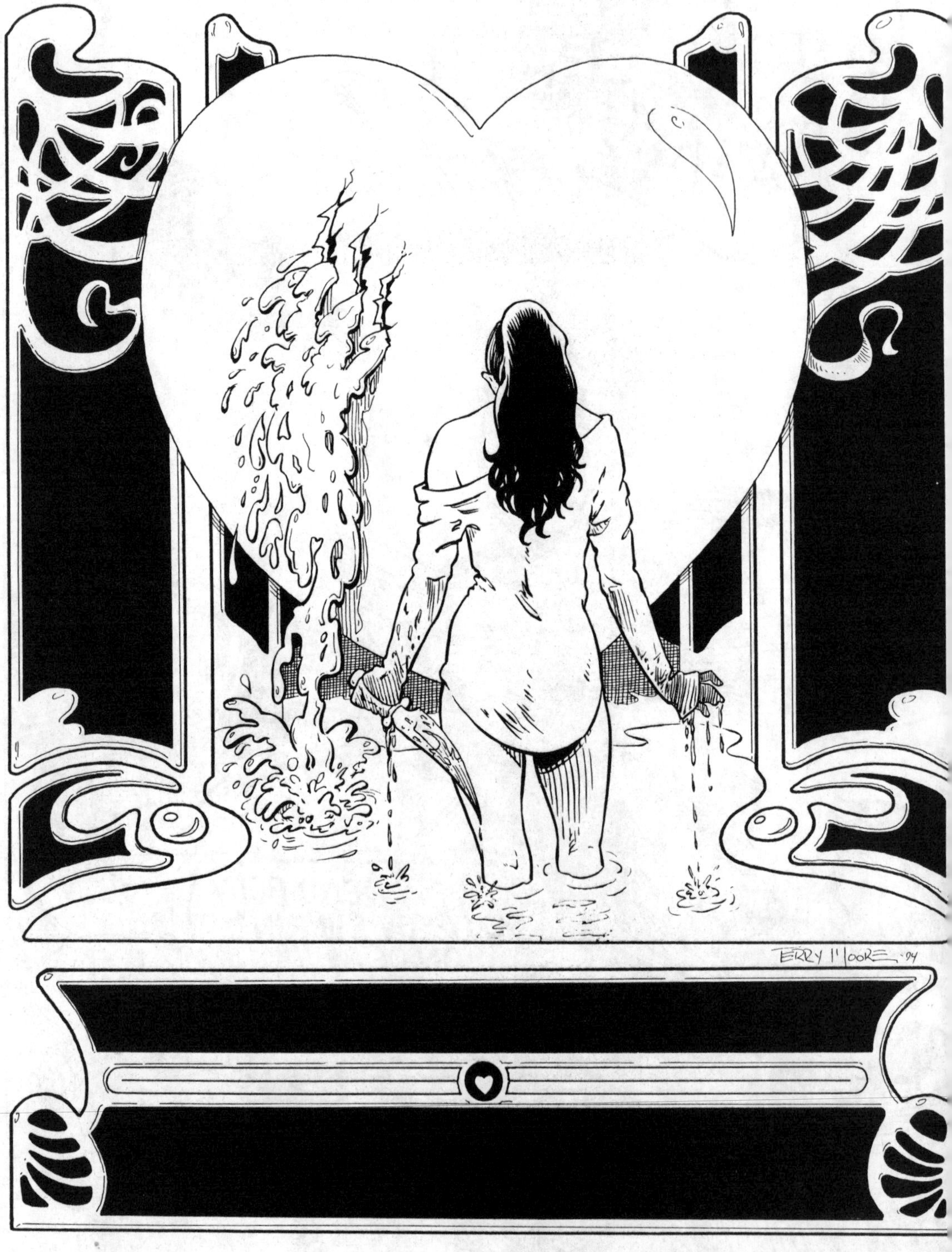
TERRY MOORE '94

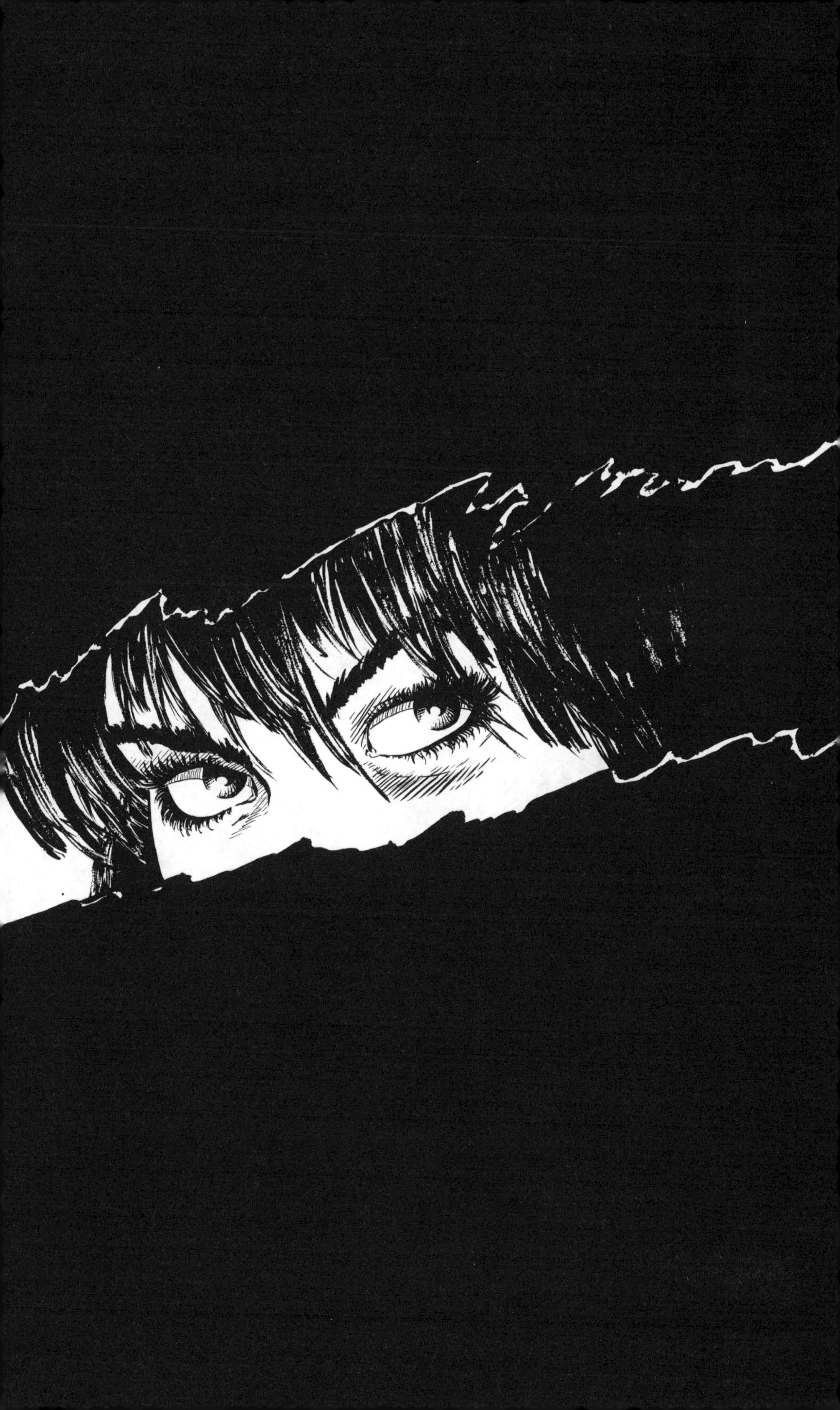

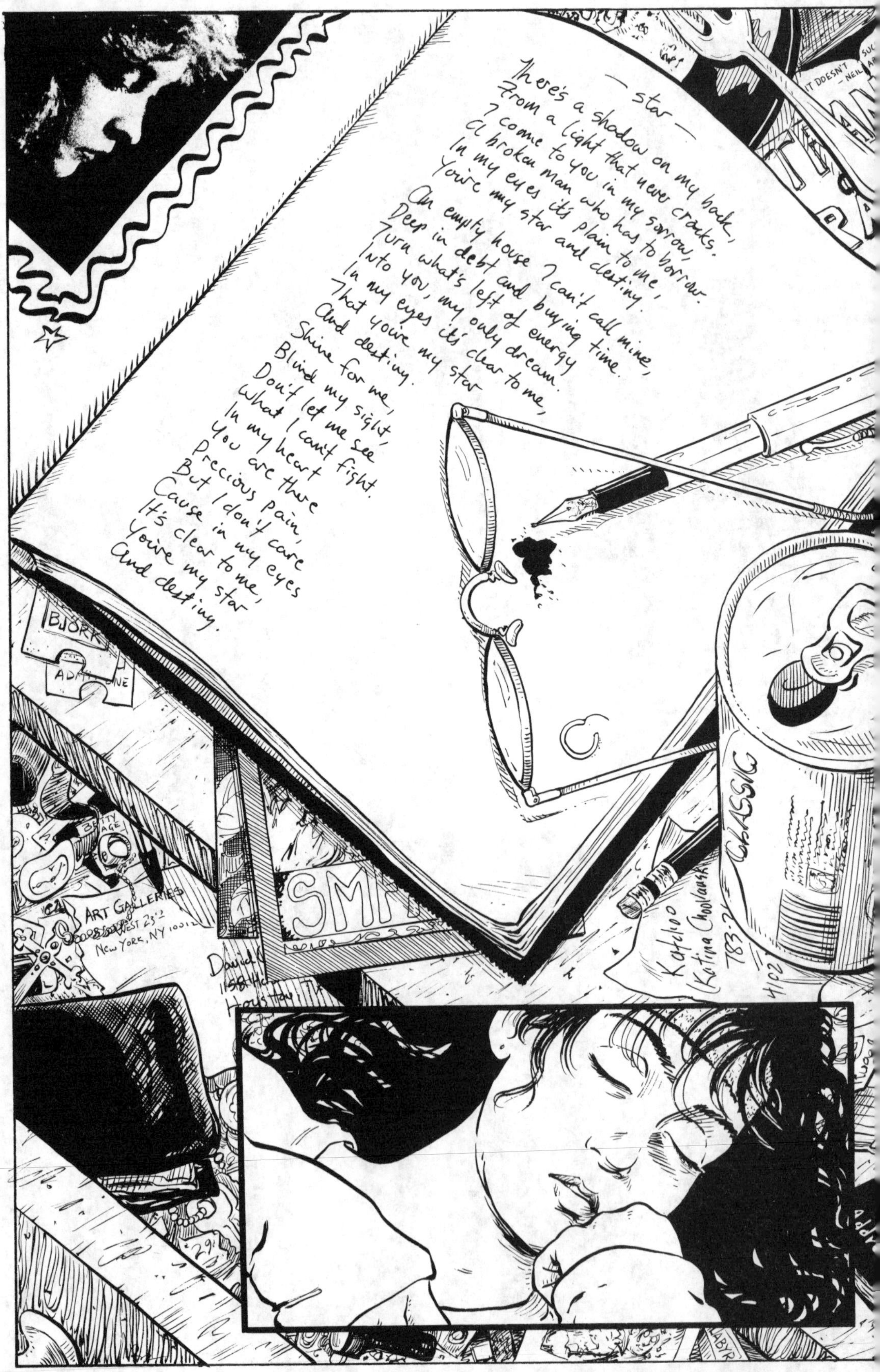

— star —
There's a shadow on my back,
From a light that never cracks.
I come to you in my sorrow,
A broken man who has to borrow.
In my eyes it's plain to me,
You're my star and destiny.
An empty house I can't call mine,
Deep in debt and buying time.
Turn what's left of energy
Into you, my only dream.
In my eyes it's clear to me,
That you're my star
And destiny.
Shine for me,
Blind my sight,
Don't let me see
What I can't fight.
In my heart
You are there
Precious pain,
But I don't care
Cause in my eyes
It's clear to me,
You're my star
And destiny.
BJORK
ART GALLERIES
CLASSIC
Katchoo

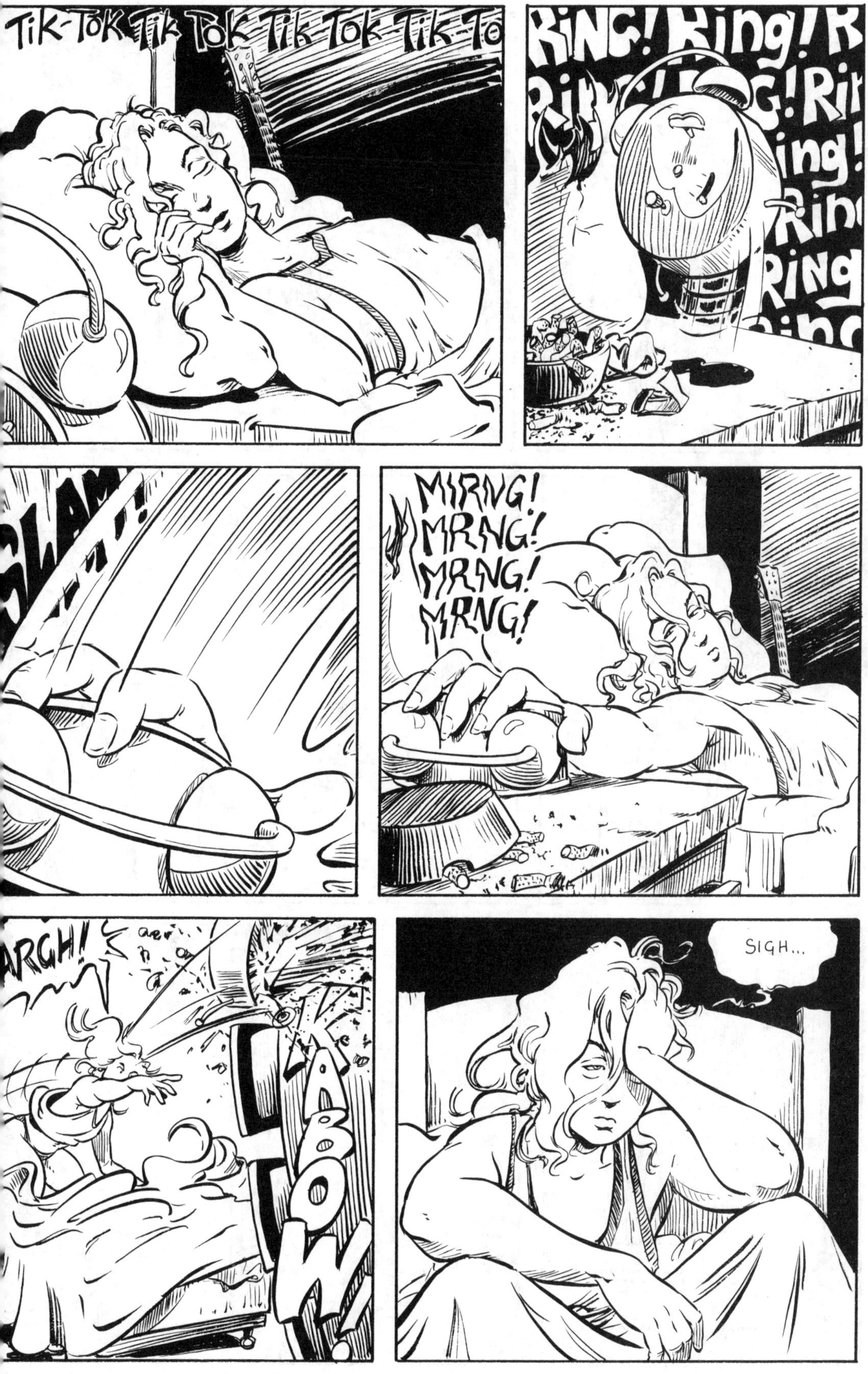
TIK-TOK TIK TOK TIK TOK TIK TO
RING! RING! R
RING!
RING
MIRNG!
MRNG!
MRNG!
MRNG!
ARGH!
SIGH...

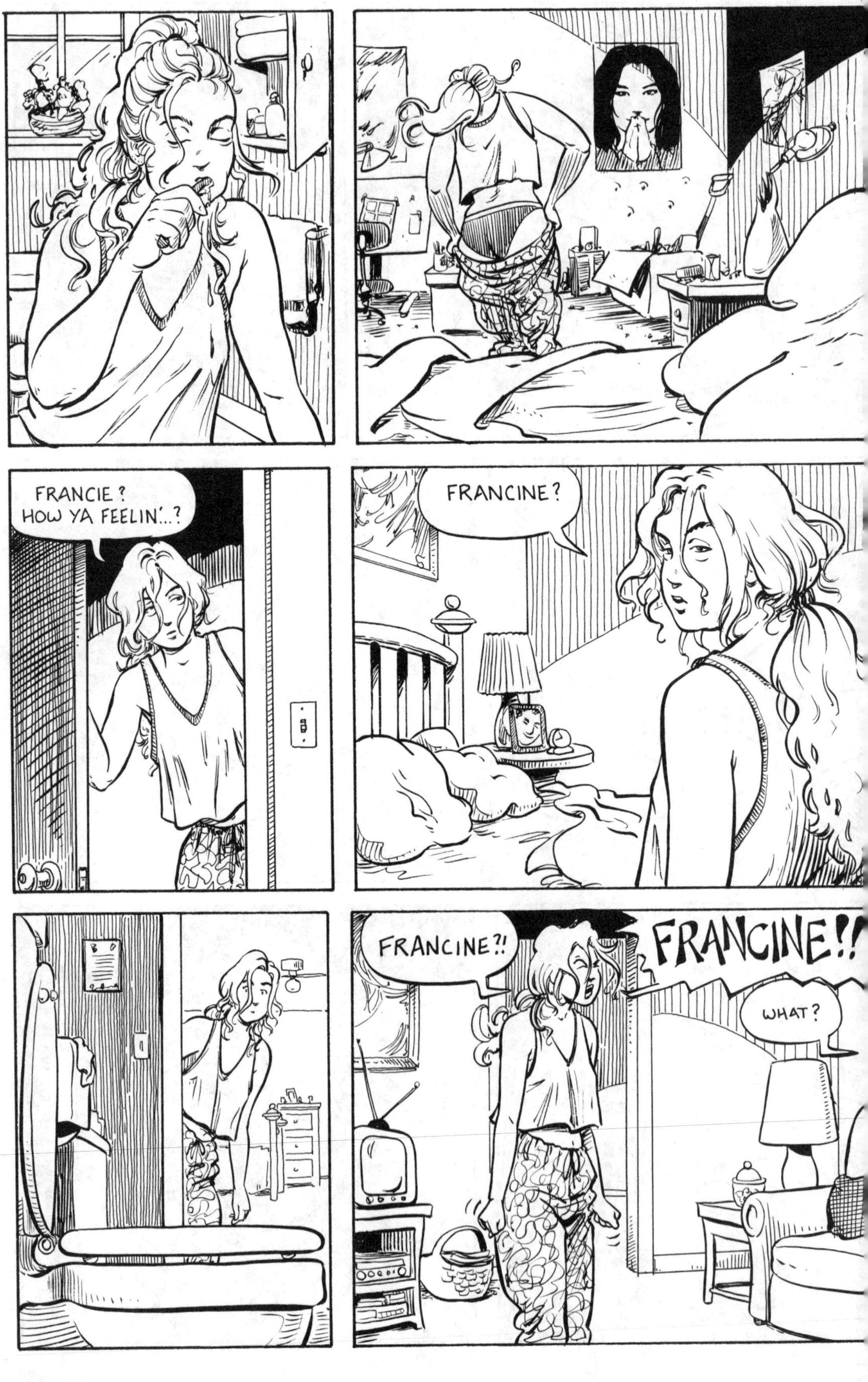
FRANCIE ? HOW YA FEELIN'...?
FRANCINE ?
FRANCINE?!
FRANCINE!!
WHAT ?

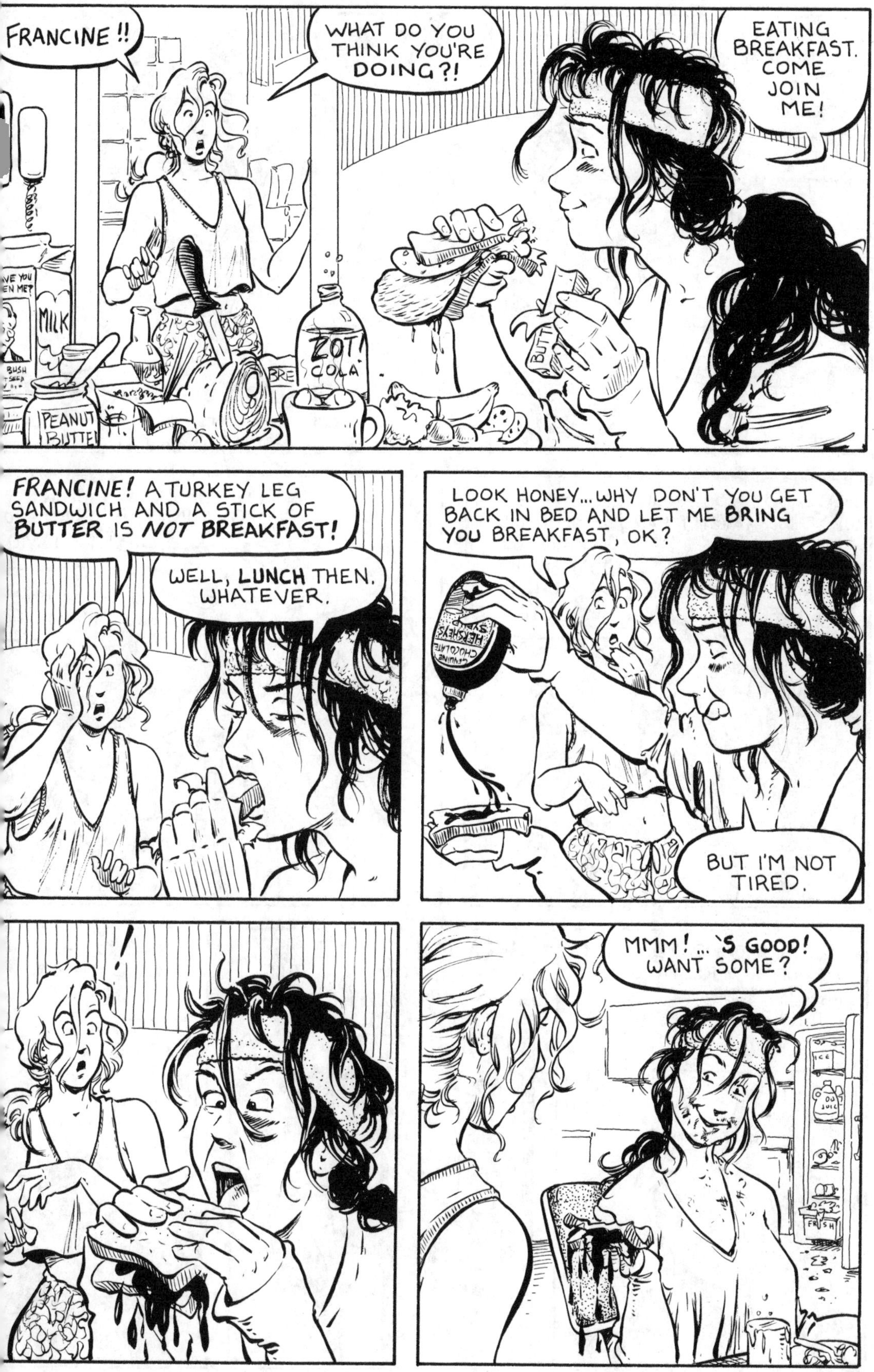
FRANCINE !!
WHAT DO YOU THINK YOU'RE DOING?!
EATING BREAKFAST. COME JOIN ME!
MILK
PEANUT BUTTE
ZOT! COLA
FRANCINE! A TURKEY LEG SANDWICH AND A STICK OF BUTTER IS NOT BREAKFAST!
WELL, LUNCH THEN. WHATEVER.
LOOK HONEY... WHY DON'T YOU GET BACK IN BED AND LET ME BRING YOU BREAKFAST, OK?
GENUINE CHOCOLATE HERSHEY'S SYRUP
BUT I'M NOT TIRED.
!
MMM! ...'S GOOD! WANT SOME?

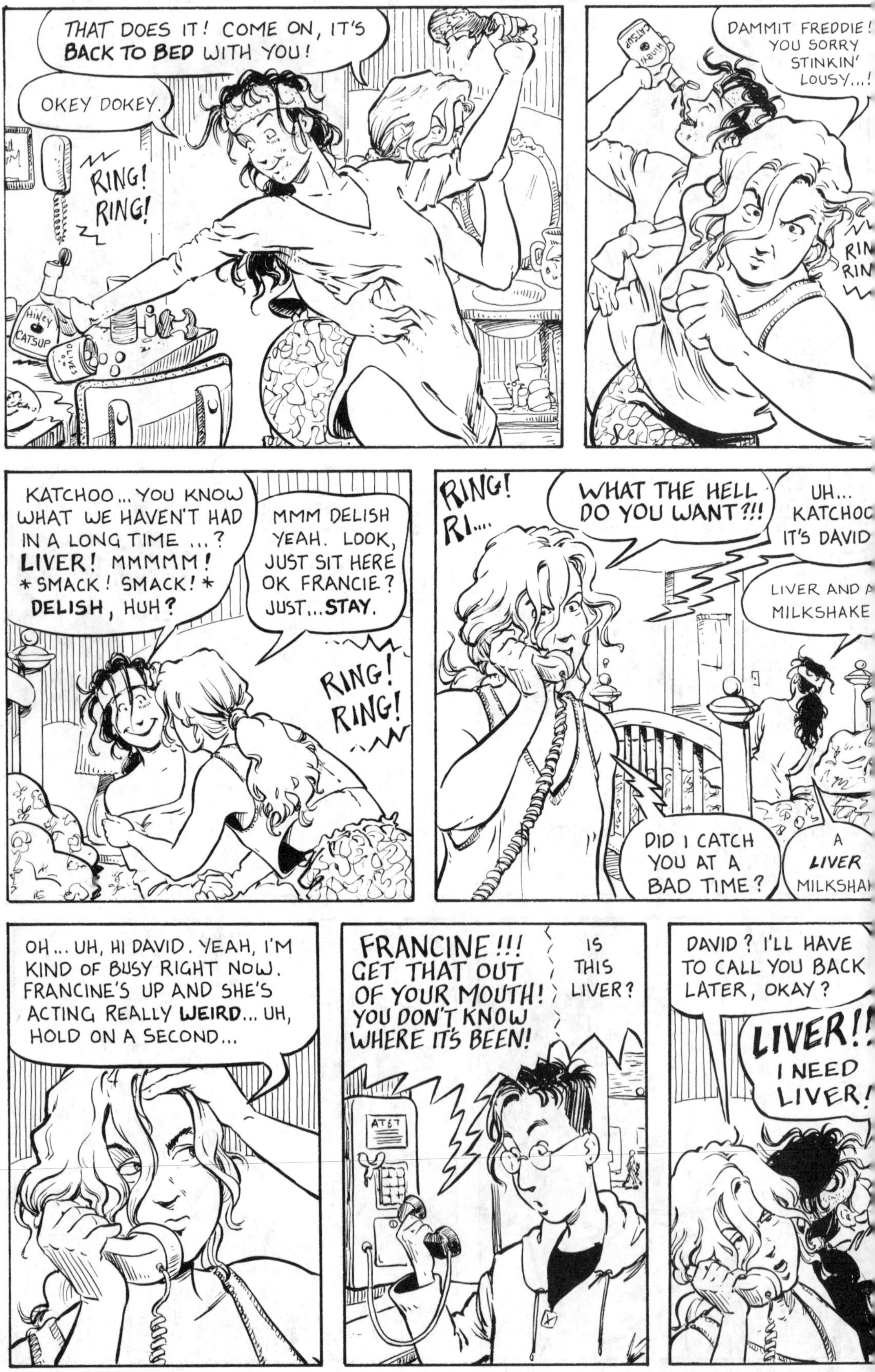
THAT DOES IT! COME ON, IT'S BACK TO BED WITH YOU!
OKEY DOKEY.
RING! RING!
HINEY CATSUP
OLIVES
DAMMIT FREDDIE! YOU SORRY STINKIN' LOUSY...!
CATSUP
KATCHOO... YOU KNOW WHAT WE HAVEN'T HAD IN A LONG TIME ...? LIVER! MMMMM! *SMACK! SMACK!* DELISH, HUH?
MMM DELISH YEAH. LOOK, JUST SIT HERE OK FRANCIE? JUST... STAY.
RING! RING!
RING! RI....
WHAT THE HELL DO YOU WANT?!!
UH... KATCHOO IT'S DAVID
LIVER AND A MILKSHAKE
DID I CATCH YOU AT A BAD TIME?
A LIVER MILKSHA
OH... UH, HI DAVID. YEAH, I'M KIND OF BUSY RIGHT NOW. FRANCINE'S UP AND SHE'S ACTING REALLY WEIRD... UH, HOLD ON A SECOND...
FRANCINE!!! GET THAT OUT OF YOUR MOUTH! YOU DON'T KNOW WHERE IT'S BEEN!
IS THIS LIVER?
AT&T
DAVID? I'LL HAVE TO CALL YOU BACK LATER, OKAY?
LIVER!! I NEED LIVER!

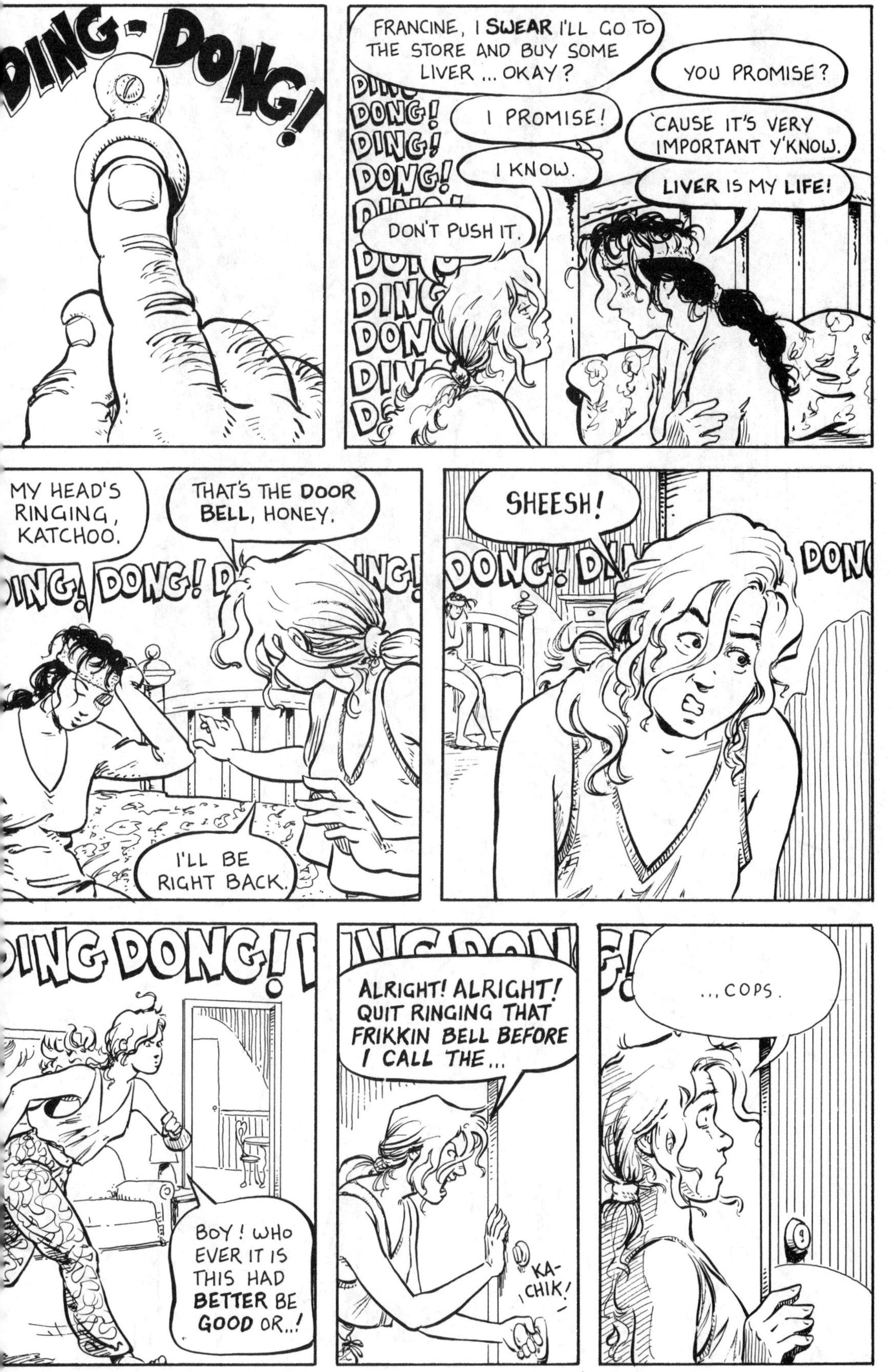
DING-DONG!
FRANCINE, I SWEAR I'LL GO TO THE STORE AND BUY SOME LIVER ... OKAY?
YOU PROMISE?
I PROMISE!
`CAUSE IT'S VERY IMPORTANT Y'KNOW.
I KNOW.
LIVER IS MY LIFE!
DON'T PUSH IT.
DONG! DING! DONG!
MY HEAD'S RINGING, KATCHOO.
THAT'S THE DOOR BELL, HONEY.
DONG!
I'LL BE RIGHT BACK.
SHEESH!
DONG!
DING DONG!
ALRIGHT! ALRIGHT! QUIT RINGING THAT FRIKKIN BELL BEFORE I CALL THE...
BOY! WHO EVER IT IS THIS HAD BETTER BE GOOD OR..!
KA-CHIK!
...COPS.

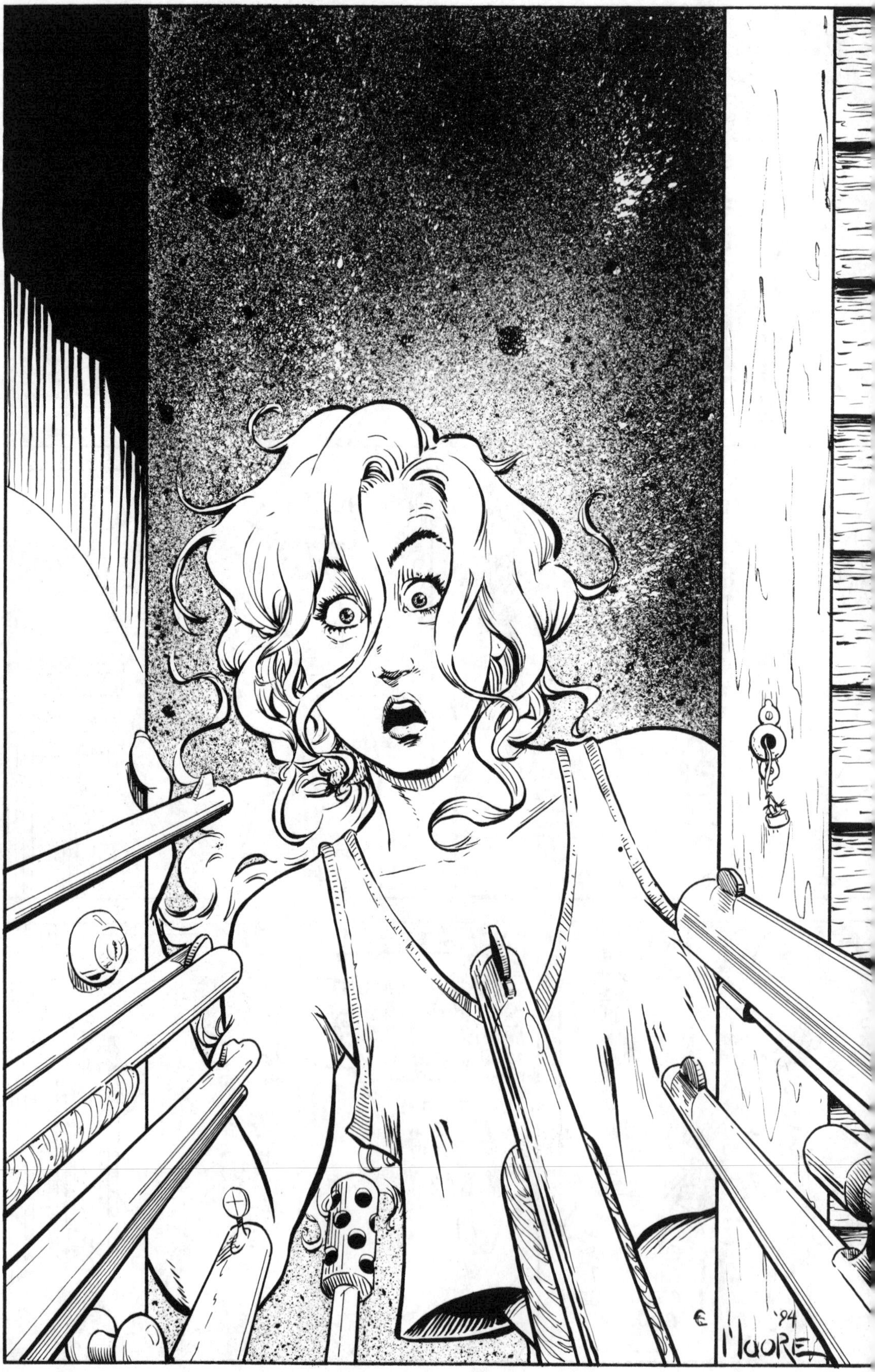
© '94
MOORE

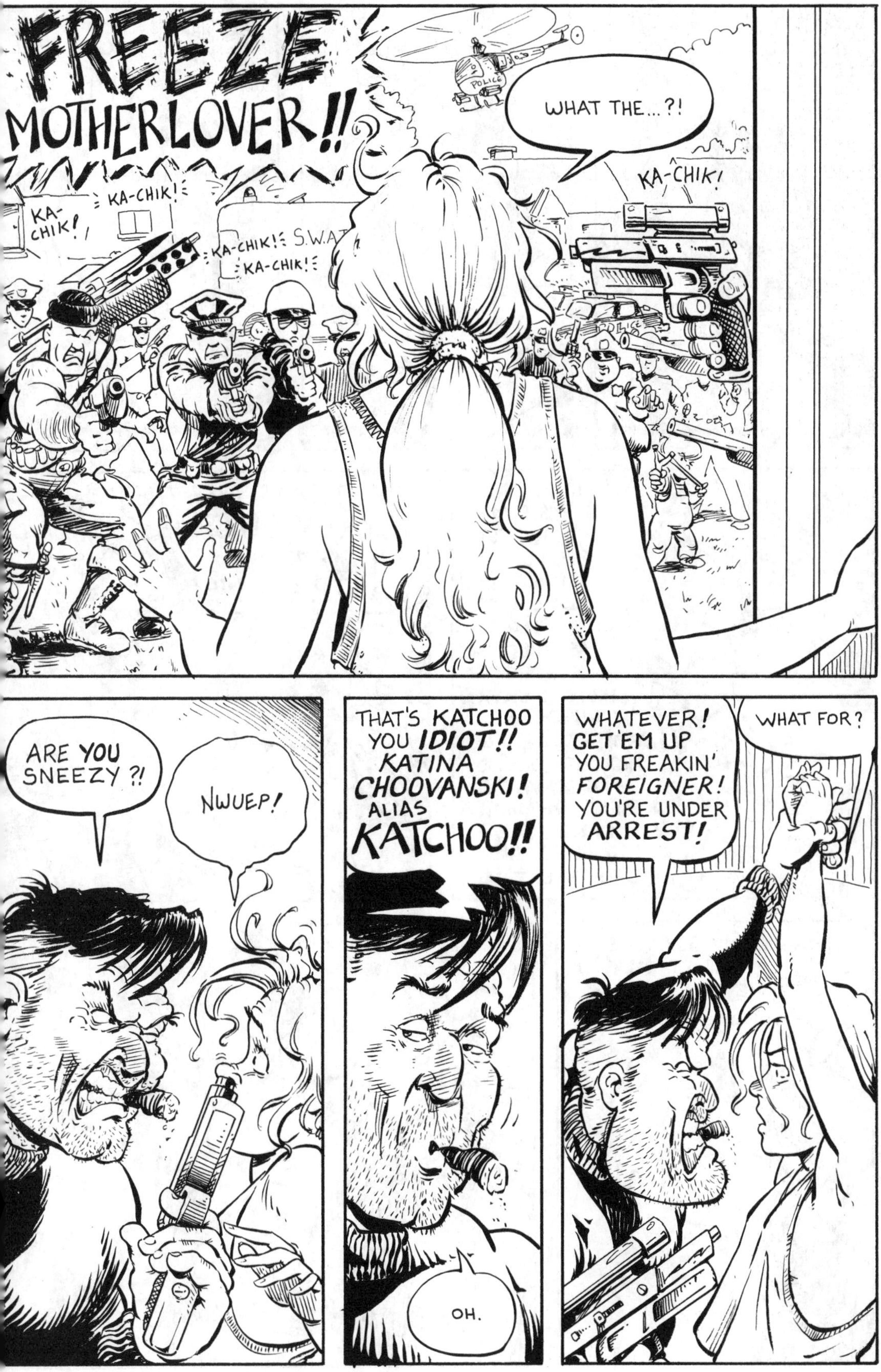

FREEZE MOTHERLOVER!!
WHAT THE...?!
KA-CHIK!
KA-CHIK!
KA-CHIK!
KA-CHIK!
KA-CHIK!
S.W.A.T
POLICE
ARE YOU SNEEZY?!
NWUEP!
THAT'S KATCHOO YOU IDIOT!! KATINA CHOOVANSKI! ALIAS KATCHOO!!
OH.
WHATEVER! GET'EM UP YOU FREAKIN' FOREIGNER! YOU'RE UNDER ARREST!
WHAT FOR?

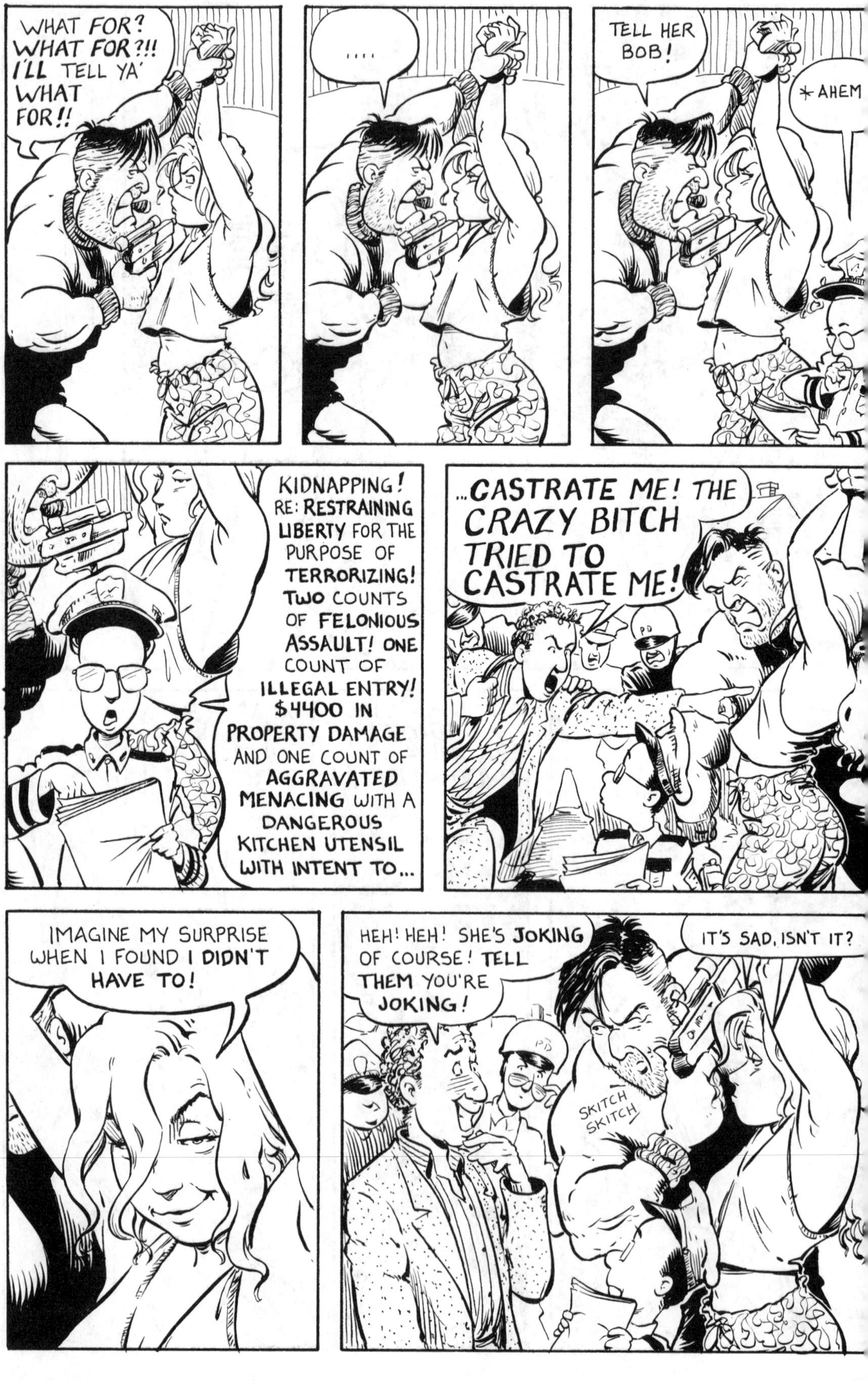
WHAT FOR? WHAT FOR?!! I'LL TELL YA' WHAT FOR!!
....
TELL HER BOB!
*AHEM
KIDNAPPING! RE: RESTRAINING LIBERTY FOR THE PURPOSE OF TERRORIZING! TWO COUNTS OF FELONIOUS ASSAULT! ONE COUNT OF ILLEGAL ENTRY! $4400 IN PROPERTY DAMAGE AND ONE COUNT OF AGGRAVATED MENACING WITH A DANGEROUS KITCHEN UTENSIL WITH INTENT TO...
...CASTRATE ME! THE CRAZY BITCH TRIED TO CASTRATE ME!
PD
IMAGINE MY SURPRISE WHEN I FOUND I DIDN'T HAVE TO!
HEH! HEH! SHE'S JOKING OF COURSE! TELL THEM YOU'RE JOKING!
IT'S SAD, ISN'T IT?
PD
SKITCH SKITCH

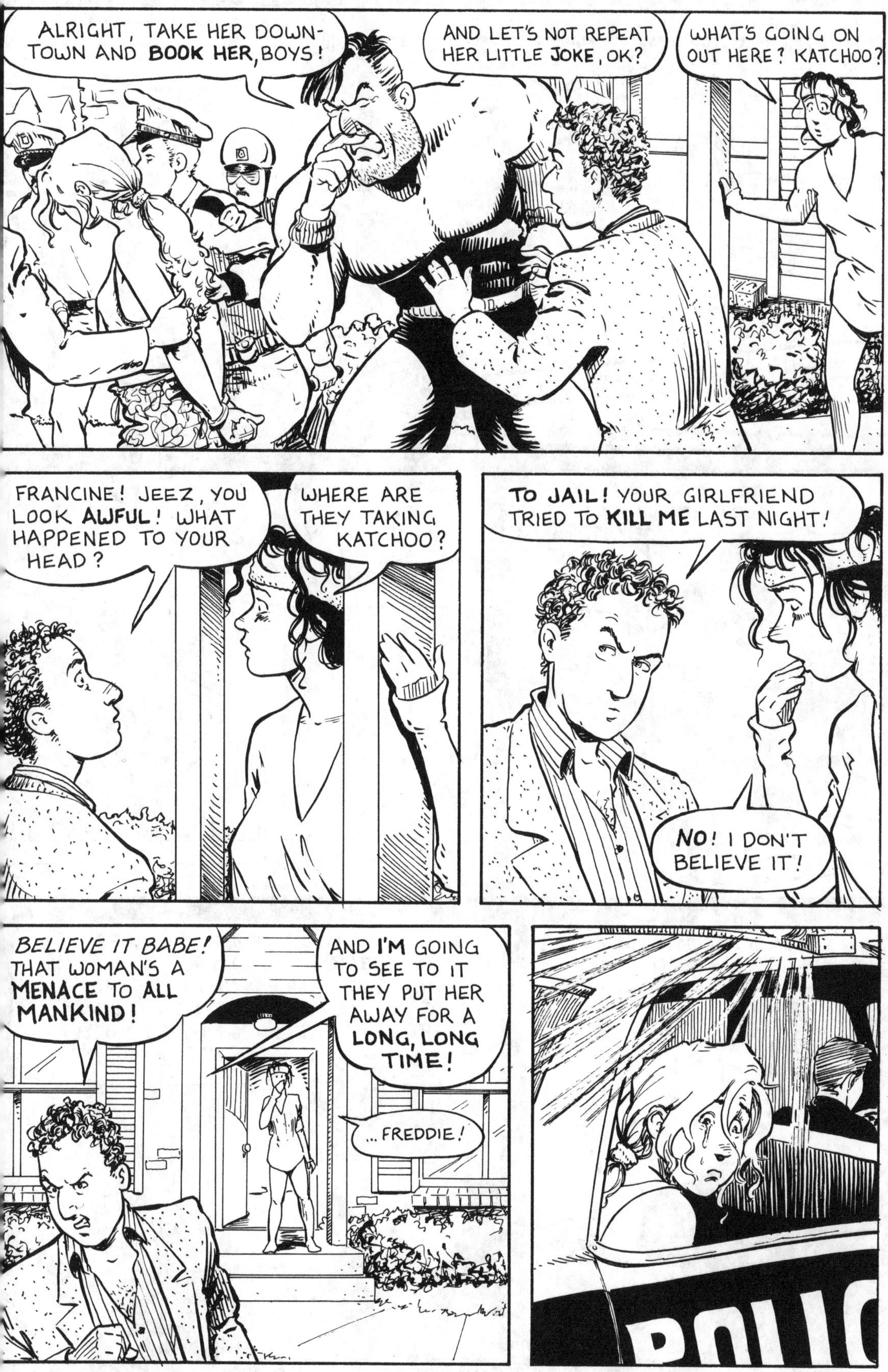

ALRIGHT, TAKE HER DOWN-TOWN AND BOOK HER, BOYS!
AND LET'S NOT REPEAT HER LITTLE JOKE, OK?
WHAT'S GOING ON OUT HERE? KATCHOO?
FRANCINE! JEEZ, YOU LOOK AWFUL! WHAT HAPPENED TO YOUR HEAD?
WHERE ARE THEY TAKING KATCHOO?
TO JAIL! YOUR GIRLFRIEND TRIED TO KILL ME LAST NIGHT!
NO! I DON'T BELIEVE IT!
BELIEVE IT BABE! THAT WOMAN'S A MENACE TO ALL MANKIND!
AND I'M GOING TO SEE TO IT THEY PUT HER AWAY FOR A LONG, LONG TIME!
...FREDDIE!
POLIC

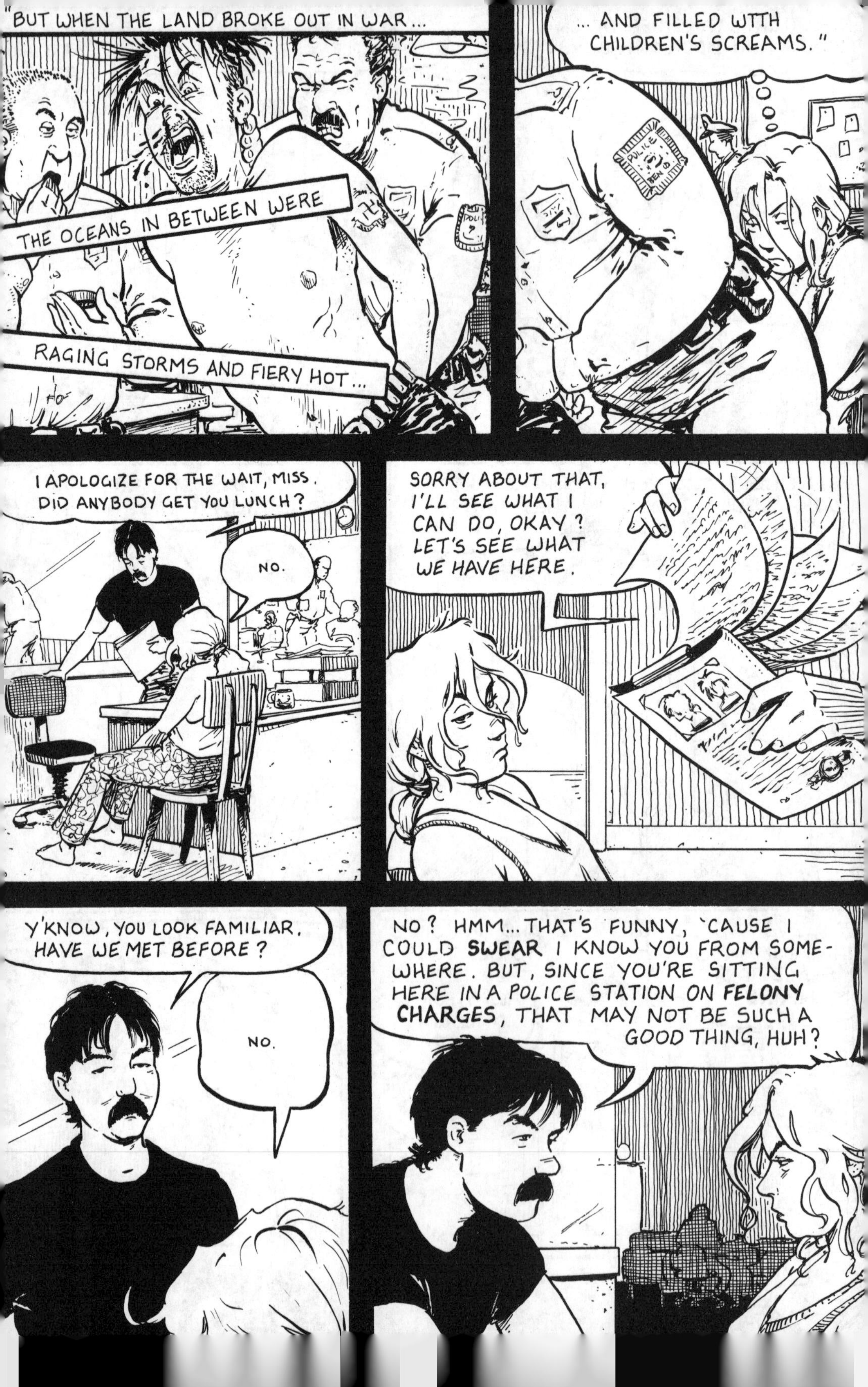
"BUT WHEN THE LAND BROKE OUT IN WAR...
THE OCEANS IN BETWEEN WERE
RAGING STORMS AND FIERY HOT...
...AND FILLED WTTH CHILDREN'S SCREAMS."
I APOLOGIZE FOR THE WAIT, MISS. DID ANYBODY GET YOU LUNCH?
NO.
SORRY ABOUT THAT, I'LL SEE WHAT I CAN DO, OKAY? LET'S SEE WHAT WE HAVE HERE.
Y'KNOW, YOU LOOK FAMILIAR. HAVE WE MET BEFORE?
NO.
NO? HMM... THAT'S FUNNY, 'CAUSE I COULD SWEAR I KNOW YOU FROM SOMEWHERE. BUT, SINCE YOU'RE SITTING HERE IN A POLICE STATION ON FELONY CHARGES, THAT MAY NOT BE SUCH A GOOD THING, HUH?

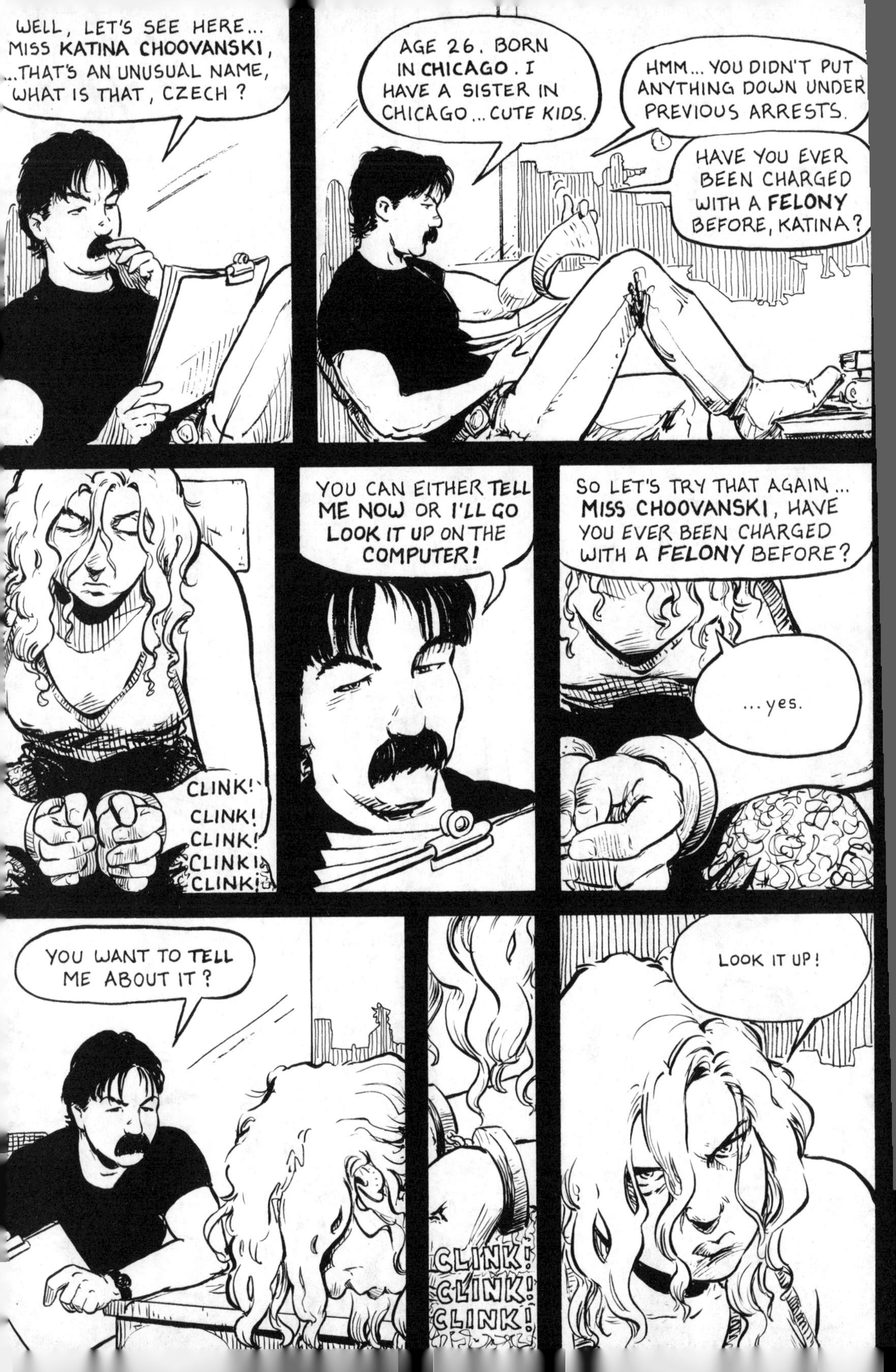
WELL, LET'S SEE HERE... MISS KATINA CHOOVANSKI, ...THAT'S AN UNUSUAL NAME, WHAT IS THAT, CZECH?
AGE 26. BORN IN CHICAGO. I HAVE A SISTER IN CHICAGO... CUTE KIDS.
HMM... YOU DIDN'T PUT ANYTHING DOWN UNDER PREVIOUS ARRESTS.
HAVE YOU EVER BEEN CHARGED WITH A FELONY BEFORE, KATINA?
CLINK! CLINK! CLINK! CLINK! CLINK!
YOU CAN EITHER TELL ME NOW OR I'LL GO LOOK IT UP ON THE COMPUTER!
SO LET'S TRY THAT AGAIN... MISS CHOOVANSKI, HAVE YOU EVER BEEN CHARGED WITH A FELONY BEFORE?
...yes.
YOU WANT TO TELL ME ABOUT IT?
CLINK! CLINK! CLINK!
LOOK IT UP!

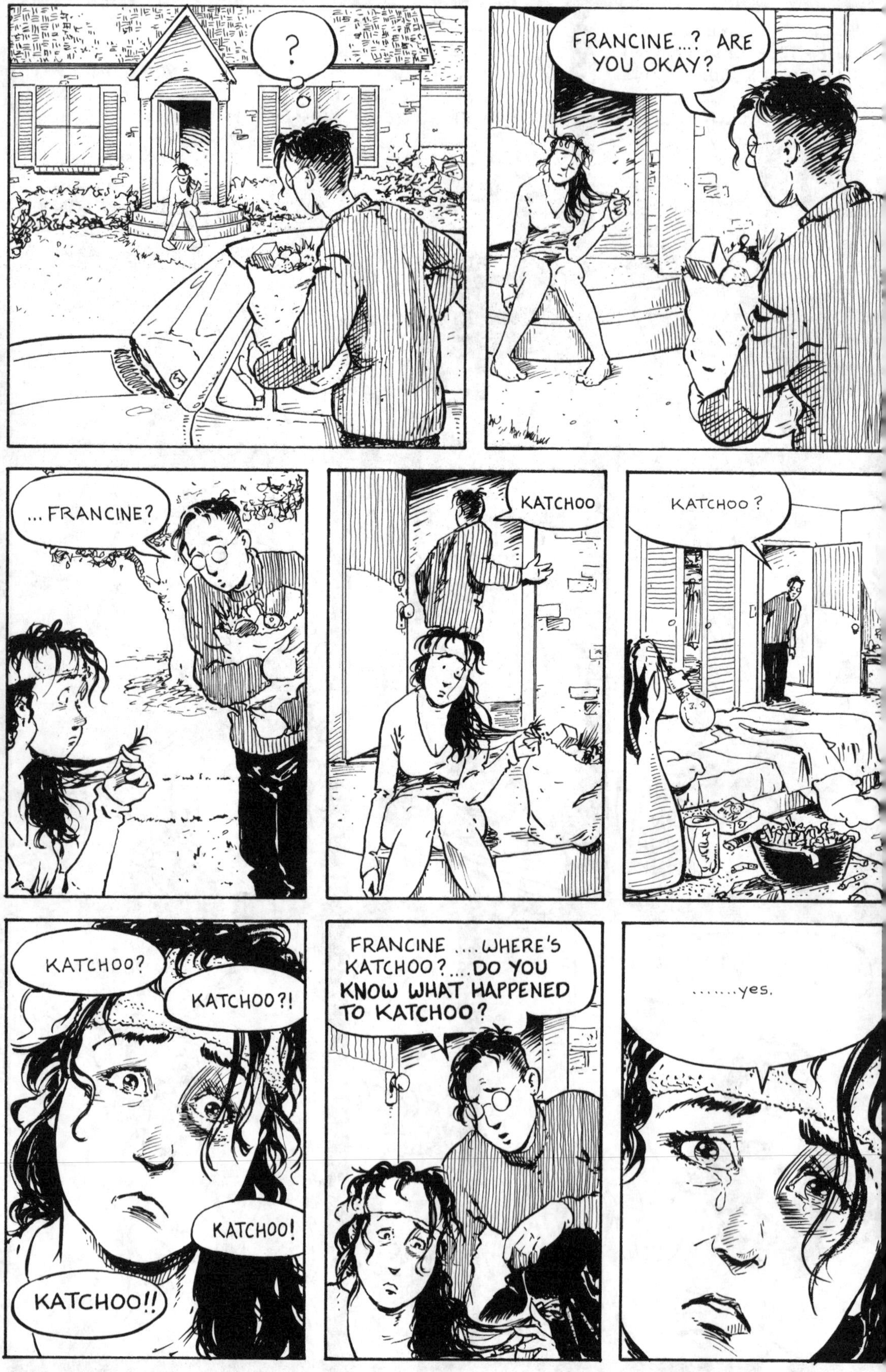
?
FRANCINE...? ARE YOU OKAY?
...FRANCINE?
KATCHOO
KATCHOO?
KATCHOO?
KATCHOO?!
KATCHOO!
KATCHOO!!
FRANCINE ....WHERE'S KATCHOO?....DO YOU KNOW WHAT HAPPENED TO KATCHOO?
.......yes.

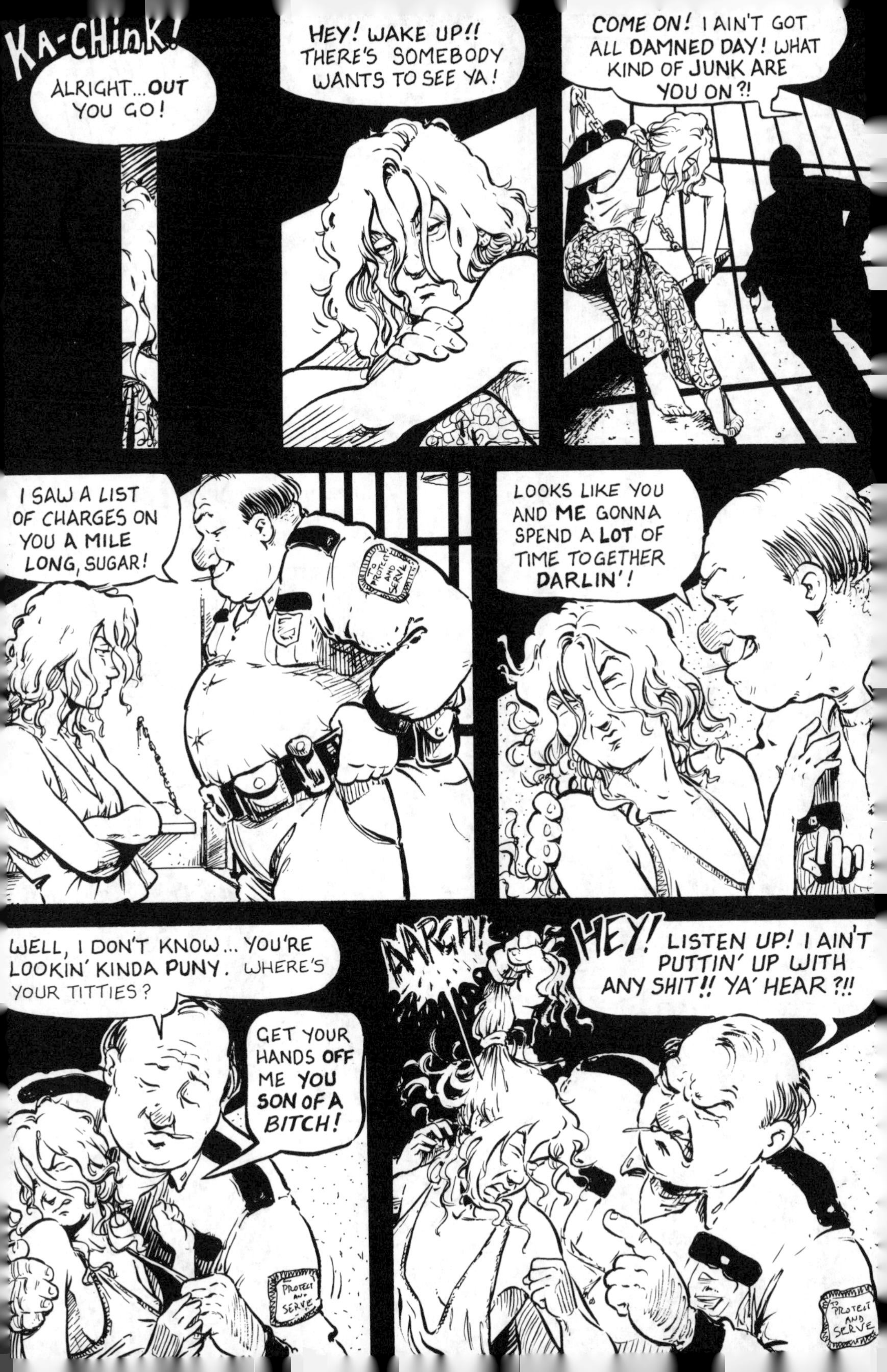
KA-CHINK!
ALRIGHT... OUT YOU GO!
HEY! WAKE UP!! THERE'S SOMEBODY WANTS TO SEE YA!
COME ON! I AIN'T GOT ALL DAMNED DAY! WHAT KIND OF JUNK ARE YOU ON?!
I SAW A LIST OF CHARGES ON YOU A MILE LONG, SUGAR!
TO PROTECT AND SERVE
LOOKS LIKE YOU AND ME GONNA SPEND A LOT OF TIME TOGETHER DARLIN'!
WELL, I DON'T KNOW... YOU'RE LOOKIN' KINDA PUNY. WHERE'S YOUR TITTIES?
GET YOUR HANDS OFF ME YOU SON OF A BITCH!
AARGH!
HEY!
LISTEN UP! I AIN'T PUTTIN' UP WITH ANY SHIT!! YA' HEAR?!!
TO PROTECT AND SERVE

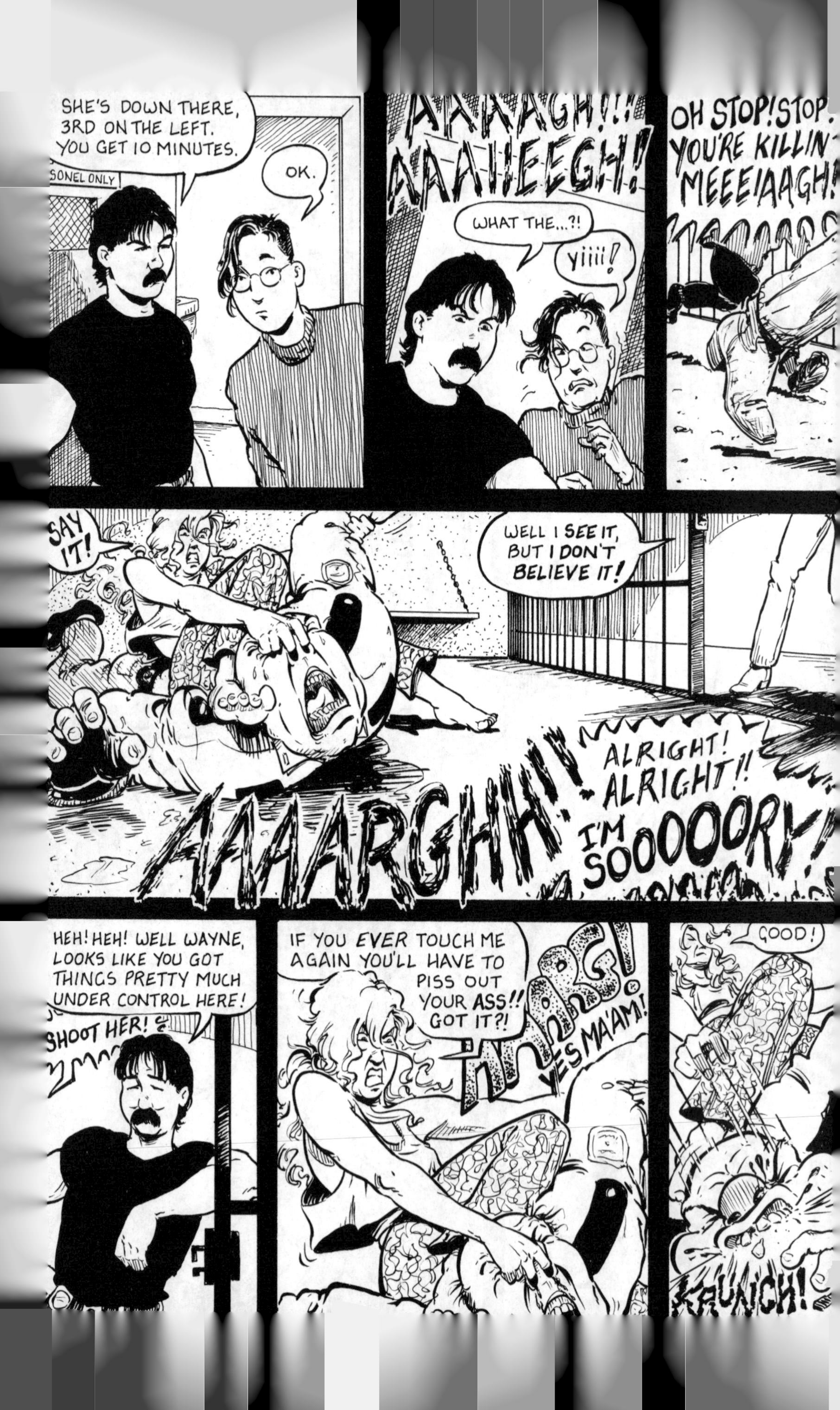
SHE'S DOWN THERE, 3RD ON THE LEFT. YOU GET 10 MINUTES.
SONEL ONLY
OK.
AAAAGH!!!
AAAIIEEGH!
WHAT THE...?!
yiiii!
OH STOP! STOP! YOU'RE KILLIN MEEE! AAGH!
SAY IT!
WELL I SEE IT, BUT I DON'T BELIEVE IT!
AAAARGHH!!
ALRIGHT! ALRIGHT!! I'M SOOOOORY!
HEH! HEH! WELL WAYNE, LOOKS LIKE YOU GOT THINGS PRETTY MUCH UNDER CONTROL HERE!
SHOOT HER!
IF YOU EVER TOUCH ME AGAIN YOU'LL HAVE TO PISS OUT YOUR ASS!! GOT IT?!
HNARG!
YES MA'AM!
GOOD!
KRUNCH!

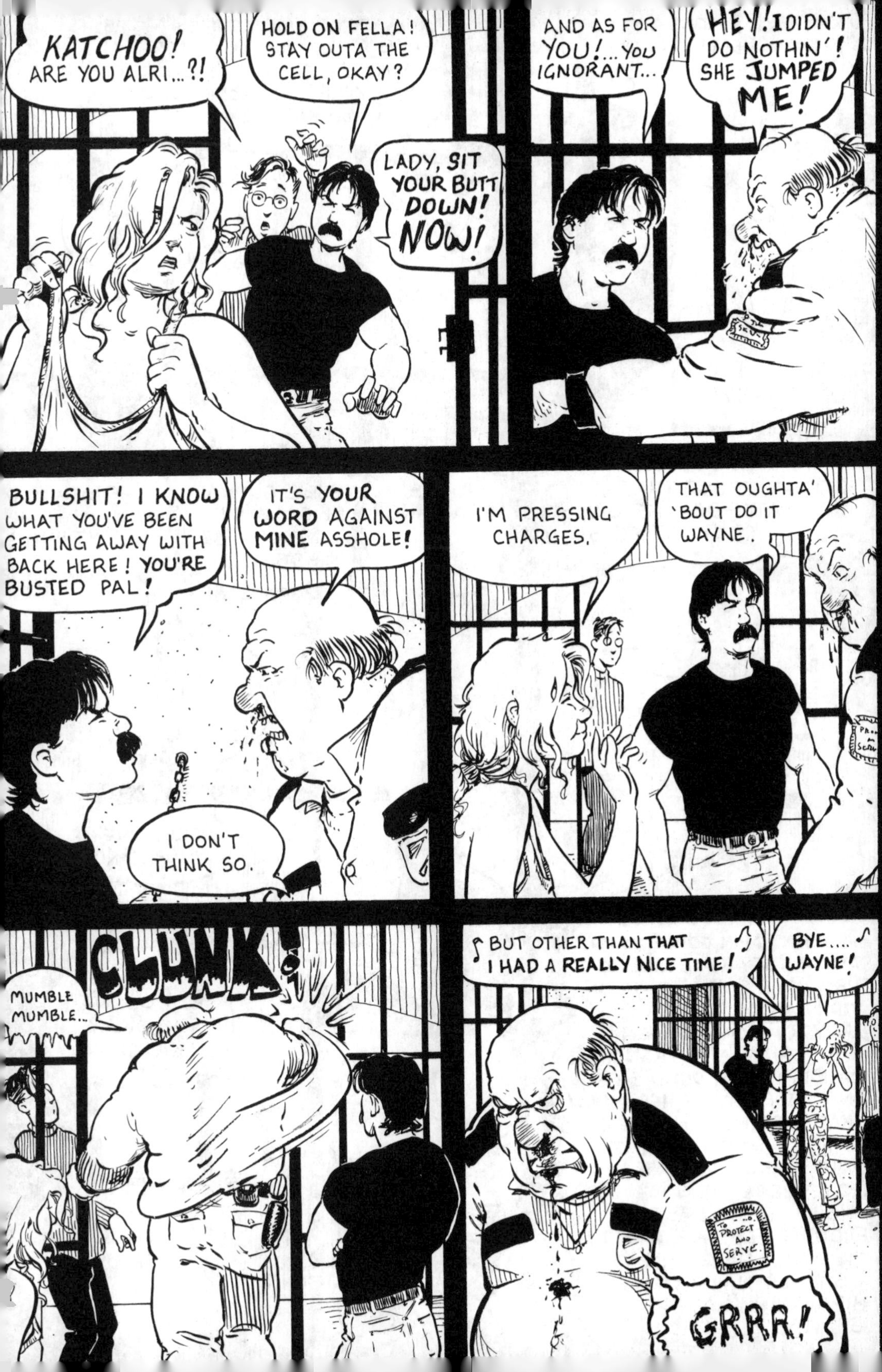

KATCHOO! ARE YOU ALRI...?!
HOLD ON FELLA! STAY OUTA THE CELL, OKAY?
LADY, SIT YOUR BUTT DOWN! NOW!
AND AS FOR YOU!... YOU IGNORANT...
HEY! I DIDN'T DO NOTHIN'! SHE JUMPED ME!
BULLSHIT! I KNOW WHAT YOU'VE BEEN GETTING AWAY WITH BACK HERE! YOU'RE BUSTED PAL!
IT'S YOUR WORD AGAINST MINE ASSHOLE!
I DON'T THINK SO.
I'M PRESSING CHARGES.
THAT OUGHTA' 'BOUT DO IT WAYNE.
CLUNK!
MUMBLE MUMBLE...
BUT OTHER THAN THAT I HAD A REALLY NICE TIME!
BYE.... WAYNE!
TO PROTECT AND SERVE.
GRRR!

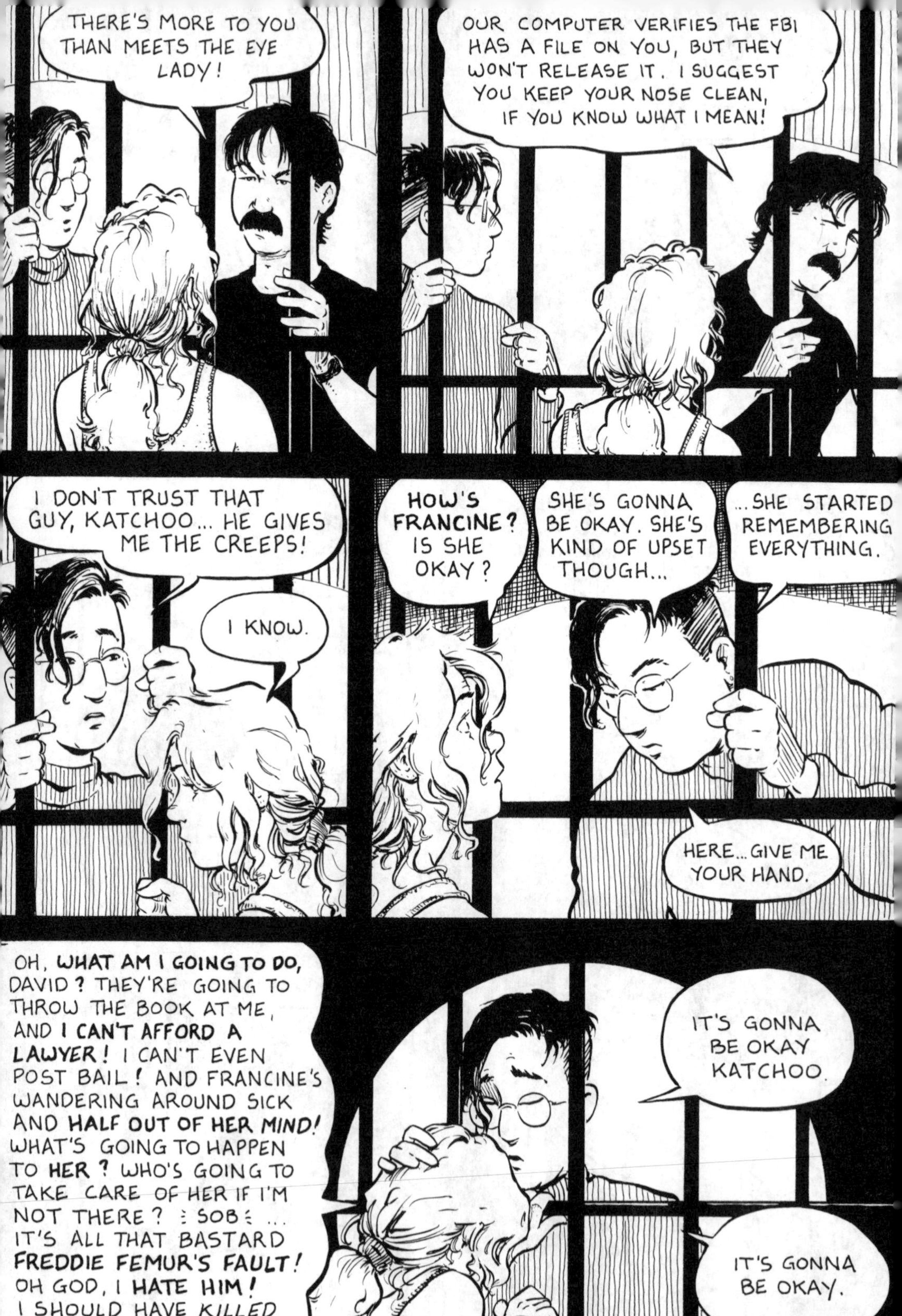
THERE'S MORE TO YOU THAN MEETS THE EYE LADY!
OUR COMPUTER VERIFIES THE FBI HAS A FILE ON YOU, BUT THEY WON'T RELEASE IT. I SUGGEST YOU KEEP YOUR NOSE CLEAN, IF YOU KNOW WHAT I MEAN!
I DON'T TRUST THAT GUY, KATCHOO... HE GIVES ME THE CREEPS!
I KNOW.
HOW'S FRANCINE? IS SHE OKAY?
SHE'S GONNA BE OKAY. SHE'S KIND OF UPSET THOUGH...
...SHE STARTED REMEMBERING EVERYTHING.
HERE... GIVE ME YOUR HAND.
OH, WHAT AM I GOING TO DO, DAVID? THEY'RE GOING TO THROW THE BOOK AT ME, AND I CAN'T AFFORD A LAWYER! I CAN'T EVEN POST BAIL! AND FRANCINE'S WANDERING AROUND SICK AND HALF OUT OF HER MIND! WHAT'S GOING TO HAPPEN TO HER? WHO'S GOING TO TAKE CARE OF HER IF I'M NOT THERE? :SOB: ... IT'S ALL THAT BASTARD FREDDIE FEMUR'S FAULT! OH GOD, I HATE HIM! I SHOULD HAVE KILLED HIM WHEN I HAD THE CHANCE! ... :SOB:
IT'S GONNA BE OKAY KATCHOO.
IT'S GONNA BE OKAY.

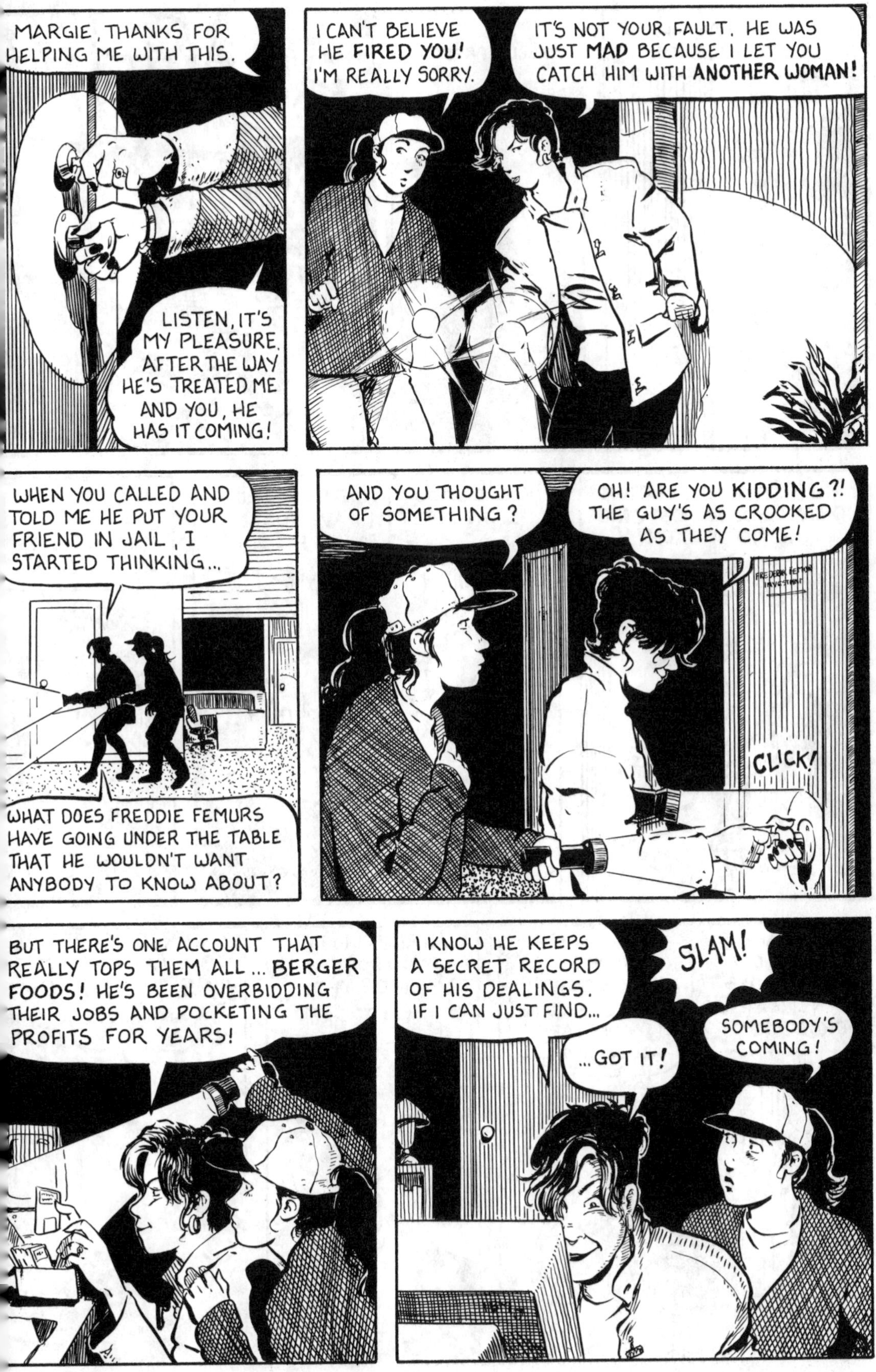

MARGIE, THANKS FOR HELPING ME WITH THIS.
LISTEN, IT'S MY PLEASURE. AFTER THE WAY HE'S TREATED ME AND YOU, HE HAS IT COMING!
I CAN'T BELIEVE HE FIRED YOU! I'M REALLY SORRY.
IT'S NOT YOUR FAULT. HE WAS JUST MAD BECAUSE I LET YOU CATCH HIM WITH ANOTHER WOMAN!
WHEN YOU CALLED AND TOLD ME HE PUT YOUR FRIEND IN JAIL, I STARTED THINKING...
WHAT DOES FREDDIE FEMURS HAVE GOING UNDER THE TABLE THAT HE WOULDN'T WANT ANYBODY TO KNOW ABOUT?
AND YOU THOUGHT OF SOMETHING?
OH! ARE YOU KIDDING?! THE GUY'S AS CROOKED AS THEY COME!
CLICK!
BUT THERE'S ONE ACCOUNT THAT REALLY TOPS THEM ALL... BERGER FOODS! HE'S BEEN OVERBIDDING THEIR JOBS AND POCKETING THE PROFITS FOR YEARS!
I KNOW HE KEEPS A SECRET RECORD OF HIS DEALINGS. IF I CAN JUST FIND...
SLAM!
...GOT IT!
SOMEBODY'S COMING!

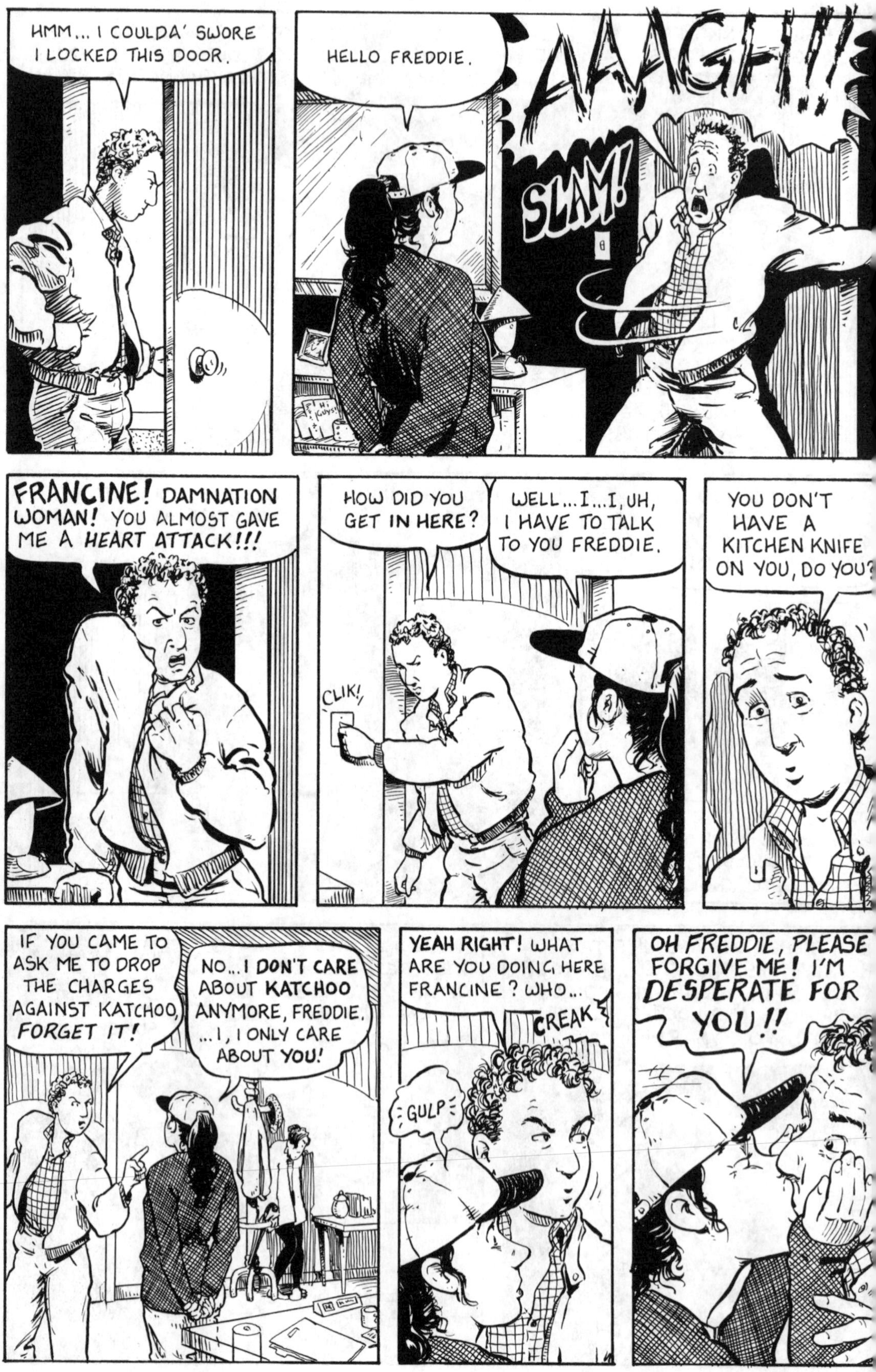
HMM... I COULDA' SWORE I LOCKED THIS DOOR.
HELLO FREDDIE.
AAAGH!!!
SLAM!
HI GUYS!
FRANCINE! DAMNATION WOMAN! YOU ALMOST GAVE ME A HEART ATTACK!!!
HOW DID YOU GET IN HERE?
CLIK!
WELL... I... I, UH, I HAVE TO TALK TO YOU FREDDIE.
YOU DON'T HAVE A KITCHEN KNIFE ON YOU, DO YOU?
IF YOU CAME TO ASK ME TO DROP THE CHARGES AGAINST KATCHOO, FORGET IT!
NO... I DON'T CARE ABOUT KATCHOO ANYMORE, FREDDIE. ...I, I ONLY CARE ABOUT YOU!
YEAH RIGHT! WHAT ARE YOU DOING HERE FRANCINE? WHO...
CREAK
GULP
OH FREDDIE, PLEASE FORGIVE ME! I'M DESPERATE FOR YOU!!

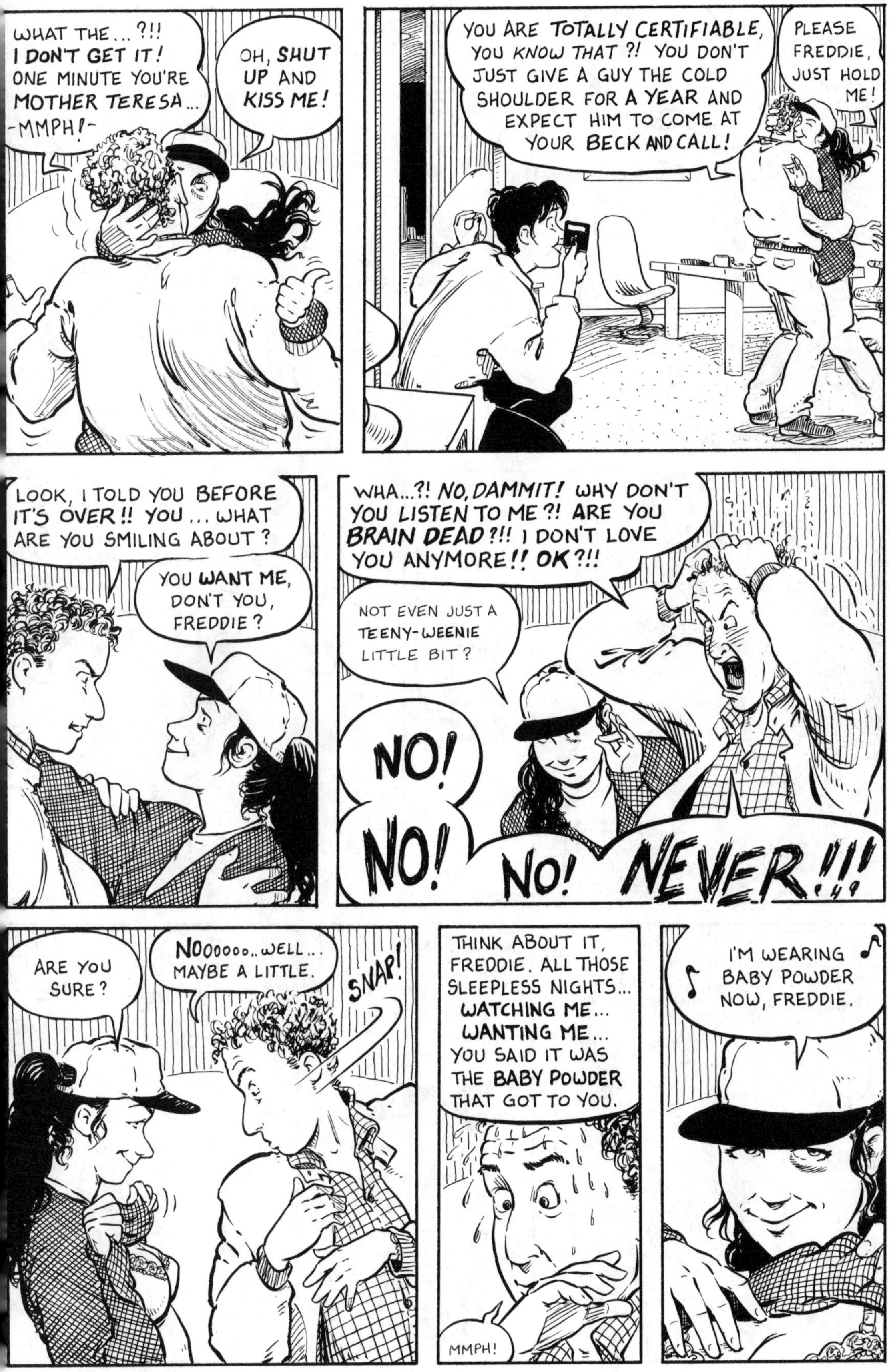
WHAT THE...?!! I DON'T GET IT! ONE MINUTE YOU'RE MOTHER TERESA... -MMPH!-
OH, SHUT UP AND KISS ME!
YOU ARE TOTALLY CERTIFIABLE, YOU KNOW THAT?! YOU DON'T JUST GIVE A GUY THE COLD SHOULDER FOR A YEAR AND EXPECT HIM TO COME AT YOUR BECK AND CALL!
PLEASE FREDDIE, JUST HOLD ME!
LOOK, I TOLD YOU BEFORE IT'S OVER!! YOU... WHAT ARE YOU SMILING ABOUT?
YOU WANT ME, DON'T YOU, FREDDIE?
WHA...?! NO, DAMMIT! WHY DON'T YOU LISTEN TO ME?! ARE YOU BRAIN DEAD?!! I DON'T LOVE YOU ANYMORE!! OK?!!
NOT EVEN JUST A TEENY-WEENIE LITTLE BIT?
NO!
NO!
NO! NEVER!!!
ARE YOU SURE?
NOOOOOO.. WELL... MAYBE A LITTLE.
SNAP!
THINK ABOUT IT, FREDDIE. ALL THOSE SLEEPLESS NIGHTS... WATCHING ME... WANTING ME... YOU SAID IT WAS THE BABY POWDER THAT GOT TO YOU.
MMPH!
I'M WEARING BABY POWDER NOW, FREDDIE.

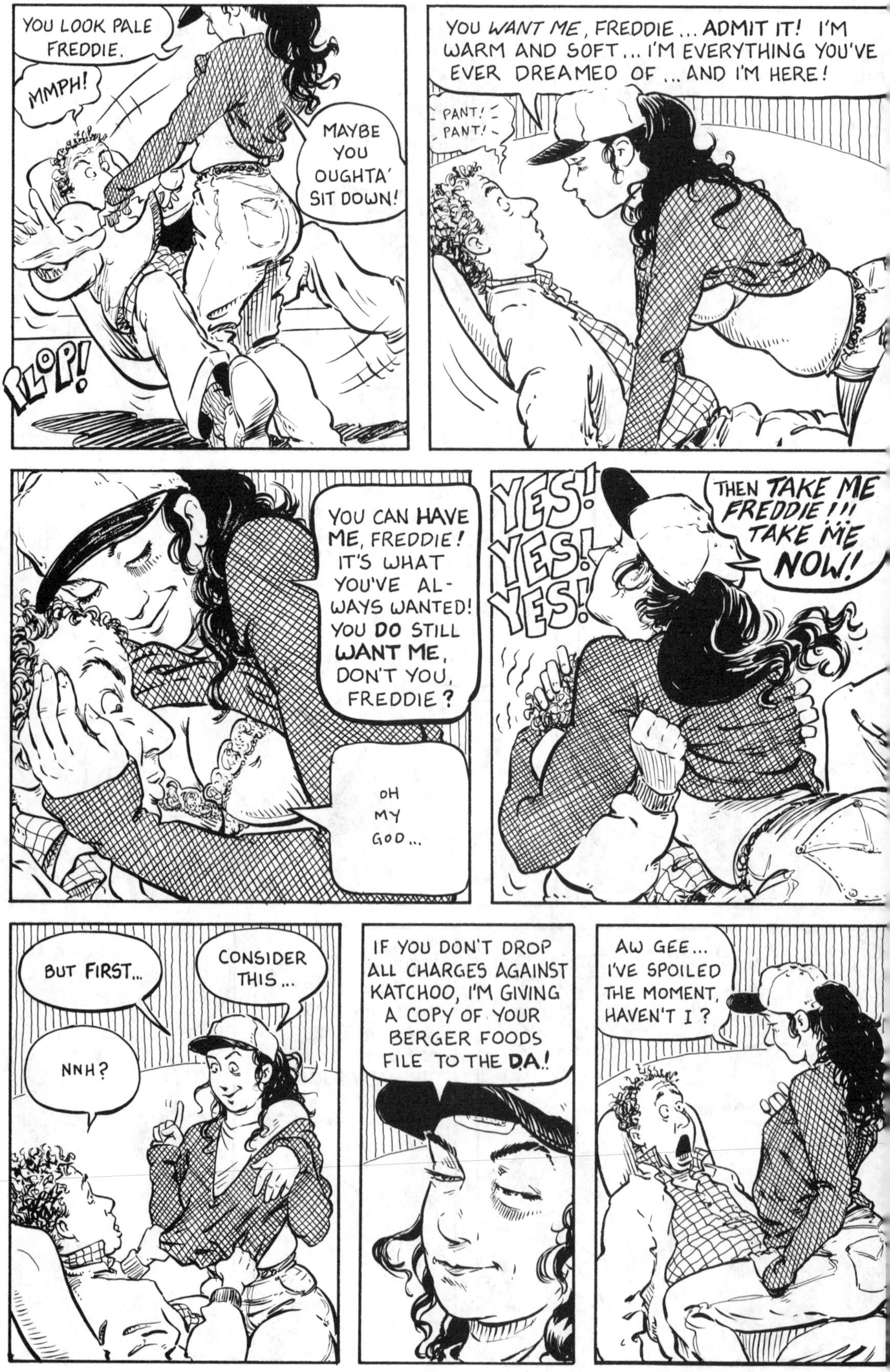
YOU LOOK PALE FREDDIE.
MMPH!
MAYBE YOU OUGHTA' SIT DOWN!
PLOP!
YOU WANT ME, FREDDIE... ADMIT IT! I'M WARM AND SOFT... I'M EVERYTHING YOU'VE EVER DREAMED OF... AND I'M HERE!
PANT! PANT!
YOU CAN HAVE ME, FREDDIE! IT'S WHAT YOU'VE ALWAYS WANTED! YOU DO STILL WANT ME, DON'T YOU, FREDDIE?
OH MY GOD...
YES! YES! YES!
THEN TAKE ME FREDDIE!!! TAKE ME NOW!
BUT FIRST...
CONSIDER THIS...
NNH?
IF YOU DON'T DROP ALL CHARGES AGAINST KATCHOO, I'M GIVING A COPY OF YOUR BERGER FOODS FILE TO THE D.A.!
AW GEE... I'VE SPOILED THE MOMENT, HAVEN'T I?

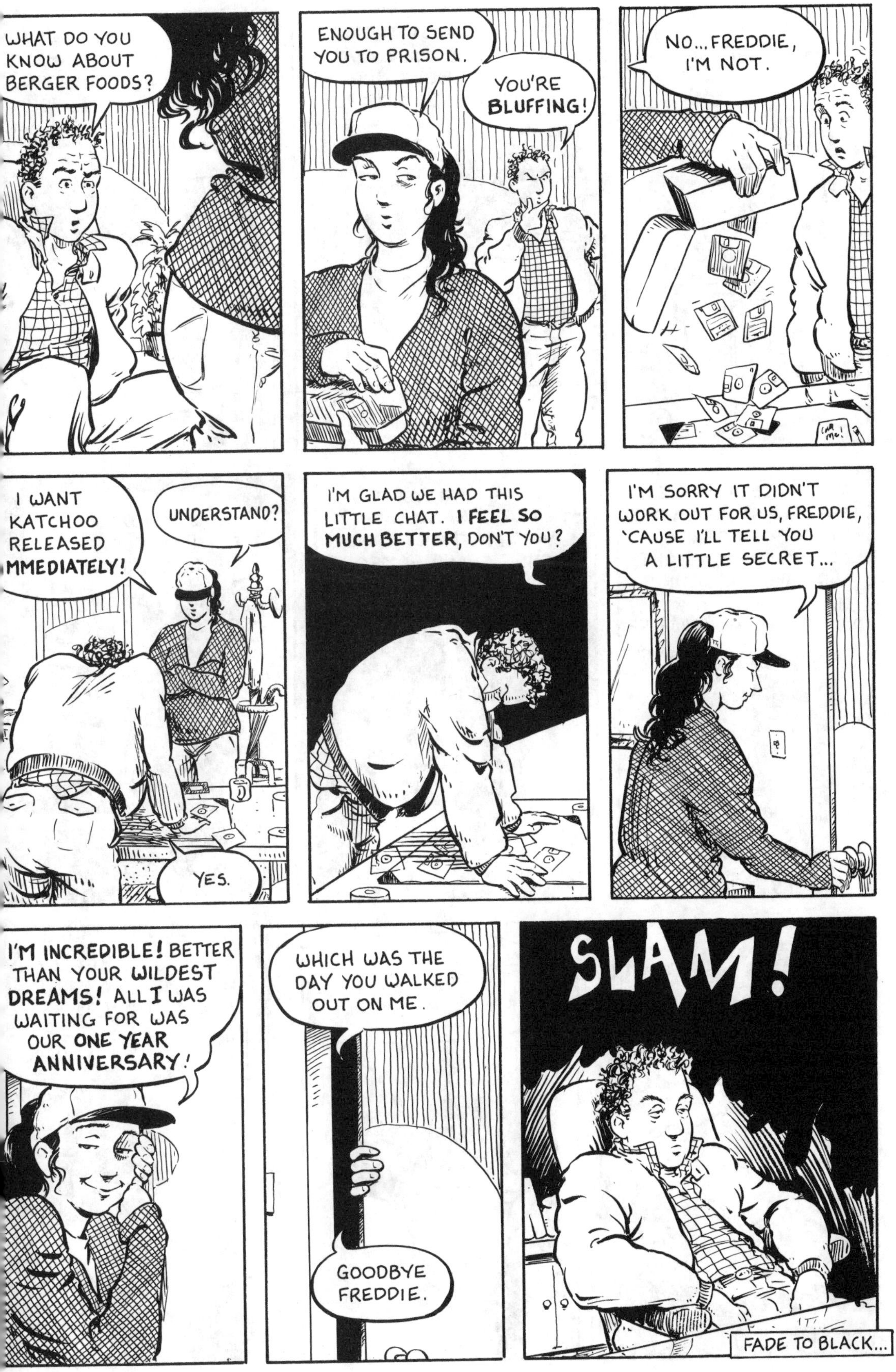
WHAT DO YOU KNOW ABOUT BERGER FOODS?
ENOUGH TO SEND YOU TO PRISON.
YOU'RE BLUFFING!
NO... FREDDIE, I'M NOT.
I WANT KATCHOO RELEASED MMEDIATELY!
UNDERSTAND?
YES.
I'M GLAD WE HAD THIS LITTLE CHAT. I FEEL SO MUCH BETTER, DON'T YOU?
I'M SORRY IT DIDN'T WORK OUT FOR US, FREDDIE, 'CAUSE I'LL TELL YOU A LITTLE SECRET...
I'M INCREDIBLE! BETTER THAN YOUR WILDEST DREAMS! ALL I WAS WAITING FOR WAS OUR ONE YEAR ANNIVERSARY!
WHICH WAS THE DAY YOU WALKED OUT ON ME.
GOODBYE FREDDIE.
SLAM!
FADE TO BLACK...

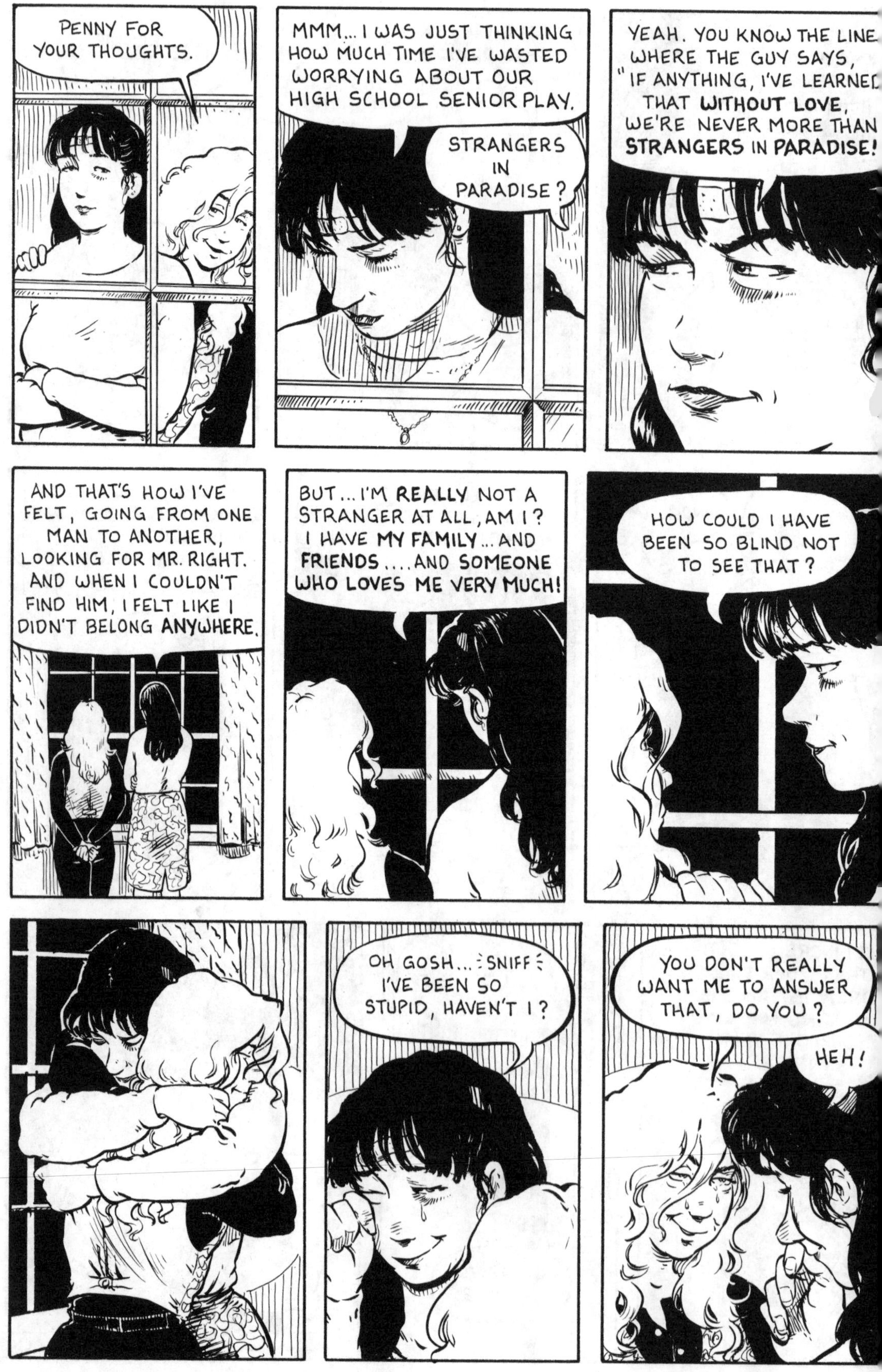
PENNY FOR YOUR THOUGHTS.
MMM... I WAS JUST THINKING HOW MUCH TIME I'VE WASTED WORRYING ABOUT OUR HIGH SCHOOL SENIOR PLAY.
STRANGERS IN PARADISE?
YEAH. YOU KNOW THE LINE WHERE THE GUY SAYS, "IF ANYTHING, I'VE LEARNED THAT **WITHOUT LOVE**, WE'RE NEVER MORE THAN **STRANGERS** IN **PARADISE**!
AND THAT'S HOW I'VE FELT, GOING FROM ONE MAN TO ANOTHER, LOOKING FOR MR. RIGHT. AND WHEN I COULDN'T FIND HIM, I FELT LIKE I DIDN'T BELONG **ANYWHERE**.
BUT... I'M **REALLY** NOT A STRANGER AT ALL, AM I? I HAVE **MY FAMILY**... AND **FRIENDS**.... AND **SOMEONE WHO LOVES ME VERY MUCH**!
HOW COULD I HAVE BEEN SO BLIND NOT TO SEE THAT?
OH GOSH... SNIFF I'VE BEEN SO STUPID, HAVEN'T I?
YOU DON'T REALLY WANT ME TO ANSWER THAT, DO YOU?
HEH!

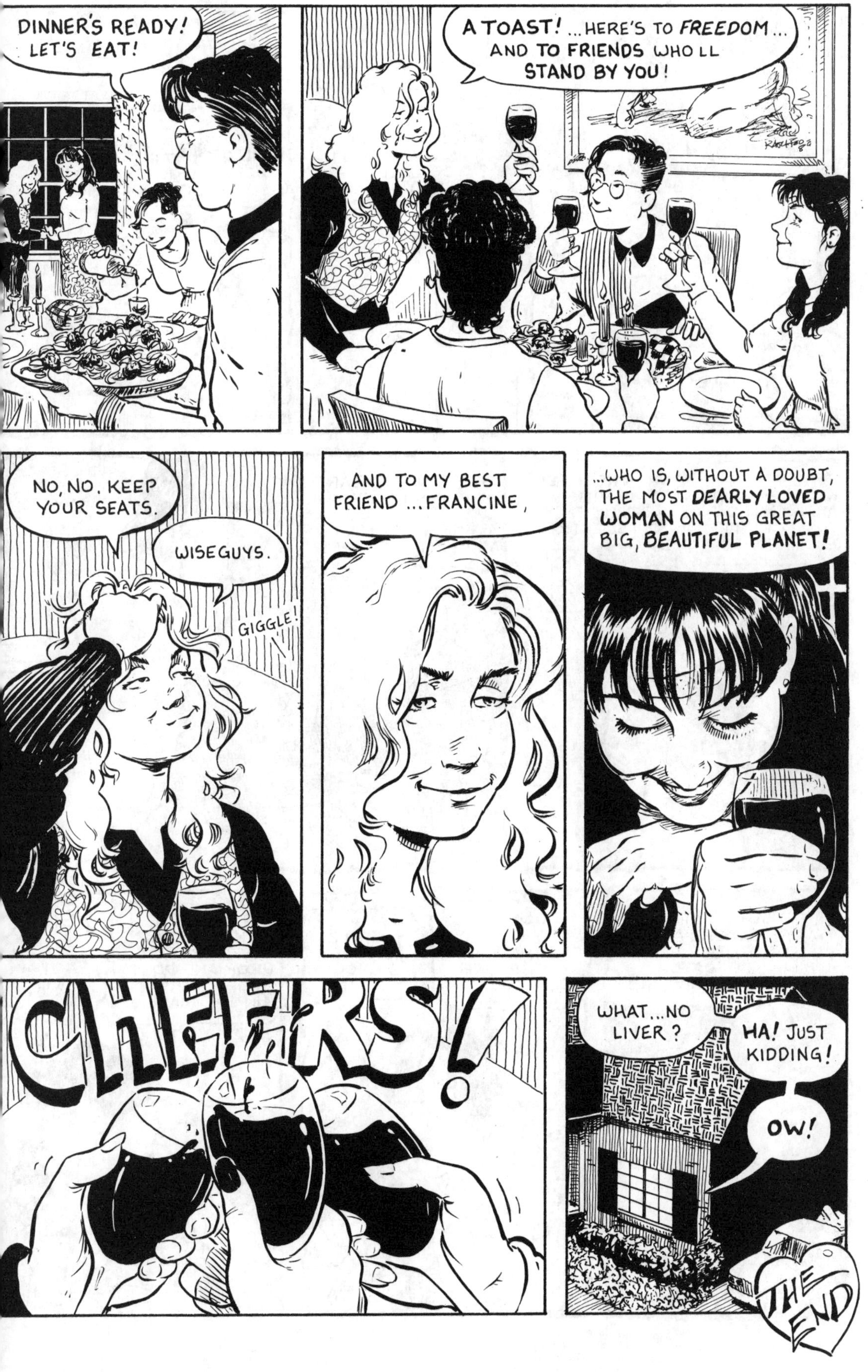
DINNER'S READY! LET'S EAT!
A TOAST! ...HERE'S TO FREEDOM... AND TO FRIENDS WHO'LL STAND BY YOU!
NO, NO. KEEP YOUR SEATS.
WISEGUYS.
GIGGLE!
AND TO MY BEST FRIEND ...FRANCINE,
...WHO IS, WITHOUT A DOUBT, THE MOST DEARLY LOVED WOMAN ON THIS GREAT BIG, BEAUTIFUL PLANET!
CHEERS!
WHAT...NO LIVER?
HA! JUST KIDDING!
OW!
THE END

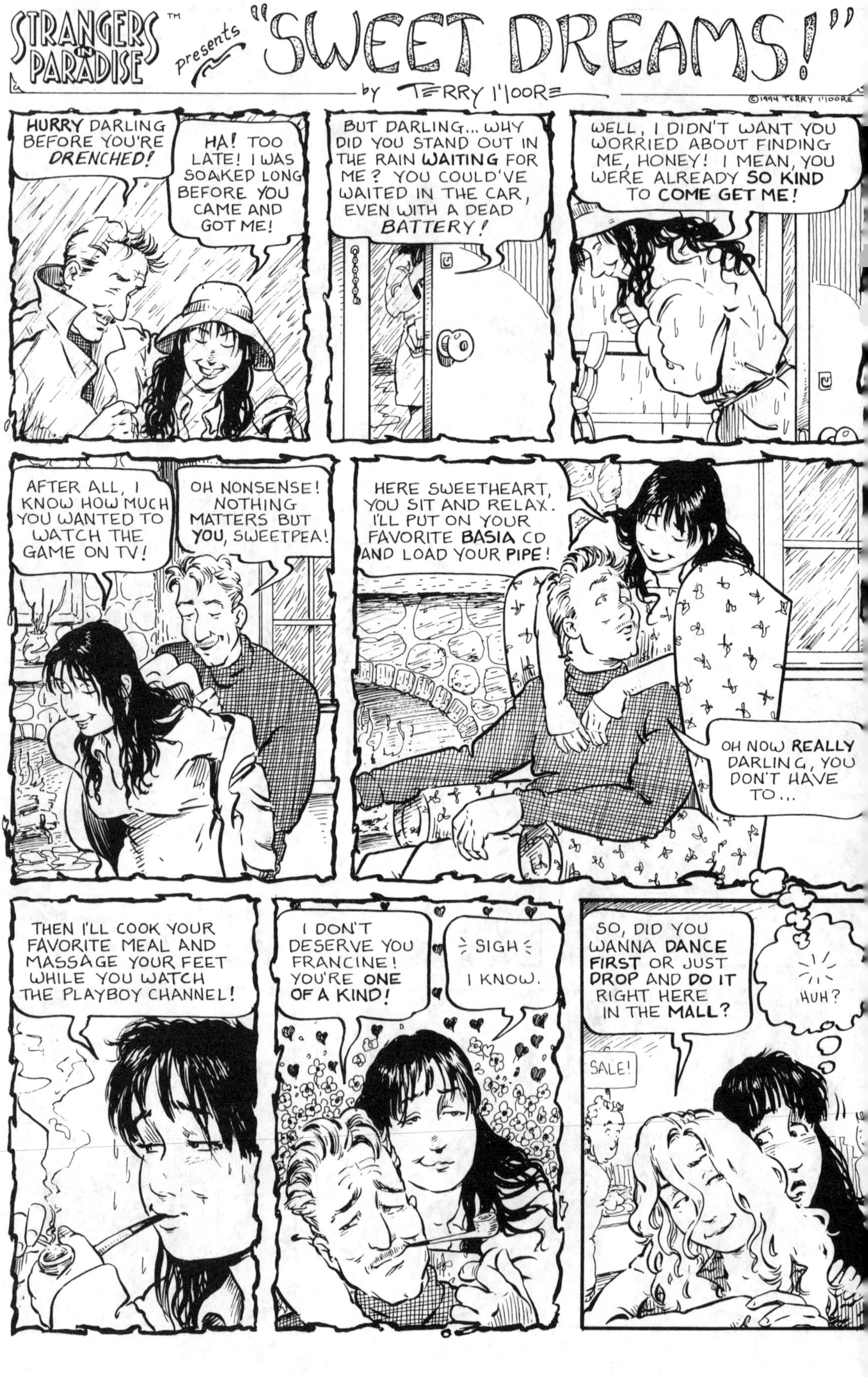
STRANGERS IN PARADISE™ presents "SWEET DREAMS!"
by TERRY MOORE
©1994 TERRY MOORE
HURRY DARLING BEFORE YOU'RE DRENCHED!
HA! TOO LATE! I WAS SOAKED LONG BEFORE YOU CAME AND GOT ME!
BUT DARLING... WHY DID YOU STAND OUT IN THE RAIN WAITING FOR ME? YOU COULD'VE WAITED IN THE CAR, EVEN WITH A DEAD BATTERY!
WELL, I DIDN'T WANT YOU WORRIED ABOUT FINDING ME, HONEY! I MEAN, YOU WERE ALREADY SO KIND TO COME GET ME!
AFTER ALL, I KNOW HOW MUCH YOU WANTED TO WATCH THE GAME ON TV!
OH NONSENSE! NOTHING MATTERS BUT YOU, SWEETPEA!
HERE SWEETHEART, YOU SIT AND RELAX. I'LL PUT ON YOUR FAVORITE BASIA CD AND LOAD YOUR PIPE!
OH NOW REALLY DARLING, YOU DON'T HAVE TO...
THEN I'LL COOK YOUR FAVORITE MEAL AND MASSAGE YOUR FEET WHILE YOU WATCH THE PLAYBOY CHANNEL!
I DON'T DESERVE YOU FRANCINE! YOU'RE ONE OF A KIND!
SIGH
I KNOW.
SO, DID YOU WANNA DANCE FIRST OR JUST DROP AND DO IT RIGHT HERE IN THE MALL?
HUH?
SALE!

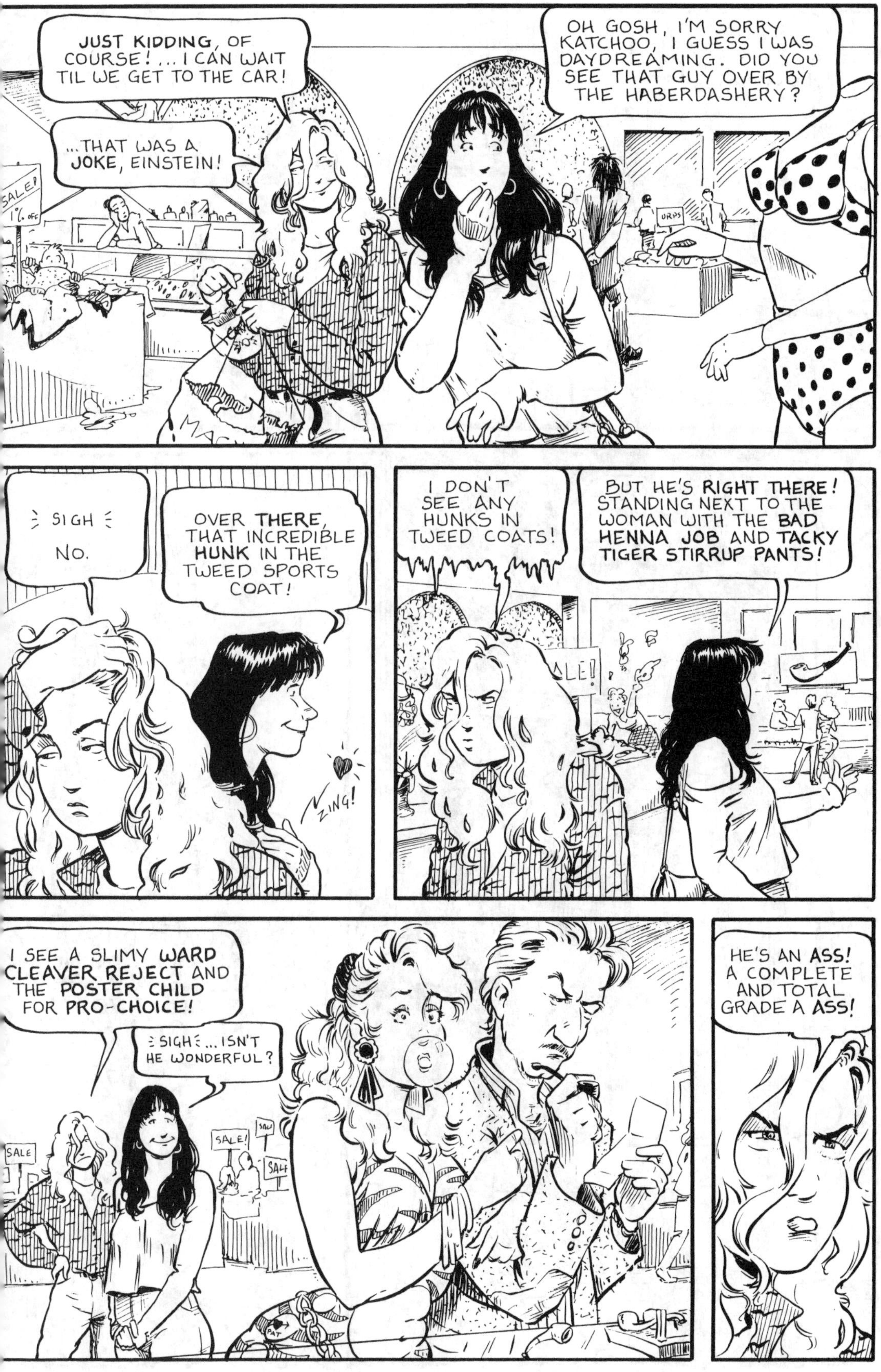
JUST KIDDING, OF COURSE! ... I CAN WAIT TIL WE GET TO THE CAR!
...THAT WAS A JOKE, EINSTEIN!
OH GOSH, I'M SORRY KATCHOO, I GUESS I WAS DAYDREAMING. DID YOU SEE THAT GUY OVER BY THE HABERDASHERY?
SIGH
No.
OVER THERE, THAT INCREDIBLE HUNK IN THE TWEED SPORTS COAT!
ZING!
I DON'T SEE ANY HUNKS IN TWEED COATS!
BUT HE'S RIGHT THERE! STANDING NEXT TO THE WOMAN WITH THE BAD HENNA JOB AND TACKY TIGER STIRRUP PANTS!
I SEE A SLIMY WARD CLEAVER REJECT AND THE POSTER CHILD FOR PRO-CHOICE!
SIGH ... ISN'T HE WONDERFUL?
SALE
SALE!
HE'S AN ASS! A COMPLETE AND TOTAL GRADE A ASS!

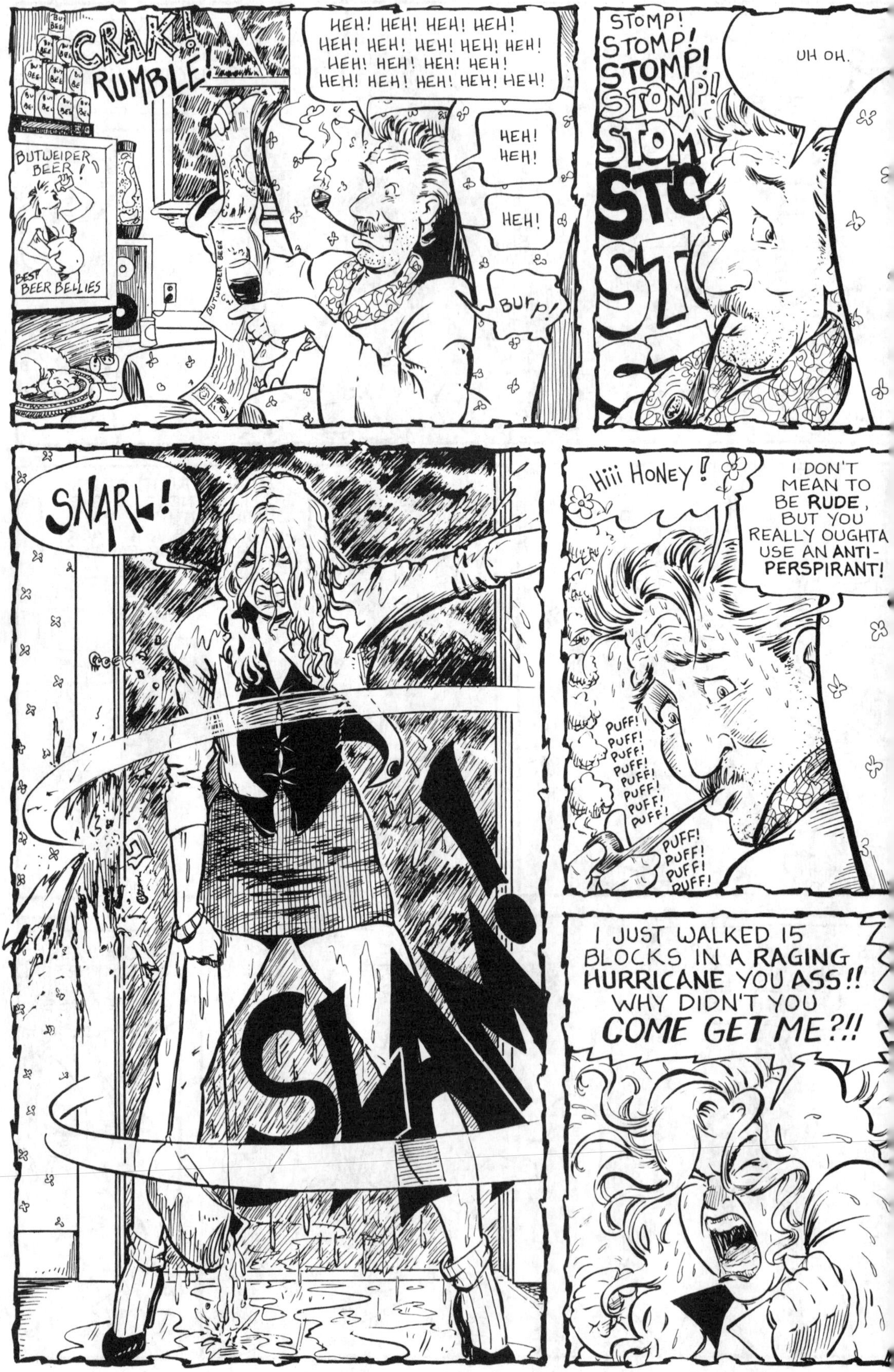
CRAK!
RUMBLE!
BUTWEIDER BEER!
BEST BEER BELLIES
HEH! HEH! HEH! HEH! HEH! HEH! HEH! HEH! HEH! HEH! HEH! HEH! HEH! HEH! HEH! HEH! HEH! HEH!
HEH! HEH!
HEH!
Burp!
STOMP! STOMP! STOMP! STOMP! STOM STO STO
UH OH.
SNARL!
SLAM!
Hiii HONEY!
I DON'T MEAN TO BE RUDE, BUT YOU REALLY OUGHTA USE AN ANTI-PERSPIRANT!
PUFF! PUFF! PUFF! PUFF! PUFF! PUFF! PUFF! PUFF!
PUFF! PUFF! PUFF! PUFF!
I JUST WALKED 15 BLOCKS IN A RAGING HURRICANE YOU ASS!! WHY DIDN'T YOU COME GET ME?!!

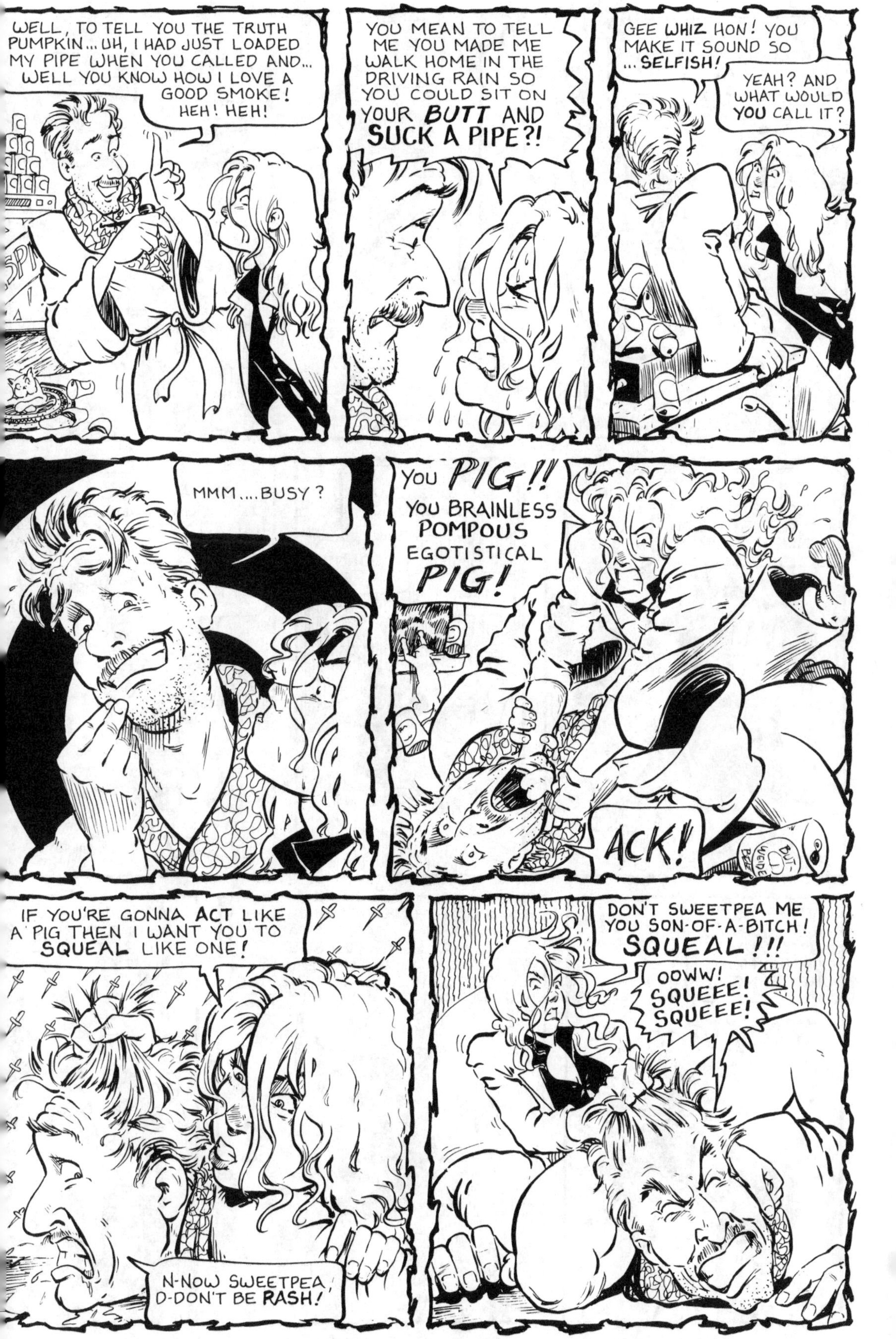
WELL, TO TELL YOU THE TRUTH PUMPKIN... UH, I HAD JUST LOADED MY PIPE WHEN YOU CALLED AND... WELL YOU KNOW HOW I LOVE A GOOD SMOKE! HEH! HEH!
YOU MEAN TO TELL ME YOU MADE ME WALK HOME IN THE DRIVING RAIN SO YOU COULD SIT ON YOUR BUTT AND SUCK A PIPE?!
GEE WHIZ HON! YOU MAKE IT SOUND SO ...SELFISH!
YEAH? AND WHAT WOULD YOU CALL IT?
MMM....BUSY?
YOU PIG!! YOU BRAINLESS POMPOUS EGOTISTICAL PIG!
ACK!
IF YOU'RE GONNA ACT LIKE A PIG THEN I WANT YOU TO SQUEAL LIKE ONE!
N-NOW SWEETPEA D-DON'T BE RASH!
DON'T SWEETPEA ME YOU SON-OF-A-BITCH! SQUEAL!!!
OOWW! SQUEEE! SQUEEE!

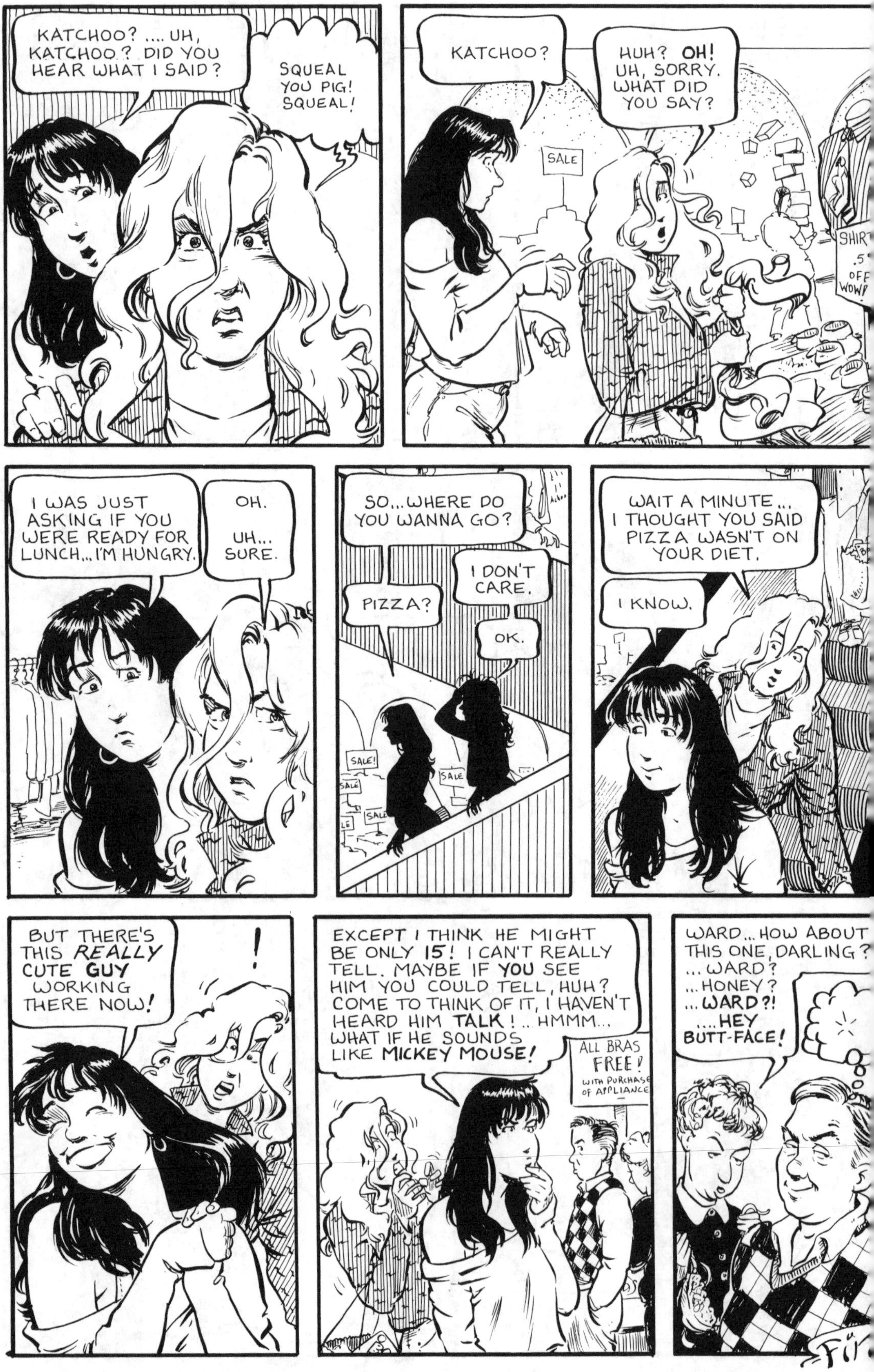
KATCHOO? .... UH, KATCHOO? DID YOU HEAR WHAT I SAID?
SQUEAL YOU PIG! SQUEAL!
KATCHOO?
HUH? OH! UH, SORRY. WHAT DID YOU SAY?
SALE
I WAS JUST ASKING IF YOU WERE READY FOR LUNCH... I'M HUNGRY.
OH. UH... SURE.
SO... WHERE DO YOU WANNA GO?
PIZZA?
I DON'T CARE.
OK.
SALE!
SALE
SALE
WAIT A MINUTE... I THOUGHT YOU SAID PIZZA WASN'T ON YOUR DIET.
I KNOW.
BUT THERE'S THIS REALLY CUTE GUY WORKING THERE NOW!
!
EXCEPT I THINK HE MIGHT BE ONLY 15! I CAN'T REALLY TELL. MAYBE IF YOU SEE HIM YOU COULD TELL, HUH? COME TO THINK OF IT, I HAVEN'T HEARD HIM TALK!... HMMM... WHAT IF HE SOUNDS LIKE MICKEY MOUSE!
ALL BRAS FREE! WITH PURCHASE OF APPLIANCE
WARD... HOW ABOUT THIS ONE, DARLING? ...WARD? ...HONEY? ...WARD?! ....HEY BUTT-FACE!

Sketchbook

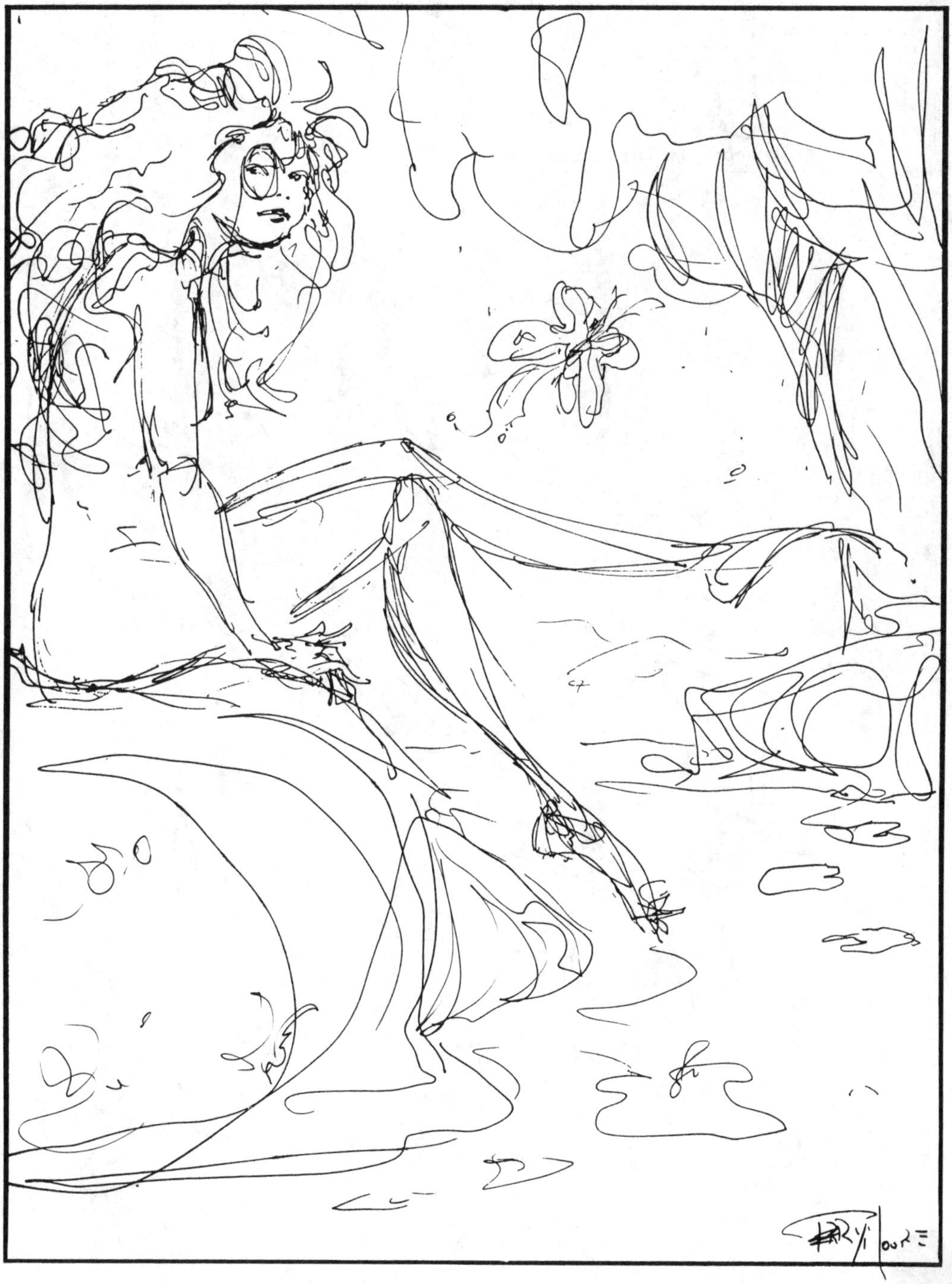

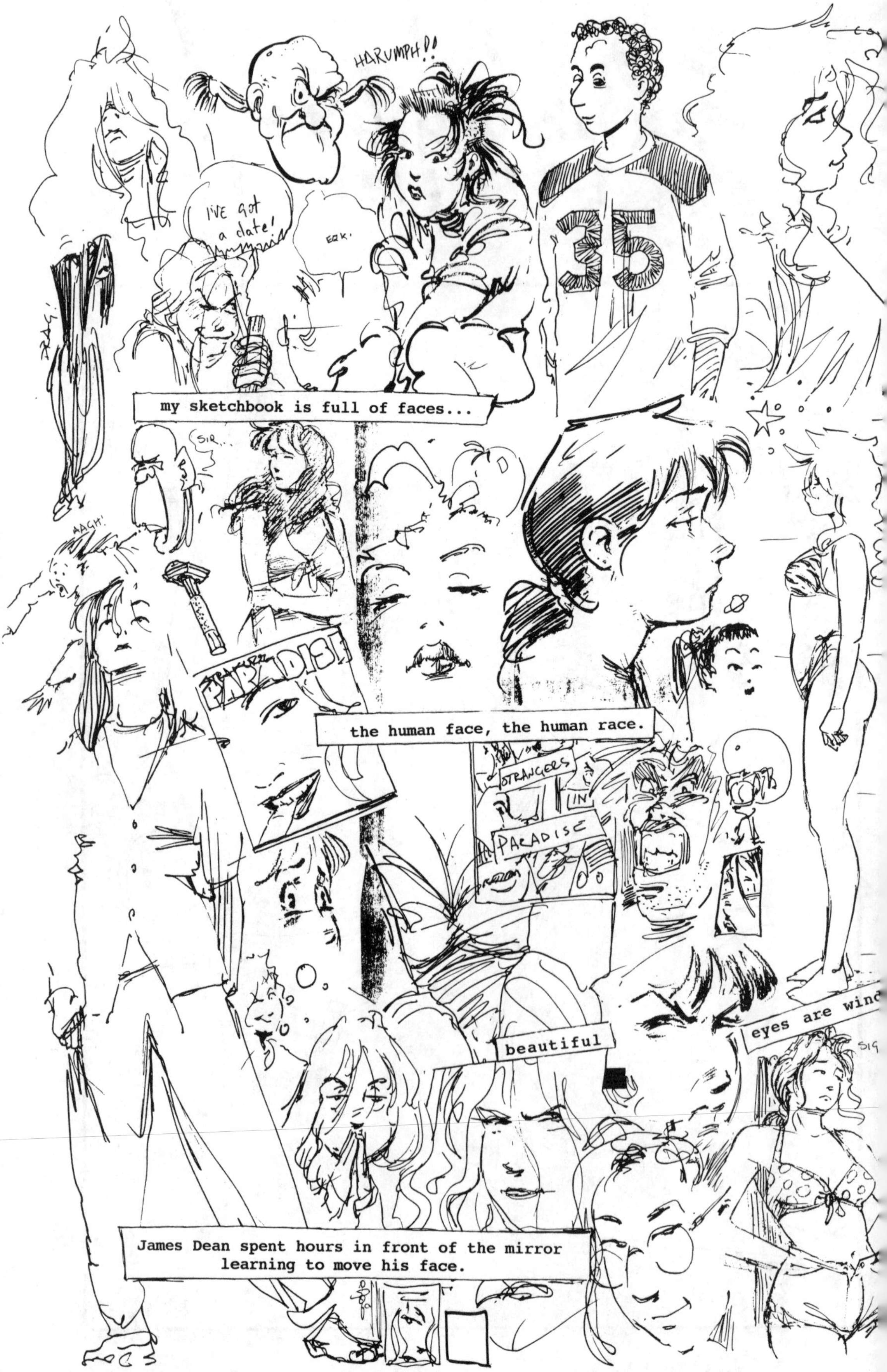
HARUMPH!!
I'VE got a date!
EEK.
my sketchbook is full of faces...
SIR..
AACH!
the human face, the human race.
STRANGERS IN PARADISE
beautiful
eyes are wind
James Dean spent hours in front of the mirror learning to move his face.

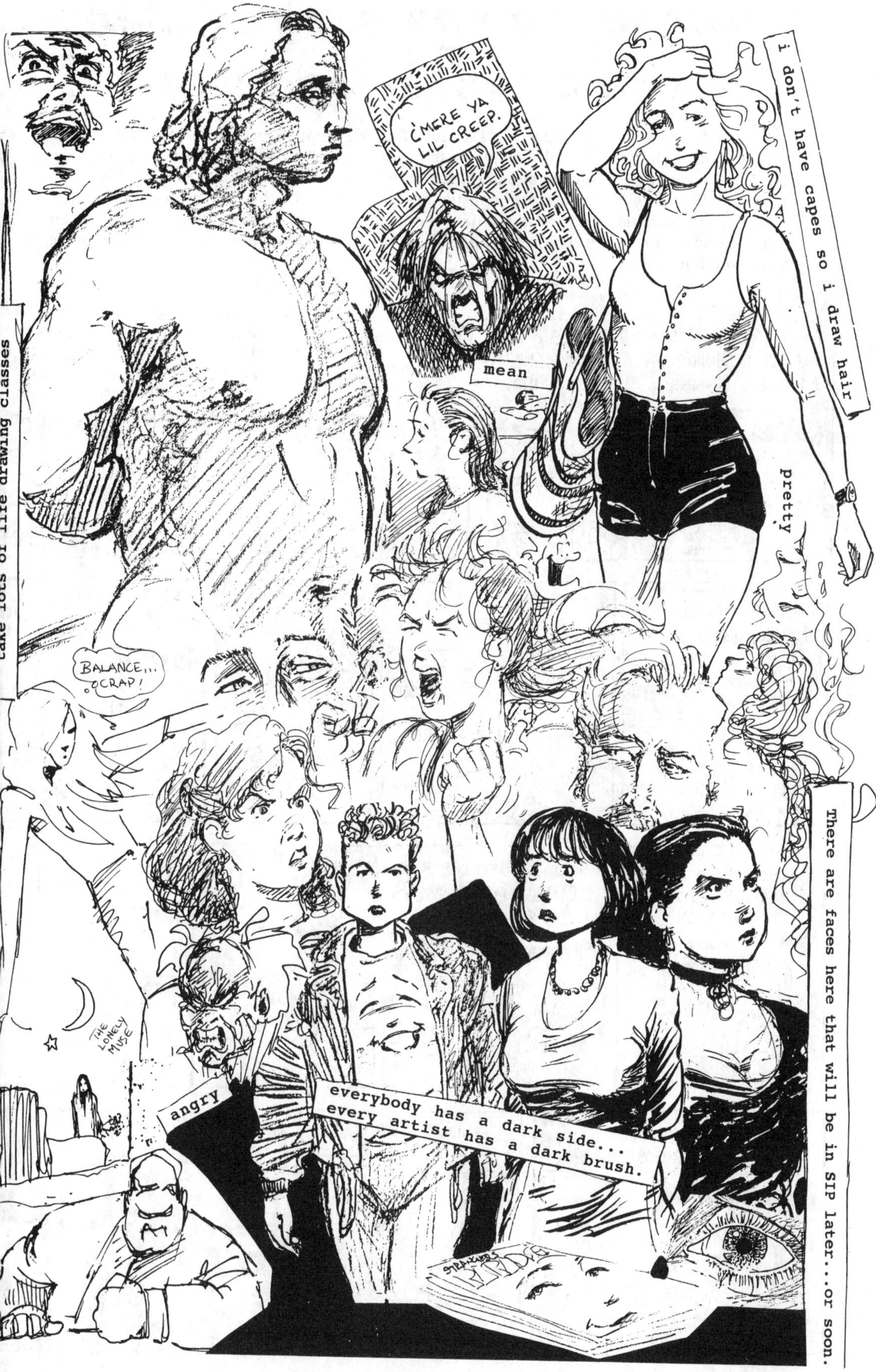

take lots of life drawing classes
C'MERE YA LIL CREEP.
i don't have capes so i draw hair
mean
pretty
BALANCE... CRAP!
There are faces here that will be in SIP later...or soon.
THE LONELY MUSE
angry
everybody has a dark side...
every artist has a dark brush.

WHERE DID YOU GET THE IDEA FOR STRANGERS IN PARADISE?

...is a question I've heard a a lot. "I dunno" I usually reply because the answer is so long and undoubtably boring I don't know where to begin. Truth is, I started out wanting to draw a newspaper comic strip and tried one idea after another before I realized I hated the gag-a-day life and really wanted to tell a story instead. Fortunately by that time I had quite an eclectic collection of characters and ideas to draw from. One of my earliest strips was about an enchanted forest filled with cigar smoking toads, wino owls, punk ducks and a beautiful blonde wood nymph named...

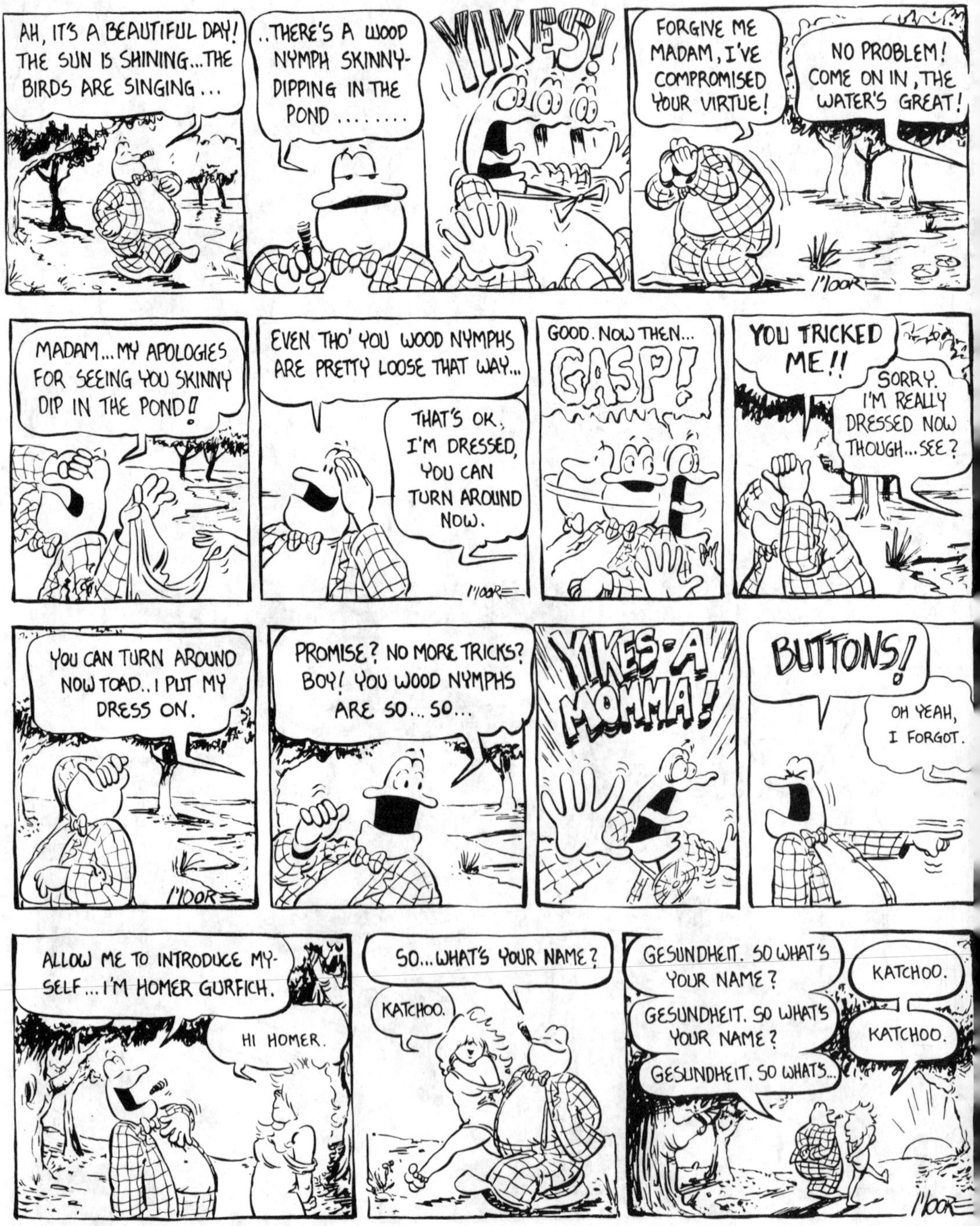

AH, IT'S A BEAUTIFUL DAY! THE SUN IS SHINING...THE BIRDS ARE SINGING...
..THERE'S A WOOD NYMPH SKINNY-DIPPING IN THE POND........
YIKES!
FORGIVE ME MADAM, I'VE COMPROMISED YOUR VIRTUE!
NO PROBLEM! COME ON IN, THE WATER'S GREAT!
MOORE
MADAM...MY APOLOGIES FOR SEEING YOU SKINNY DIP IN THE POND!
EVEN THO' YOU WOOD NYMPHS ARE PRETTY LOOSE THAT WAY...
THAT'S OK, I'M DRESSED, YOU CAN TURN AROUND NOW.
MOORE
GOOD. NOW THEN...
GASP!
YOU TRICKED ME!!
SORRY. I'M REALLY DRESSED NOW THOUGH...SEE?
YOU CAN TURN AROUND NOW TOAD.. I PUT MY DRESS ON.
MOORE
PROMISE? NO MORE TRICKS? BOY! YOU WOOD NYMPHS ARE SO...SO...
YIKES-A MOMMA!
BUTTONS!
OH YEAH, I FORGOT.
ALLOW ME TO INTRODUCE MY-SELF...I'M HOMER GURFICH.
HI HOMER.
SO...WHAT'S YOUR NAME?
KATCHOO.
GESUNDHEIT. SO WHAT'S YOUR NAME?
KATCHOO.
GESUNDHEIT. SO WHAT'S YOUR NAME?
KATCHOO.
GESUNDHEIT. SO WHAT'S...
MOORE

So Katchoo began as a happy-go-lucky wood nymph. Weird, huh? She did have a cousin named Madison though (sorry Teri!). Her manner may seem more familiar...

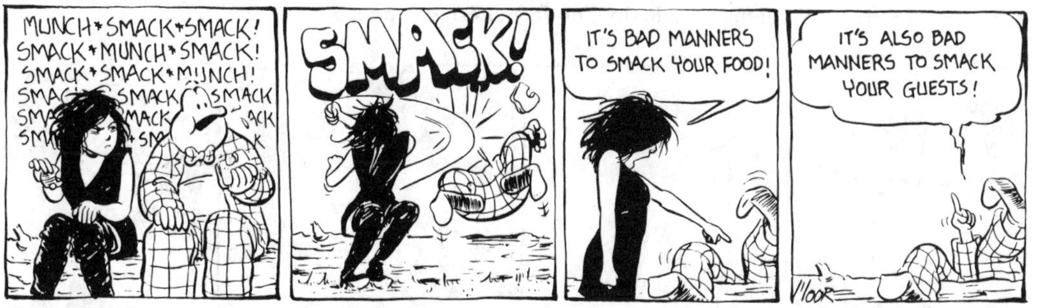
MUNCH*SMACK*SMACK!
SMACK*MUNCH*SMACK!
SMACK*SMACK*MUNCH!
SMACK!
IT'S BAD MANNERS TO SMACK YOUR FOOD!
IT'S ALSO BAD MANNERS TO SMACK YOUR GUESTS!

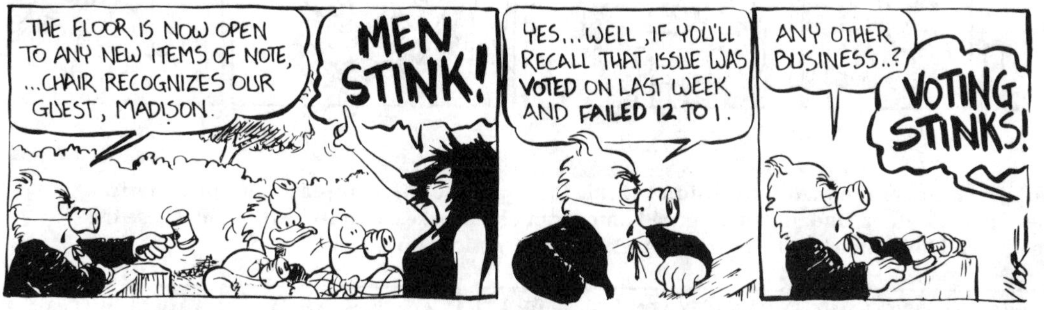
THE FLOOR IS NOW OPEN TO ANY NEW ITEMS OF NOTE, ...CHAIR RECOGNIZES OUR GUEST, MADISON.
MEN STINK!
YES... WELL, IF YOU'LL RECALL THAT ISSUE WAS VOTED ON LAST WEEK AND FAILED 12 TO 1.
ANY OTHER BUSINESS..?
VOTING STINKS!

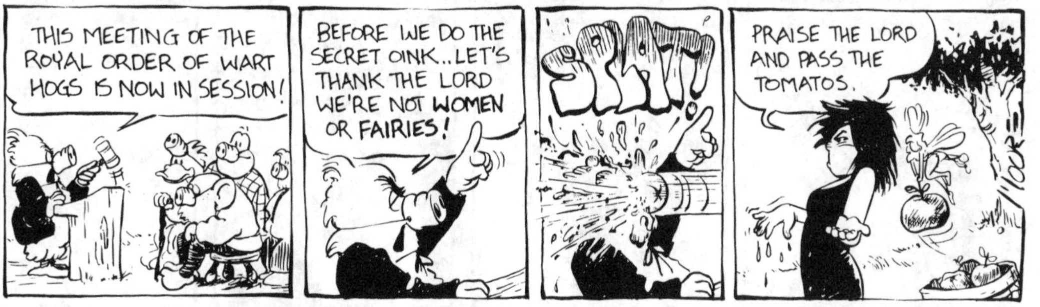
THIS MEETING OF THE ROYAL ORDER OF WART HOGS IS NOW IN SESSION!
BEFORE WE DO THE SECRET OINK...LET'S THANK THE LORD WE'RE NOT WOMEN OR FAIRIES!
SPLAT!
PRAISE THE LORD AND PASS THE TOMATOS.

When guys talk to me about SiP, they always mention Katchoo. Even when she was a wood nymph, Katchoo always had the same effect on men...

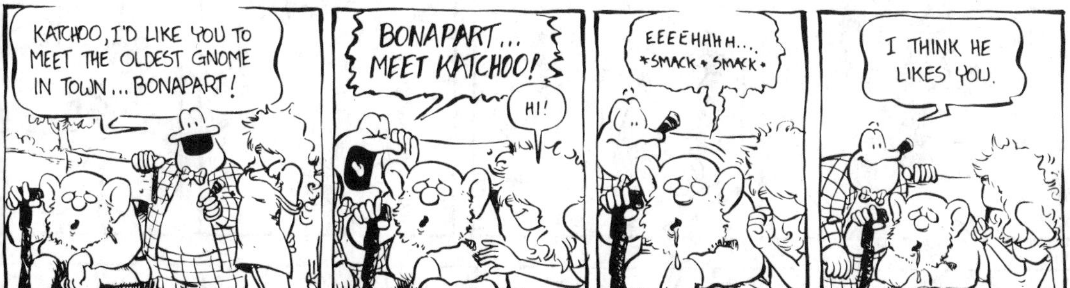
KATCHOO, I'D LIKE YOU TO MEET THE OLDEST GNOME IN TOWN... BONAPART!
BONAPART... MEET KATCHOO!
HI!
EEEEHHHH...
*SMACK*SMACK*
I THINK HE LIKES YOU.

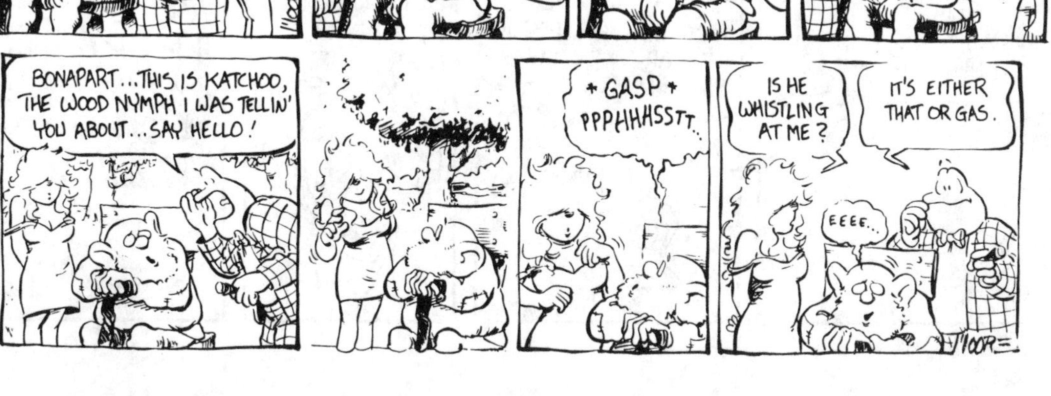
BONAPART...THIS IS KATCHOO, THE WOOD NYMPH I WAS TELLIN' YOU ABOUT...SAY HELLO!
GASP
PPPHHHSSTT..
IS HE WHISTLING AT ME?
IT'S EITHER THAT OR GAS.
EEEE...

For some reason, the syndicates didn't think my fantasy forest strip was wholesome enough. Hmm...I thought, wholesome. I resolved to create the ultimate wholesome comic strip, and what could be more wholesome than the all-American couple? I started a strip about the typical American domestic family of the 90's...loving, understanding, supportive, axe-weilding.

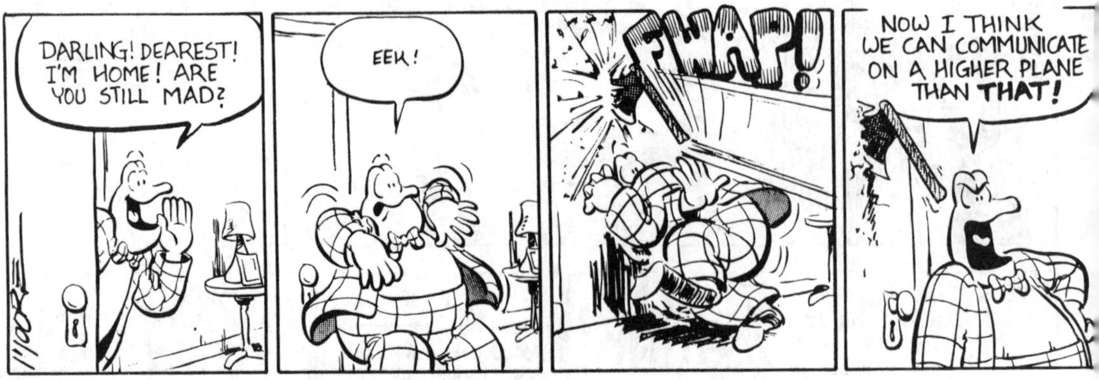

DARLING! DEAREST! I'M HOME! ARE YOU STILL MAD?
EEK!
FWAP!
NOW I THINK WE CAN COMMUNICATE ON A HIGHER PLANE THAN THAT!

To my surprise, the syndicates didn't think that approach was appropriate for Americas newspapers either. Undaunted, I figured hmm...can't be the axe....it must be the toads. Lose the toads. And love, there's gotta be more love. Typical American love...

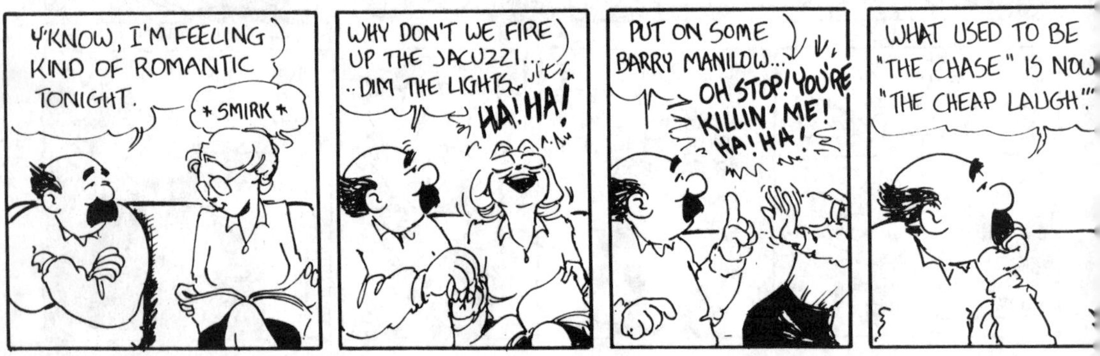

Y'KNOW, I'M FEELING KIND OF ROMANTIC TONIGHT.
SMIRK
WHY DON'T WE FIRE UP THE JACUZZI... ..DIM THE LIGHTS...
HA! HA!
PUT ON SOME BARRY MANILOW...
OH STOP! YOU'RE KILLIN' ME! HA! HA!
WHAT USED TO BE "THE CHASE" IS NOW "THE CHEAP LAUGH".

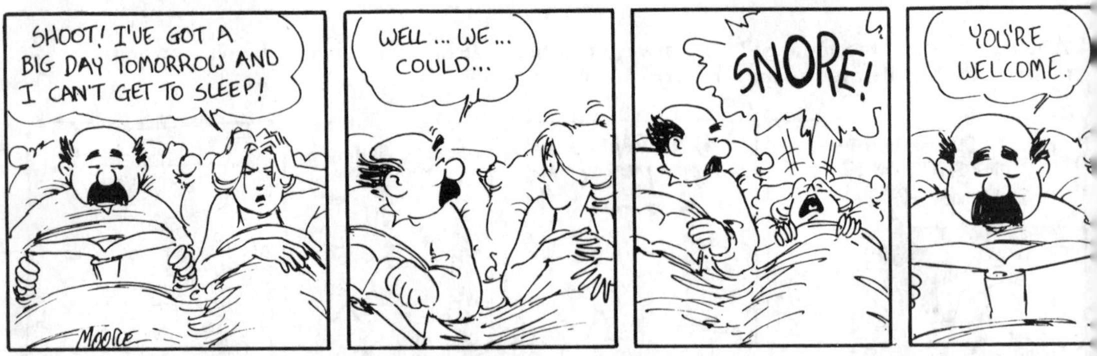

SHOOT! I'VE GOT A BIG DAY TOMORROW AND I CAN'T GET TO SLEEP!
MOORE
WELL ... WE ... COULD...
SNORE!
YOU'RE WELCOME.

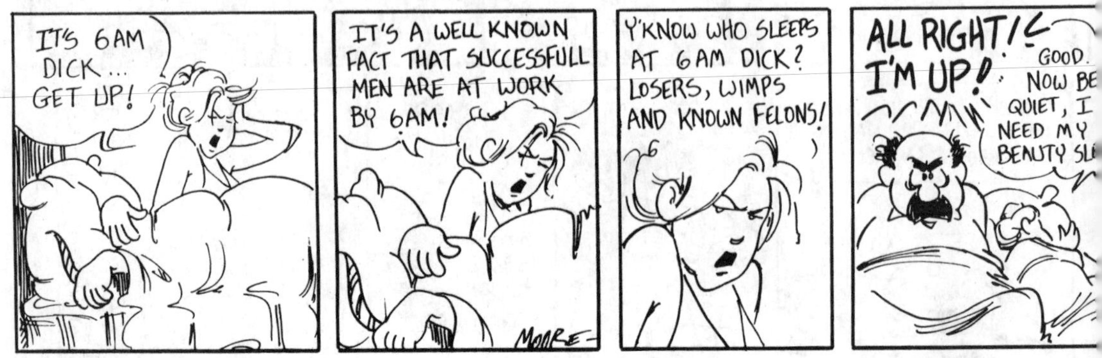

IT'S 6AM DICK... GET UP!
IT'S A WELL KNOWN FACT THAT SUCCESSFULL MEN ARE AT WORK BY 6AM!
MOORE
Y'KNOW WHO SLEEPS AT 6AM DICK? LOSERS, WIMPS AND KNOWN FELONS!
ALL RIGHT! I'M UP!
GOOD. NOW BE QUIET, I NEED MY BEAUTY SL

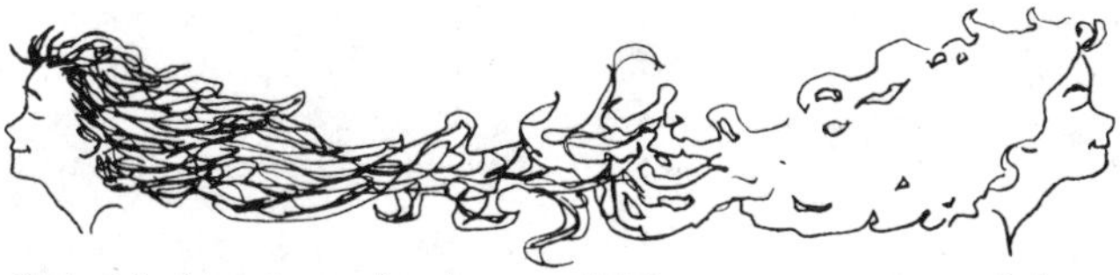

Needless to say, that strip is not running in over 2300 newspapers around the world today. Something about beds and inference. Hmph!

I was about ready to give it up when I tried one last idea. I had this Walter Mitty type guy, a chronic daydreamer, married to a patient and understanding wife named Francine. See, he's really out of touch with reality, see? And he lives in his own world most of the time...and if I have to explain it this much it must have been a really bad idea...but I did get Francine out of it.

If this strip didn't work though, I vowed to never do another comic strip again! Forget it! Blow it off! Burn the newspapers!...maybe I'd draw a comic book or something...

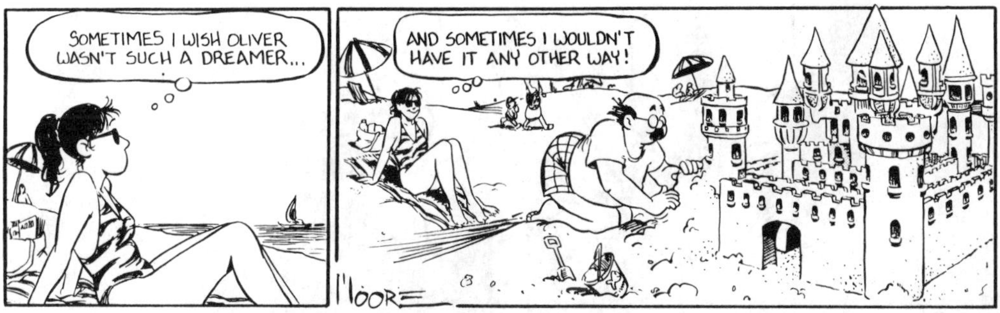
SOMETIMES I WISH OLIVER WASN'T SUCH A DREAMER...
AND SOMETIMES I WOULDN'T HAVE IT ANY OTHER WAY!

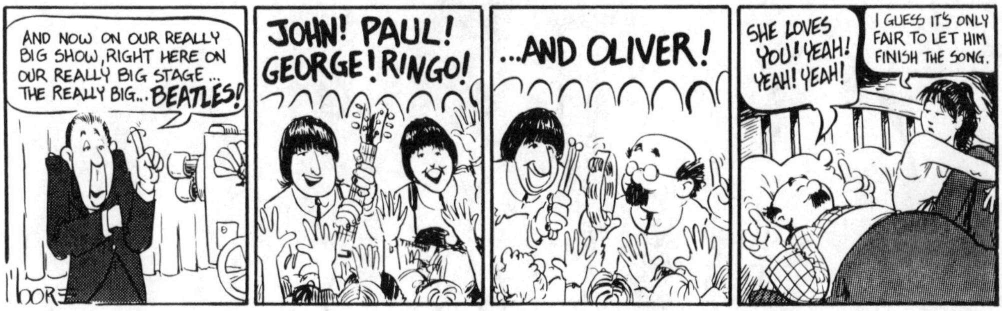
AND NOW ON OUR REALLY BIG SHOW, RIGHT HERE ON OUR REALLY BIG STAGE... THE REALLY BIG... BEATLES!
JOHN! PAUL! GEORGE! RINGO!
...AND OLIVER!
SHE LOVES YOU! YEAH! YEAH! YEAH!
I GUESS IT'S ONLY FAIR TO LET HIM FINISH THE SONG.

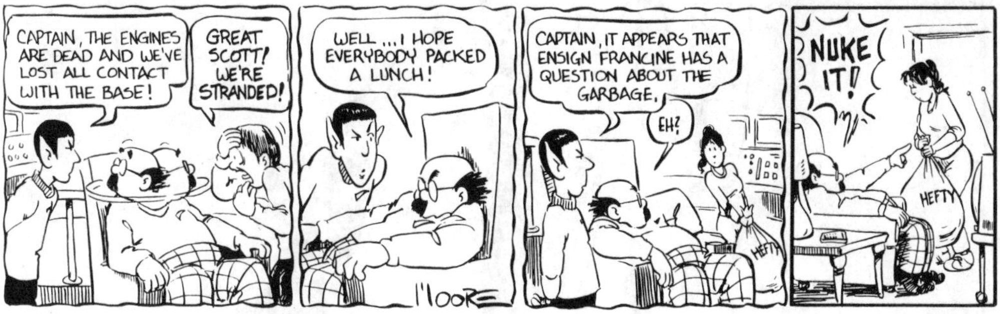
CAPTAIN, THE ENGINES ARE DEAD AND WE'VE LOST ALL CONTACT WITH THE BASE!
GREAT SCOTT! WE'RE STRANDED!
WELL... I HOPE EVERYBODY PACKED A LUNCH!
CAPTAIN, IT APPEARS THAT ENSIGN FRANCINE HAS A QUESTION ABOUT THE GARBAGE,
EH?
NUKE IT!
HEFTY

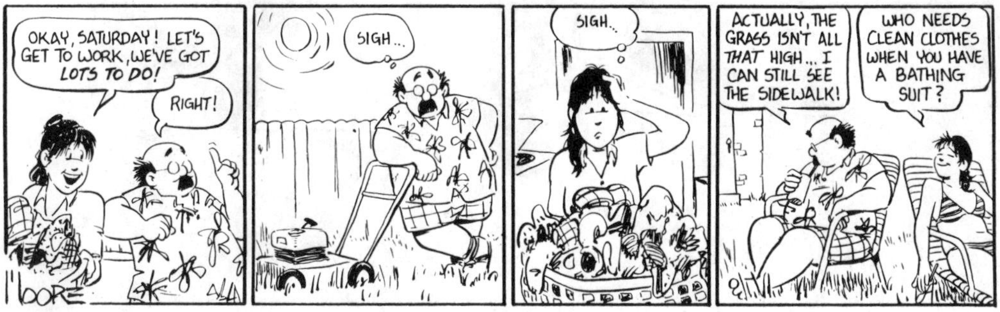
OKAY, SATURDAY! LET'S GET TO WORK, WE'VE GOT LOTS TO DO!
RIGHT!
SIGH...
SIGH..
ACTUALLY, THE GRASS ISN'T ALL THAT HIGH... I CAN STILL SEE THE SIDEWALK!
WHO NEEDS CLEAN CLOTHES WHEN YOU HAVE A BATHING SUIT?

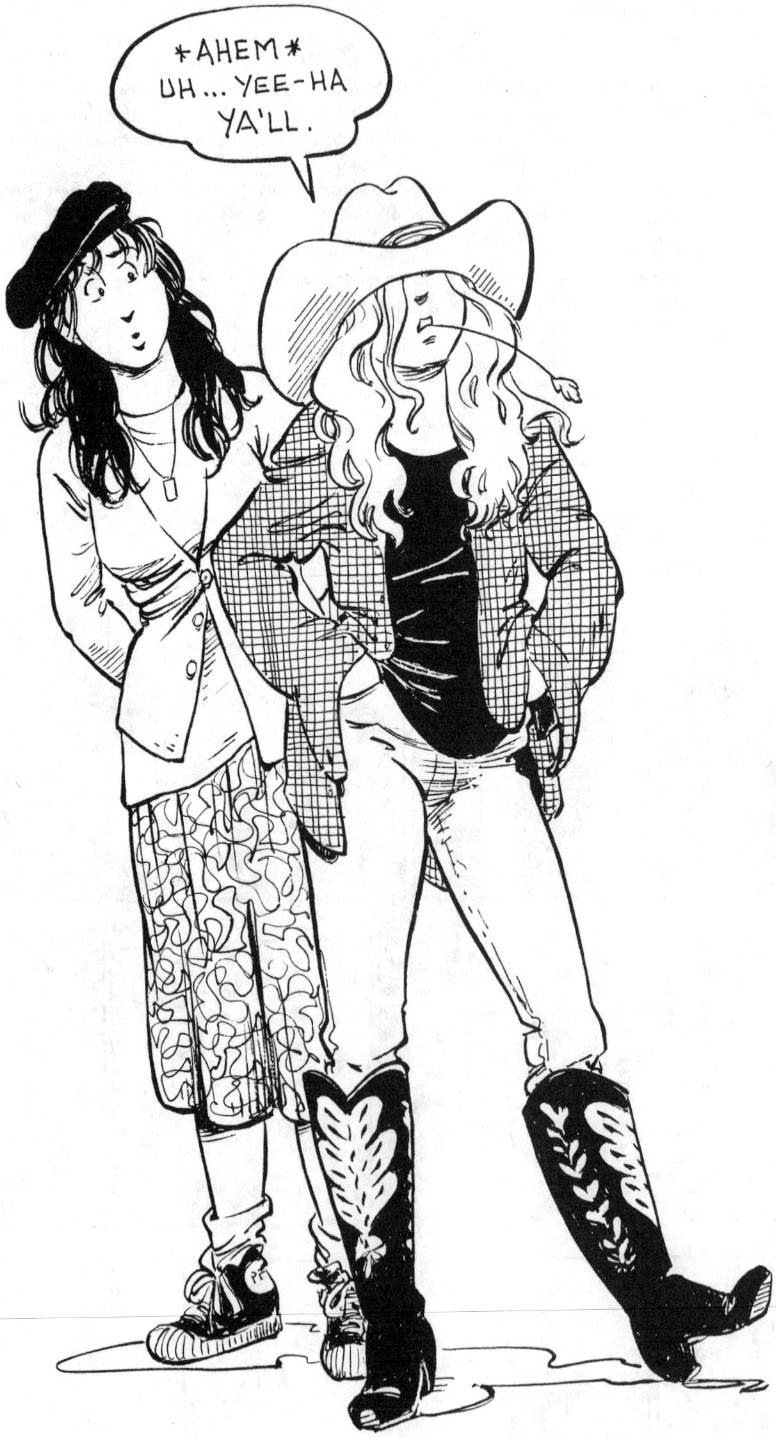
AHEM UH... YEE-HA YA'LL.